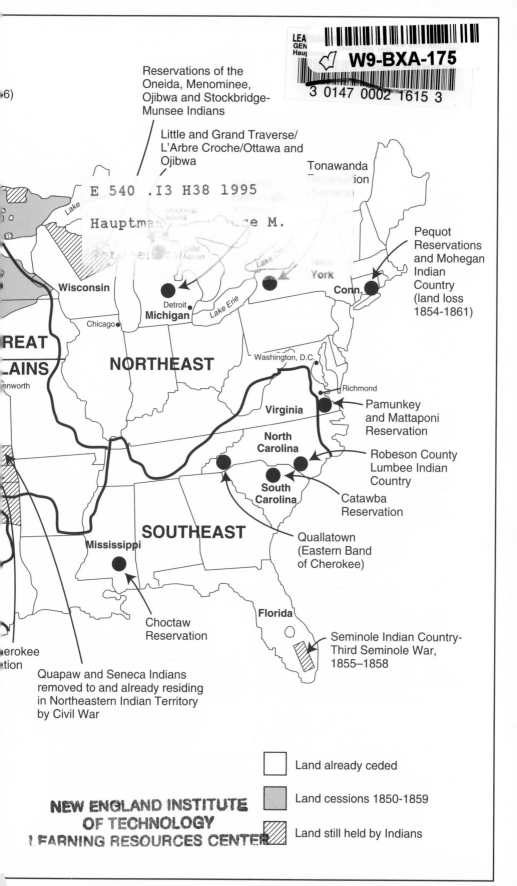

Reservations of the Oneida, Menominee, Ojibwa and Stockbridge-Munsee Indians

Little and Grand Traverse/L'Arbre Croche/Ottawa and Ojibwa

Tonawanda Reservation (Seneca)

Pequot Reservations and Mohegan Indian Country (land loss 1854-1861)

Lake

Lake Huron

Lake On...

Wisconsin

New York

Conn.

Detroit

Michigan

Lake Erie

Chicago

GREAT PLAINS

...enworth

NORTHEAST

Washington, D.C.

Richmond

Virginia

Pamunkey and Mattaponi Reservation

North Carolina

Robeson County Lumbee Indian Country

South Carolina

Catawba Reservation

SOUTHEAST

Mississippi

Quallatown (Eastern Band of Cherokee)

Choctaw Reservation

Florida

Seminole Indian Country-Third Seminole War, 1855–1858

...erokee ...tion

Quapaw and Seneca Indians removed to and already residing in Northeastern Indian Territory by Civil War

	Land already ceded
	Land cessions 1850-1859
	Land still held by Indians

BETWEEN TWO FIRES

American Indians
in the Civil War

LAURENCE M. HAUPTMAN

THE FREE PRESS

New York London Toronto Sydney Tokyo Singapore

The Free Press
A Division of Simon & Schuster Inc.
866 Third Avenue, New York, N.Y. 10022

Printed in the United States of America

printing number

1 2 3 4 5 6 7 8 9 10

Library of Congress Cataloging-in-Publication Data
Hauptman, Laurence M.
Between two fires: American Indians in the Civil War/Laurence M. Hauptman.
       p.   cm.
Includes bibliographical references (p.   ).
ISBN 0–02–914180–X
1. Indians of North America—History—Civil War, 1861–1865. 2. United States—History—
Civil War, 1861–1865—Participation, Indian. 3. Indians of North America—History—
19th century.
I. Title.
E540.I3H38   1995   94–42217
973.7'3—dc20   CIP

For the following Iroquois veterans:

Roy Black

Duwayne "Duce" Bowen

Gordie McLester

Barney Waterman

Contents

PART THREE. THE NORTH

Acknowledgments

BETWEEN TWO FIRES IS A BOOK THAT WAS TEN YEARS IN THE MAKING and owes much to the contributions of many people who are too numerous to thank individually; however, certain individuals deserve special acknowledgment. Mr. Bruce Nichols, Senior Editor at The Free Press, helped shape my thesis with his insightful comments about the Civil War's impact upon American Indians. Mr. Carlo De Vito, now of Simon and Schuster, and Ms. Joyce Seltzer, now of Harvard University Press, encouraged the project at The Free Press before leaving for new pastures. Mr. William Evans of the New York State Archives first introduced me to the world of military records. Through numerous discussions with Mr. Evans, the idea and structure for this book were born. Mr. James Corsaro, Head of the Manuscript Division of the New York State Library, as well as George Hamell and Craig Williams of the New York State Museum, have also aided me in this project in a variety of ways. Mr. Michael Meier, Mr. Michael Pilgrim, and Ms. DeAnne Blanton of the Military Service Branch of the National Archives answered my numerous questions and guided my research at that national treasure. Two National Park Service historians—Christopher Calkins of Petersburg National Battlefield and Ted Alexander of Antietam National Battlefield— helped me understand their specific sites. Dr. Jack Campisi of Wellesley College and Dr. Kevin McBride shared with me their special knowledge of Pequot history. Dr. Helen Rountree of Old Dominion University supplied me with the names of Pamunkey in the Civil War. Dr. James Merrell of Vassar College recommended key readings on Catawba Indians. Dr. Adolph Dial of Pembroke State University spent time answering my inquiries about the Lowry Band and gave me an extensive tour of his beloved Lumbee Country. My friend David Jaman provided me with frank and helpful comments about this manuscript.

My wife and two children tolerated my frequent ramblings in American Indian history and my compulsive work habits. I could not have completed this project without their support. Special thanks should be given to my daughter Beth who used her photographic skills to copy some of the plates reproduced in this book.

Laurence M. Hauptman

New Paltz, New York

Prologue

CONTEMPORARY INDIAN POW-WOWS CAN BE WITNESSED FROM Memorial Day to well past Labor Day throughout the United States. After the "grand entrance dance" that initiates the doings, the "flag ceremony" begins. The announcer then invites both Indians and non-Indians who served in the United States Armed Forces to enter the circle to join the "honor dance," out of respect for their sacrifice. I have witnessed this poignant ceremony throughout the Northeast nearly fifty times over the last quarter of a century. In popular culture and even in certain scholarly writings, the stereotyped "Indian" has often been pictured as an instigator of conflict and a hostile/renegade intent on "savage war," but the sentiments expressed at the pow-wow are no mere ploys aimed at tourist dollars. Native Americans, in fact, have distinguished themselves as members of the United States Armed Forces from the Battle of Oriskany in 1777 to the Gulf War in 1991.

One war in particular forces gray meanings and colorful personal stories to shade particularly deeply to black tones of irony. In the 1860s, when white brothers fought brothers, when border states faced agonizing choices, and when one people of color finally achieved emancipation, American Indians found themselves fighting fiercely on both sides of the conflict. And in the deepest irony of all, many fought because they believed it was their last best hope to halt a genocide that had begun in the East in the early seventeenth century, one that continued throughout the Trail of Tears westward in the 1830s, and exploded again after the California Gold Rush of 1849. Yet the Civil War, rather than the last best hope, proved to be a final nail in the coffin in Indian efforts to stop the tide of American expansion.

Some twenty thousand American Indians served in the Civil War. They contributed to Union and Confederate causes on both land and sea, as "grunts" in the trenches and even as commissioned and noncommissioned officers. A casual walk through most nineteenth-century Native American cemeteries reflects this. The tombstones frequently indicate the Indian's regiment, be it in Confederate or Union service, much like their non-Indian counterparts. Indeed, monuments dedicated to American Indian Civil War service stretch from Fort Mill, South Carolina to Tahlequah, Oklahoma.

American Indians participated in many of the major battles and some of the heaviest fighting of the Civil War. Most earlier histories have simply chronicled their participation in the war in the Trans-Mississippi West, especially their important involvement at the Battle of Pea Ridge in 1862. But they also served at Second Bull Run and Antietam in 1862; at Chattanooga in 1863; at the Wilderness, Spotsylvania, Cold Harbor, and Second Cabin Creek in 1864; and in the Union assaults on Petersburg in 1864 and 1865. From the evacuation of Indian Territory in the spring of 1861 to Sherman's Carolina Campaign in the last months of the war, American Indians provided valuable service to the Union. At Appomattox, Colonel (later General) Ely S. Parker served as General Grant's Military Secretary, drawing up the articles of Lee's surrender. Meanwhile, in both the East and Trans-Mississippi West, Confederate Cherokee units were among the last troops to surrender to the federal army.

Much of the tragedy brought by the war occurred elsewhere than on the battlefield, and affected far more than just the twenty thousand Indians in uniform. As Confederate artillery pieces were aimed at Fort Sumter during the secession crisis of 1860–1861, Washington officials made plans for continued Indian removals as an option to solve the so-called "Indian Problem." The United States Army, during the years of heaviest fighting during the Civil War, undertook campaigns of "pacification" against the Indians in the Great Lakes,

Northwest, Plains, and Southwest. While the Confederate constitutional convention was meeting in February 1861 at Montgomery, Alabama, the United States Army was attempting to capture Cochise, the Chiricahua Apache leader, who resisted these efforts for two more years. At the end of the Seven Days Battles on July 1, 1862, the United States Congress passed legislation authorizing the building of the Transcontinental Railroad. When it was completed seven years later, the link contributed to the disruption of traditional Plains Indian life, resulted in the extermination of bison herds, brought massive non-Indian population westward, increased Indian–white tension and conflicts, and led to reservation existence and overall Indian dependence. Less than two weeks before the Second Battle of Bull Run in August of 1862, the "Great Sioux Uprising" began in Minnesota. The federal army eventually put down the Santee Sioux. Thirty-eight Indian leaders were subsequently executed after appeals for clemency were denied by President Lincoln.

While the Union army in March 1864 was undertaking an ambitious campaign up the Red River of Louisiana with the intention of capturing Shreveport and invading Confederate Texas, General James Carleton was ordering Kit Carson to force the Indians out of their citadel at Canyon de Chelly. Throughout 1864, eight thousand Navajos and Mescalero Apaches were removed and relocated, for a four-year stay, at a concentration camp, the Bosque Redondo at Fort Sumner, New Mexico. Two weeks after Lincoln's reelection in November, 1864, Colonel John Chivington, a crazed religious fanatic, and the troops of the First and Third Colorado Cavalry, attacked a peaceful camp of mostly Cheyenne Indians along the Sand Creek, killing about 150 men, women, and children and mutilating their bodies.

What then explains the significant presence of American Indians in the Civil War? The answer goes well beyond one simple reason. To be sure, poverty induced enlistment. And despite their separate nationhoods, some Indian communities had by 1861 been integrated into the region that surrounded them, becoming dependent on the non-Indian world for economic and political survival. For some the Civil War was inspired by wanderlust and search for adventure. In other instances, it was based on past alliances, treaty obligations, and earlier military experiences. As in olden days, participation in war validated tribal leadership and status within one's community. Moreover, Native Americans' own views about slavery led at times to internal disputes and civil wars, since some Indians were slaveholders and others were opposed to the "peculiar institution." Frequently the reasons for volunteering were simply the result of persuasive and well-respected community leaders who were committed to joining the war effort of North or South. On a few occasions in the South, American Indians were conscripted into military labor service when suddenly whites found them "useful." Most of all, it was their tenuous existence in both the North and South that brought so many of the Indian nations to the Confederate or Union sides in 1861. They were dependent peoples as a result of American wars of conquest, treaties, or economic, political, social, and religious changes introduced by the "Long Knives." From Connecticut to Indian Territory and from New York to South Carolina, they sought the "warpath" because it seemed imperative for their own and/or their Indian community's survival.

Between Two Fires tells the tales of representative American Indian communities whose men went off to serve in the Civil War. It employs first-person accounts wherever possible and focuses on key individuals in companies that had American Indians. But the fighting is only part of the story; at various points this book will put the battles in context by describing the terrible declining fortunes of Indian communities throughout the continental United States. The picture that emerges is one of separate warrior-volunteers, whose heroic actions on Civil War battlefields failed to improve the overall conditions of their peoples at home, the tragedy that is expressed throughout this book.

The first chapter describes the precariousness of American Indian life by the time of the Civil War. Part One of *Between Two Fires* then focuses on the Trans-Mississippi West. Faced with uncertainty and land loss from the mid-1850s onward as a result of the Kansas-Nebraska Act and "Bleeding Kansas," the Delaware, as shown in Chapter 2, found themselves in a tenuous situation at best. Having served the United States army in the past as scouts on the frontier, these Indians decided to "cut a deal" about their future south of Kansas. Hoping to secure a new home, most Delaware signed up with the Union. In sharp contrast, the Cherokee of Indian Territory, the focus of Chapter 3, were a sharply divided people. The pro-Confederate allied faction, led by the ambitious and brilliant military strategist Stand Watie, had long-standing grievances against Principal Chief John Ross's controversial leadership. Watie's Cherokees had diverse reasons for choosing the Confederate cause, ranging from their strong advocacy of slavery to their goal of igniting an ambitious coup d'état and seizing control of their Indian nation.

In Part Two, *Between Two Fires* moves to the South during the Civil War. Chapter 4 describes two American Indian communities—the Pamunkey of Virginia and the Lumbee of North Carolina—who reacted to the white supremacist world of the antebellum American South by serving Union interests. The Pamunkey worked as river pilots for General George McClellan's Army of the Potomac during the Peninsula campaign of 1862. The Lumbee were guerrillas fighting Confederate Home Guards in the swamp country of North Carolina during Sherman's Carolina campaign of 1865. Although the Lumbee were more aggressive in resisting the local Confederate power structure than the Pamunkey, both communities saw themselves as avengers reacting to their demeaning status as "free persons of color."

Chapters 5 and 6 treat the most significant allies of the Confederacy in the East—the Catawba of South Carolina and the Eastern Band of Cherokee. For well over one hundred years, the Catawba, described in Chapter 5, were identified with South Carolina, serving as military allies as well as catchers of runaway slaves for the white power centers at Charleston and Columbia. In order to survive in a circumscribed world after the French and Indian War, they presented themselves as cooperative southern Indian neighbors. Increasingly economically dependent on whites of the piedmont, the Catawba became the first American Indian community to join the Confederate army, serving loyally as South Carolina volunteer infantrymen in the

Army of Northern Virginia. Chapter 6 focuses on the Eastern Band of Cherokee, the largest American Indian contingent in the Confederate army east of the Mississippi. Over four hundred Indians were led into service by William Holland Thomas, a white man who had been adopted as a child by the Cherokee. The Thomas Legion of Indians and Highlanders performed immeasurable service to the South, guarding the vital mountain passes and preventing Union strikes along Confederate communications and rail links, and intimidating pro-Unionist supporters in eastern Tennessee and western North Carolina. In addition to Thomas's own grand ambitions, the "white chief" also hoped to gain concessions for continued Cherokee occupation of their lands in western North Carolina.

Part Three concentrates on American Indians of the Northeast who joined the Union. The Ottawa and Ojibwa, two culturally and historically related communities, faced removal from Michigan from the 1820s onward. As Chapter 7 shows, these Indians' world was shrinking and their status was ambiguous by the time of the Civil War, leading them to be increasingly dependent on Washington. Hoping to renegotiate their treaties to obtain a larger, more concentrated landbase in Michigan, and hoping to end talk of their removal from the state, great numbers of Ottawa and Ojibwa Indians went to war for the Union as sharpshooters. The small culturally and historically related communities of Pequot and Mohegan Indians of Connecticut, analyzed in Chapter 8, had no pretenses about noble ideals when they joined the Union Army. With the decline of whaling as their major source of economic survival in the 1850s and 1860s, they reluctantly chose another risky endeavor, almost exclusively because of their desperate condition by 1864. The Tonawanda Band of Seneca were fearful of the nefarious activities of land speculation companies after a series of disastrous treaties that led to their dispossession from their homeland. As Chapter 9 indicates, the federal government "allowed" the Seneca in 1857 to repurchase part of their homeland. By the Civil War, most Seneca saw Washington as a needed ally to guard against a recurrence of these efforts at dispossession and removal.

The goal of this book then is to recover a hidden chapter in the history of the Civil War, in all its variety, with all its heroism and all its ugliness. For starters, of course, American Indians faced many of the same battlefield horrors as their non-Indian counterparts. They were not immune to high casualty rates, poor field sanitation, improper medical care, and disease. Captured Union Indians were sent to Andersonville and Belle Isle while Confederate Indian prisoners of war were sent to Elmira and Fort Columbus. They became refugees in massive numbers in Union-held eastern Kansas and in Confederate northern Texas and the southern part of Indian Territory. Yet their participation was even more tragic. American Indian communities who lost men in combat were not replenished by massive immigration. Equally important, as diverse people caught between two fires, these same communities lost more of their self-sufficiency and became more dependent economically, legally, and politically on the "Great Father" for their survival. This loss of independence, however, did not suddenly begin in 1861, but was rooted well back in American history.

1

Not Ten Years of Peace

IN 1867, TWO YEARS AFTER THE CIVIL WAR, THE COMMISSIONER OF
Indian affairs wrote in his annual report: "... this benevolent and
bounteous government [United States] has from the onset accorded
to them [Indians] rights and possessions, and extended over them a
paternal care which is most simply and admirably acknowledged in
their appellation which styles the government 'the great father.' |"[1]
This "benevolent" father in the eighty years from 1787 to 1867 had
exhibited its "paternalism" mostly in the form of wars of "pacification," regulation of the Indian trade, removal of Indian nations to the
Trans-Mississippi West, and assimilationist strategies ranging from
Indian schooling, to support for proselytizing by missionaries, to ini-
tiatives to allot Indian lands, to efforts to extend United States citizenship to Indians with or without the Indians' consent.

By 1860, the result was to produce a precarious existence for the
overwhelming majority of American Indians. The major signposts in
the early national period are well known: Tecumseh's failed efforts to
stop westward expansion before and during the War of 1812, the
bloody Indian resistance of the Second Seminole War, and the horror
of the Trail of Tears. As early as 1831, Alexis de Tocqueville described

the process: ". . . expulsion of the Indians often takes place at the present day in a regular, and, as it were a legal manner. . . . Half convinced and half compelled, they go to inhabit new deserts, where the importunate whites will not let them remain ten years in peace. . . . In this manner do the Americans obtain, at a very low price, whole provinces, which the richest sovereigns of Europe could not purchase."[2] By the time of the Civil War, the unsettling fear of removal permeated all Indian communities, from Seneca Country in western New York to Delaware Country in eastern Kansas, from the Ottawa Country of the lower peninsula of Michigan to the Catawba Country of the South Carolina piedmont.

From 1787 until the end of federal–Indian treaty making in 1871, the federal government continuously negotiated treaties with Indian nations. These same treaties were often used to secure more and more land and/or promote the "civilization" programs of Washington. Assimilation requirements in United States treaties involved everything from individual Indian land allotments of the tribal estate (i.e., the imposition of private property) to imposition of new forms of tribal organization and government. United States treaties with the Cherokee in 1817 and 1819 provided for individual allotments of tribal lands to heads of families "who may wish to become citizens of the United States."[3] In 1830, the federal Treaty of Dancing Rabbit Creek with the Choctaw that removed them to the Trans-Mississippi West clearly specified that "each Choctaw head of a family being desirous to remain and become a citizen of the States, shall be permitted to do so, by signifying his intention to the agent within six months from the ratification of this treaty."[4] Individual Indians, in each of these treaties, had to choose between tribal membership and removal or land allotments and United States citizenship. Of course, even when Indians chose the latter, they were still not allowed full rights and guarantees of United States citizenship by a racist America.[5]

Other Indian nations were faced with more direct threats to their tribal existence through the extension of citizenship. The Stockbridge Indians of Wisconsin, in federal treaties from 1843 to 1864, "vacillated between dissolving the tribe and admitting all members or retaining the separate organization and allowing individuals to choose either citizenship or tribal membership."[6] Federal treaties with the Wyandot and Ottawa in 1855 and 1862 required relinquishment of tribal government in exchange for allotment and the rights of United States citizenship. By the 1860s, certain treaties with Indian nations gave the President and the federal courts the power to determine Indian competency to warrant admission to United States citizenship.[7]

Throughout much of the nineteenth century, Washington policymakers adhered to the belief that the Indians' continued insistence on and maintenance of tribal organization prevented their becoming United States citizens. Many leading legal scholars and jurists in the country saw Indians as members of nations apart and "not capable" of attaining this goal. The famous jurist, Chancellor James Kent, in the New York Court of Errors in 1823 insisted that individual Indians did not qualify as United States citizens because of their own tribal allegiance.[8] Six years later, the South Carolina court of appeals rejected the appeal by a Pamunkey Indian to allow him to vote. The Pamunkey was a veteran of the Continental Army, who had taken an oath of allegiance and had received a federal pension. The judge insisted that the Indian was not a citizen but belonged to a "race of people, who have always been considered as a separate and distinct class, never having been incorporated into the body politic."[9]

In 1835, Indians in North Carolina were redefined into a new peculiarly American and ugly category with the adoption of a state constitution that designated them as "free persons of color." From 1826 onward, restrictive laws—the "Free Negro Code"—were passed that led to Indians being denied the right to vote, legally bear arms without a license, or serve in the militia. Similar racist restrictions on Indian citizenship occurred from Virginia to Louisiana and were a feature of southern life well into the twentieth century.[10]

In the era of Jacksonian removal policies, the United States Supreme Court in the 1830s had a dramatic impact on defining the status of American Indian nations. Chief Justice John Marshall in *Cherokee Nation v. Georgia* (1831) defined Indian tribes within the

United States as "domestic dependent nations" occupying a "state of pupilage" with respect to the United States resembling the relationship "of a ward to a guardian."[11] Significantly, in *Worcester v. Georgia* (1832), Marshall insisted that the relation of the Cherokees to the federal government "was that of a nation claiming and receiving the protection of one more powerful, not that of individuals abandoning their national character, and submitting as subjects to the laws of a master."[12] To Marshall, American Indian nations were not nations such as Great Britain or France but were sovereign enough to demand loyalty from tribal members. Regardless of their dependency on the United States, they were aliens holding quasi-sovereign status. The Marshall court thus helped create a "twilight zone" status for American Indians. Since Indian nations remained separate no matter how dependent or limited their sovereignty, their individual members could not successfully claim to be American citizens by birthright. According to legal scholar James Kettner, the Marshall court's decisions "ultimately served the purposes of those who wished to maintain control over Indians without fully incorporating them into the community of citizens."[13]

The precariousness of American Indian existence often had ironic twists. At times, American Indians were even barred from achieving United States citizenship through the naturalization process as well because that procedure was often restricted to "free white aliens."[14] Only after the ratification of the Fourteenth Amendment did Congress pass specific "naturalization acts" affecting certain American Indian nations, including in one instance allowing Winnebago male Indians, considered "aliens," to apply for citizenship![15]

The single biggest factor affecting American Indian life leading up to the Civil War was the constant threat of their removal from their homelands. In 1830, the United States Congress passed the Indian Removal Act which gave the President the authorization to exchange unorganized public-domain land in the Trans-Mississippi West for Indian land in the East. The Indian nations "emigrating" would allegedly receive perpetual title to these new lands as well as compensation and assistance in emigrating. Congress also appropriated moneys to the executive department to further this objective.[16]

American Indians from New York to Georgia and from Ohio to Wisconsin were all affected by this piece of legislation. Although many Indians and their communities had been removed to the Trans-Mississippi region from before 1829, presidents Andrew Jackson and Martin Van Buren in the 1830s "clearly shifted federal policy toward final and irrevocable removal."[17] Although largely surrounding the policy with benevolence and philanthropic rhetoric, the two presidents' records indicate otherwise. Between 20 and 25 percent of the Cherokee died in their "trail of tears."[18] Although statistics vary, 10,138 more Cherokee according to demographer Russell Thornton "would have been alive in 1840 if removal to the West had not taken place."[19] As a result of the Second Seminole War which involved thirty thousand American troops, the Indian population of Florida was reduced to approximately five hundred; four thousand had been removed to Indian Territory on an allotment north of the Creek Indians, and as many as fifteen hundred had been killed.[20] Long before the current moral indictment of Euroamericans during the Columbian Quincentennary, historian William T. Hagan observed that Indian removal of the Cherokee and other members of the Five Civilized Tribes approached the "horrors created by the Nazi handling of subject peoples."[21]

Indian removal did not just affect the Cherokee and other members of the Five Civilized Tribes. It had an impact across sections. Even in Jackson's first annual address to Congress, the President made reference to Maine, New York, Ohio, as well as Alabama and Georgia and their needs to establish jurisdiction over the Indians within their borders.[22] Jacksonian-Van Buren removal policies had far-reaching results well beyond the Southeast. Besides the Five Civilized Tribes, Indian nations affected included the Catawba, Chippewa, Delaware, Menominee, Miami, Osage, Ottawa, Potawatomi, Quapaw, Shawnee, the Six Nations of New York State, Winnebago, and Wyandot. By 1850, nearly a decade after Van Buren left the office of the presidency, 84,000 eastern Indians had been removed to the Trans-Mississippi.[23]

After the Mexican War, the official direction in Indian policy largely shifted from removing Indians in the East to the "pacification" of the Trans-Mississippi frontier. The frontier was redefined in 1848 with the signing of the Treaty of Guadeloupe Hidalgo which ended the Mexican War. With this treaty, the United States received California, Arizona, New Mexico, and Utah; over 100,000 American Indians lived in California alone. With the discovery of gold at Sutter's Mill in 1848, nearly a quarter of a million settlers came to California within the next four years. What followed has been described by historian Hubert H. Bancroft as "one of the last human hunts of civilization, and the basest and most brutal of them all."[24] By 1860, only 35,000 Indians remained alive in the entire state. By the turn of the twentieth century, there were between 12,000 and 20,000 Indians who had survived the slaughter.[25] These same Indians had been dispossessed without any compensation for more than 100,000 square miles "of the most beautiful and valuable country in the world."[26]

To be sure, there were many previous wars of conquest and pacification—the War of 1812; the First (1813–1814) and Second (1836) Creek Wars; the First (1817–1818), Second (1835–1842), and Third Seminole Wars (1855–1858); and the Black Hawk War (1832). But none compared to what transpired in northern California in the decade prior to the Civil War. Many California Indians were killed as a result of a systematic policy of extermination, although a significant number died as a result of disease, exposure, and starvation. Frederick Law Olmsted, the noted landscape architect, who traveled to the region during the Civil War, documented these heinous acts in his writings. Olmsted, no friend of the Indian, claimed "whites discriminate but imperfectly between hostile and peaceable indians, and are always suspicious of and rancorous toward the latter." Some whites planted evidence or made false reports "calculated to turn attention to the Indians" which directed "the aim of public vengeance or justice toward them." Most disturbingly, Olmsted observed: "I myself have seen men who simply with the apology that Indians were troublesome neighbors, did not shrink from stating that they had taken part in the distribution of clothes and blankets to them, which carried the infection of smallpox." Olmsted insisted that these acts occurred "within the last ten years."[27]

Although the federal government began to create a series of Indian reservations in 1853, the natives were never adequately protected by Washington from marauding whites, nor fed, clothed, or housed. Conflicts over federal or state jurisdiction also restricted American military efforts to protect the Indians. To make matters worse, corrupt Indian agents frequently misappropriated federal funds which were set aside for the Indians' welfare.[28] California whites stereotyped the Indians as "ignorant, bestial savages who deserved no rights" and lobbied for total removal of the Indians from the state borders in order to do away with the "Indian menace."[29]

The rapid destruction of the state's Indian population was most evident in northern California. The Indians were denied access to ancestral lands to fish, hunt, or gather roots. Hoopa, Nisenan, Shasta, Yana, Yuki, Yurok, Wintu, Wiyot, and others were soon starving refugees hiding out in the mountains. In order to survive, they periodically came down from the mountains, stole horses and cattle, or retaliated by killing their dispossessors, which only gave impetus to more organized "hunts" of the Indians. By the late summer of 1859, J. Y. McDuffie, Superintendent of Indian Affairs for California, reported: "The killing of Indians is a daily occurrence there." He continued in his report to the Commissioner of Indian Affairs: "If some means be not speedily devised, by which the unauthorized expeditions that are constantly out in search of them can be restrained, they will soon be exterminated."[30]

Brutal attacks occurred even after reservations were established to protect and feed the Indians. Most Indians remained outside the reservations for fear they would be kidnapped and enslaved. Indian children and women found themselves unsafe even when they were on reservations. Historian Albert Hurtado has shown that forced concubinage and rape of Indian women by white men were common features of the violent youth subculture of the mines in California.

The official "sanctioning" of these immoral activities stemmed from a California state statute of 1850 authorizing the indenture of Indians, a law that soon became a thinly disguised substitute for slavery, which had formally been abolished in the state in 1850. Kidnapping of Indian children and women became an especially profitable trade in the 1850s.[31] As late as the fall of 1862, G. M. Hanson, the superintending agent of Indian Affairs for the Northern District of California, blamed this situation of the indenture law "under cover of which all this trouble exists" and urged its repeal.[32]

Officials at every level of state government were directly or indirectly involved in this genocide. What befell the Yuki Indians was a case in point. In the 1850s, these northern California Indians were set upon and hunted down by William S. Jarboe and his Eel River Rangers, a motley assortment of Mendocino County ruffians. In a letter to the Governor of California, Captain Jarboe stated that the "ukas [Yuki] are without doubt, the most degraded, filthy, miserable thieving lot of anything living that comes under the head of and rank of human being. . . . They are inferior in intelect so devoid of feeling. . . ." Despite evidence to the contrary, Jarboe rationalized his state-sanctioned policy of "nothing short of extermination" because of these Indians' alleged thieving and murderous ways.[33]

J. Ross Browne, a special treasury agent who investigated the California situation in the late 1850s, reported: "a man name Jarboe now holds a commission from the governor of the state, in virtue of which he has raised a company, and has been engaged for some months past in a cruel and relentless pursuit of the Indians in this vicinity, slaughtering miscellaneously all with whom he comes in contact, without regard to age or sex. . . ."[34] Browne then graphically described the atrocities: "In the history of Indian races I have seen nothing so cruel and relentless as the treatment of these unhappy people by the authorities constituted by law for their protection." The treasury agent continued: "Instead of receiving aid and succor, they have been starved and driven away from the reservations, and then followed into their remote hiding places where they sought to die in peace, and cruelly slaughtered, till but few are left, and that few without hope."[35]

Browne suggested that "nothing short of military force could restrain the settlers" and save the Indians from destruction.[36]

At times the militia, not just the settlers, played a direct part in the genocide. In the early spring of 1853, Colonel Ethan Allen Hitchcock of the Second United States Infantry, later Union general during the Civil War, reported to the Adjutant General of the United States about the Indian war in northern California. A contingent of Indians was invited into the camp of Captain Ben Wright under a white flag to negotiate a peace; instead, the Indians were set upon and thirty-eight were killed in a planned trap. Wright took their scalps and later "was received with a general welcome by the local citizens of Yreka [Eureka]."[37]

The mass murder of Indians in this decade was well known in Washington and led to the federal "solution" of creating reservations in the region, including Nome Lackee (1854), Mendocino (1855), Klamath (1855), and Round Valley (1856)—which did little to stop the violence from intensifying there and elsewhere. Unauthorized white-owned businesses were established on the reservations; these included a sawmill which adversely affected salmon fishing on the Mendocino Reservation. At Round Valley Reservation, squatters literally overran the place, and, by the end of the decade, four-fifths of the reservation was in white hands.[38] By 1861, William P. Dole, the commissioner of Indian affairs, wrote in his annual report about the events taking place in Humboldt and Mendocino counties, that the "crimes that are committed in the wake" present "a picture of the perversion of power and of cruel wrong, from which humanity instinctively recoils." Dole continued: "This so-called 'Indian war' appears to be a war in which the whites alone are engaged. The Indians are hunted like wild and dangerous beasts of prey; the parents are 'murdered,' and the children 'kidnapped.'"[39]

Despite Commissioner Dole's concerns, Interior Department personnel were participants in the crimes taking place in northern California. A new height of graft was established by Colonel Thomas J. Henley, the postmaster of San Francisco, who in 1854 was appointed Superintendent of California Indians. Henley's disregard for his charges included his selling off cattle herds intended to provide food for the starving Indians, allowing his sons and other partners to establish illegal businesses on the reservations at Nome Lackee and Mendocino, and permitting white squatters to overrun the Round Valley Reservation.[40] To justify his actions, Henley insisted that the solution to the "Indian problem" was to refuse to allow the feeding of any Indian off the reservation which he deemed "injurious to the policy of colonization, as contemplated by the system now in operation."[41] Despite criticisms of his actions from 1855 onward, Henley retained his office until the late spring of 1859, by backing up squatters' claims and by having powerful allies in Sacramento and Washington.[42]

Nor were underlings in the Interior and War departments alone in their involvement in the crimes. The top echelons of the United States government at times abdicated responsibility in keeping order. While atrocities were frequently reported to them, the United States Army high command refused to budge, insisting that the federal government had no exclusive jurisdiction in the matter.[43] General John E. Wool, a hero of the Mexican War who later headed the Eighth Corps of the Union Army, insisted in 1856 that since "California is in no respect considered an Indian country," the military had no control of whites or Indians there. He maintained that California state laws applied even in the case where whites kidnapped "from the reserve one or more squaws, or one or more Indian children."[44]

By 1860, California state militia in cooperation with federal troops forced many of the Indians onto nine temporary enclaves in the northern part of the state. Militia troops hunted down the Indians while federal troops guarded the prisoners, an understanding worked out by the Indian superintendent. Yet even with this federal presence, Indian crops continued to be burned and Indian women continued to be kidnapped. Congress, which had never ratified eighteen treaties guaranteeing California Indians lands, later reimbursed the state for bonds California issued in the hunting of Indians during the decade of the 1850s.[45]

By 1860, American Indians' apprehension about the future was not simply caused by the genocidal events happening in northern

California. In 1854, the United States Congress, in the Kansas-Nebraska Act, had sharply reduced the size of Indian Territory by creating Kansas and Nebraska territories. This landmark legislation stimulated the further settlement of the Trans-Mississippi West and, with it, led to sectional violence between pro-slavery and abolitionist forces. White settlement and railroad politics also resulted in calls by Governor Robert J. Walker of Kansas Territory and James K. Lane, the most prominent Republican ally of Lincoln in Kansas and later senator from that state, for removal of the Indians to lands south of Kansas. "Bleeding Kansas" from 1856 onward was not merely a mini-Civil War between pro-Northern and pro-Southern forces; a new era of frontier violence and intimidation, especially directed at the Indians of eastern Kansas, was also occurring and aimed at forcing the Indians out of the region from Kansas City to Topeka.

During the presidential campaign of 1860, William H. Seward, the powerful Republican governor of New York State, delivered a major speech, "The National Idea: Its Perils and Triumphs," in Chicago on October 3. Calling for an end to the "irrepressible conflict" of sectionalism by urging voters to support the free soil creed of the Republican Party, Seward insisted that the destiny of the country rested with the "people of the great west." He labeled Chicago, the upstart railroad center, the "last and most wonderful of all marvelous creations of civilization in North America." Seward maintained that for the overall betterment of the country, the "Indian territory, also, south of Kansas must be vacated by the Indians."[46] Hence, in the governor's mind, as was true of most major Democrat and Republican leaders of the day, America's idea of progress had no place for Indians. The speech and Seward's subsequent appointment to be Lincoln's secretary of state did not allay Indian fears of further land cessions and/or removals.

The unsettling world of the American Indian was made even more precarious with the secession crisis and the creation of two American nations by February, 1861. Two veterans of the Indian Wars—Lincoln and Jefferson Davis—were now in charge of their respective nations. Although Lincoln saw no combat duty in the

Black Hawk War of 1832, he had volunteered for frontier service. Lincoln, who had little contact with American Indians, often highlighted his record as a captain in the Black Hawk War, despite his brief and uneventful service. Overall, in the years before entering the White House, Lincoln "apparently never challenged the American consensus on the necessity for Indian removal to make way for white progress."[47] To American Indians, there was nothing in Lincoln's background to assure them fairness and an improvement of Indian policies.

Davis, Lincoln's fellow Kentuckian, had had more involvement with American Indian affairs. The Confederate President could even trace his genealogy back to the great Powhatan chieftain Opechancanough of early seventeenth-century Virginia. A graduate of West Point, Davis had served seven years on the frontier, removing squatters from Indian lands in Michigan. Yet he had also been a second lieutenant in a company of dragoons in the Black Hawk War. After the Mexican War, as a major political figure with landed interests in Mississippi, Davis had pushed for Indian removal from the state. On March 27, 1850, as a member of Congress, he wrote: "It is an object of great importance to us that the Choctaws should be removed and prevented from returning" to Mississippi.[48] Later, in 1853, President Franklin Pierce appointed Davis secretary of war, at a time of growing white–Indian conflict in California. His major responsibilities in this post included substantially increasing the size of the frontier army.[49]

Thus, at a time when sectionalism was intensifying, American Indian existence was becoming more and more tenuous. The removal of eastern woodlands Indians westward and America's rush to the Pacific had created a continental nation, but at a heavy price for indigenous peoples. By incorporating Indians into the "American system" by wars of pacification, removal, extending American law and jurisdiction, and through assimilationist policies, United States' officials were not attempting to live side by side with or even understand American Indian cultures. A nation of thirty-one million people was content to ignore the land claims and overall wishes of several hundred thousand Indians in its rush headlong to fill in what it considered to be its physiognomic destiny. The Indian nations were slowly becoming aliens in their own land.

Now with the election of Lincoln, they were caught between two fires which threatened totally to bring down their universe. Nowhere was this tension more clearly apparent than among eastern woodlands Indians—Delaware and Cherokee—who had earlier been removed to the Trans-Mississippi West. Each had to develop the leadership and survival strategies to deal with the whirlwind caused by talk and threats of secession, not an easy objective as the conflagration began to heat up in the spring of 1861.

Part One

The Trans-Mississippi West

2

Union Scouts and Home Guards

The Delaware of the Western Border

By MID-CENTURY, WELL OVER EIGHTY THOUSAND AMERICAN INDIANS, mostly agriculturalists, had been uprooted from their eastern homelands and removed to the Trans-Mississippi West. Although the most famous of these Indians were members of the Five Civilized Tribes of the Southeast—the Cherokee, Choctaw, Chickasaw, Creek, and Seminole—many other smaller and less powerful groups were also placed on lands west of the ninety-fifth meridian. These included the Cayuga, Delaware, Seneca, and Shawnee, Indian communities that had been "relocated" from the Northeast during the 1830s. Not only did these northeastern and southeastern Indian peoples have to overcome the psychological trauma of removal and adjustment to a new homeland, but they also had to contend with an almost equal number of buffalo-hunting Indians of the Plains, including the powerful Arapaho, Cheyenne, Comanche, Kiowa, and Pawnee. The newcomers, nineteenth-century eastern refugees, had little in common with the nomadic traditions of the Plains, resulting in tense relations between the two groups. Many of these eastern Indians in the West had to adjust constantly to their new Indian and non-Indian neighbors and/or cut deals with Washington in order to survive. No better ex-

17

ample of this strategy of survival can be found than the Delaware Indians of eastern Kansas and southwestern Indian Territory on the eve of the Civil War.

The Delaware of Kansas and Indian Territory were largely pro-Union Indians who contributed significantly to the federal war effort in the Trans-Mississippi West. They primarily served as scouts and home guards. Four of their number—Black Beaver, Captain Falleaf [Fall Leaf], Ben Simon, and Jim Ned—are well-chronicled in the records of the war. The Delaware, much like other American Indians, including their Wisconsin relatives the Stockbridge, chose to volunteer for Union service because of their precarious existence. Their tragic history since the arrival of the Europeans led to these Indians' peripatetic existence right through the Civil War.

The Delaware, also known as Lenape, Munsee, Stockbridge, or Unami, are originally a Middle Atlantic coastal people, who once lived in an area stretching from Delaware Bay in the south to the Mid-Hudson River Valley of New York in the north and from western Long Island in the east to the second branch of the Delaware River in the west. These Indians' existence was frequently undermined by disease, wars, and colonial, state, and federal policies.[1] Delaware communities were on numerous occasions uprooted and moved further and further west right through the post-Civil War era.

Although a significant portion of the Delaware fought against the Americans during the French and Indian War, Pontiac's Rebellion, the American Revolution, and the War of 1812, an equal if not greater number joined the Americans as allies.[2] They served as scouts for Roger's Rangers in the French and Indian War; received commendations from George Washington for their heroism during the American Revolution; signed the first Indian treaty of alliance with the fledgling United States in 1778; helped the Americans against Tecumseh in the War of 1812; joined the United States army fighting Florida's Indians in the Second Seminole War in the 1830s; and aided the American cause in the Mexican War. Delaware and Stockbridge leaders such as Captain George White Eyes in the 1770s and Captain Hendrick Aupaumut in 1812, sought cooperation as a survival strategy. As dependent peoples who realized they had little power to resist the Americans, some of their chiefs developed an accommodationist strategy, often cutting deals in order to insure tribal survival as a people. As a result, they often were forced to agree to migrate to new lands, hoping that one day they would be left alone to rebuild their nation.[3]

In the nineteenth century, the Delawares were constantly forced to adjust to new surroundings in order to survive as a people. They were also often recruited by Americans to serve as go-betweens and cultural mediators with other Indians, who were less disposed to deal peacefully with the "Long Knives." Moreover, because of their long experience in the fur trade dating back to the early seventeenth century, the Delaware were hired as trappers in the Rocky Mountains by the American Fur Company after the War of 1812. In the 1840s, after the decline of the Rocky Mountain fur trade, they were hired as Indian interpreters as well as guides for the emigrant wagon trains on the overland trail west.[4]

While individual Delaware were busy in these entrepreneurial pursuits, American policymakers were busy removing their communities. Their migrations read as a disorganized road map of the North American heartland: Ohio, Indiana, Missouri, Texas, Indian Territory, Kansas, Wisconsin, Ontario. By the 1820s, American officials had resettled the largest body of Delaware along the James Fork, the major tributary of the White River in the Ozarks of southwestern Missouri. As a result of the swampy nature of this environment and incursions by the Osage who claimed this land as their own, some of the Delaware left the region during the same decade and settled in eastern Texas along the Sabine River, after receiving an invitation to do so by the Mexican government. These Delaware became known as the "Absentee Band." Later, after allying themselves with the United States' cause in the Mexican War, they were rewarded for service with lands along the Brazos River in Texas in 1853; however, white Texans, in part as a reaction to Comanche raids in this region, soon initiated a movement to expel all Indians from the state. In 1859, at the urging of the Texans, the United States officials removed these Absentee Delaware from their lands in Texas and transplanted them to the "Leased District," in the Wichita Indian Agency in Indian Territory near present Anandarko, Oklahoma, the site of a contemporary Delaware Indian community. By 1860, nearly five hundred Delawares were living within the Wichita Agency on the north side of the Washita River on Sugar Tree Creek.[5]

The majority of the Delaware in southwestern Missouri, after signing a treaty with the federal government in September, 1829, exchanged their lands for nearly two million acres in eastern Kansas, then part of the Indian Territory, in the environs of Fort Leavenworth, the first military outpost in the immediate region. Besides providing the Delaware with rich farm and pasture lands along the Kaw River, American officials pledged the "faith of the government to guarantee to the said Delaware Nation forever, the quiet and peaceful possession and undisturbed enjoyment of the same against the claims and assaults of all and every other people whatsoever."[6] For the next quarter century, the Delaware flourished in Kansas largely as a result of the richness of their lands and their excellence as ranchers, breeding excellent horses, cattle, sheep, and hogs. Their population swelled as a result of Delaware migrations from Missouri, Wisconsin, and even Ontario; however, this tribal renaissance was to come to a sudden halt in the 1850s when Kansas became center stage for sectional white politics. Eventually, as a result of four scandalous treaties written, signed, and ratified between May 1854 and July 1866, the Delaware were dispossessed of their Kansas lands. These Kansas Delaware, the so-called "Registered Delaware," also known as Cherokee Delaware, were removed for the last time in 1867—to their present community near Dewey, Oklahoma—on allotted lands obtained from the Cherokee Nation.[7]

In the 1850s, the Delawares in Kansas faced a repetition of what had happened to them in New York, Pennsylvania, Ohio, and Indiana. With the Gold Rush in California, a massive migration westward began. The debate over organizing the northern part of Indian Territory began in 1853, culminating the following year in the creation of two territories—Kansas and Nebraska. Under this Kansas-Nebraska Act, the people of both territories were to decide for themselves about whether to accept or reject slavery. Opponents and proponents of the extension of slavery attempted to colonize Kansas and win the day through force; this sectionalism and the resulting mini-civil war known as "Bleeding Kansas" obscured what was happening to American Indians and their lands in the eastern part of Kansas Territory.

The Delaware were prohibited by treaty and by congressional acts to sell their lands to anyone except the federal government. Even before new treaty negotiations and new congressional legislation, land speculators as well as homesteaders were already lining up to get at the Delaware estate. By 1854, building lots were laid out on Indian lands near Leavenworth, even before a new Delaware federal treaty was signed and before land companies had obtained legal title to the property. Other towns, specifically Lawrence and Topeka, were soon founded in this manner. By the time of the South's secession in 1860–1861, Leavenworth had a population of five thousand non-Indian people and town officials had ambitious plans to make it the leading city west of St. Louis.[8]

The Delaware were faced with increasing numbers of intruders, squatters, and even horse thieves. Aggressive traders encouraged Delaware indebtedness and plied alcohol into the community. By 1857, over one thousand whites were trespassing on Delaware lands.[9] The following year, Delaware leaders complained to President James Buchanan: "Since the opening of the Territory, thieves (white men) have come in and are constantly stealing our horses, and in many instances have stripped some of our people of almost everything they owned."[10] To make matters worse for the Indians, railroad promoters saw that the most practical freight route through Kansas Territory ran directly through Delaware lands. This was some of the choicest farm and ranch lands in Kansas.[11]

The Delaware were unable to withstand these pressures. From 1854 onward, tribal leaders who included members of the Conner, Journeycake, Ketcham, and Sarcoxie families, agreed to repeated concessions. Labeled by their political enemies as "government chiefs," these tribal leaders put their names on the four treaties made between 1854 and 1866. To be sure, the Delaware in eastern

Kansas were extremely divided during the chaos of the 1850s and 1860s. They came to Kansas from different refugee communities in the Midwest, spoke two dialects of the Delaware language—Munsee and Unami—and practiced different religious traditions—Baptist, Presbyterian, Mormon, Moravian, and the Delaware traditional religion known as the "Big House." Sadly, the Delaware's fractionated existence and the growing power of the territory's land and railroad interests combined to make eastern Kansas's tribal lands ripe for the taking.[12]

In the Treaty of 1854, the Delaware ceded a tract of more than one million acres for $10,000 distributed in equal shares to five Delaware chiefs. This questionable agreement allowed the President to sell these lands at public auction. The Delaware kept a strip, the "diminished reserve" forty miles long and ten miles wide. By 1860, railroad interests eyed even these diminished reserve lands. In two treaties in 1860 and 1861, the Delaware agreed to the allotment of their diminished reserve. Every man, woman, and child was to be allocated a certain plot of land of eighty acres. After allocations were made for a mill, schoolhouse, store, churches, as well as for lands for Absentee Delawares, the remaining unallocated lands were to be sold off to the Leavenworth, Pawnee and Western Railroad, later consolidated with the Union Pacific Railroad, for no less than $1.25 per acre.[13] Important to note, the Delaware leadership was supplied with alcohol during the negotiations and bribed with fee simple tracts ranging from 320 to 640 acres, far in excess of the average allotment. T. B. Sykes, the Indian agent, Senator James Lane, the most prominent Kansas politico, and the House of Ewing, the major traders with the Indians, all made a financial killing with these treaties.[14]

At first glance, under these circumstances, one would hardly expect the Delaware to greet the Civil War as an opportunity for anything other than the hope that the whites would destroy each other. Yet, out of a total of 201 eligible Delaware males between eighteen and forty-five years of age in 1862, 170 had volunteered for service in the Union Army.[15] Nevertheless, it was precisely these uncertain conditions faced by both the Absentee Delaware in southwestern Indian Territory and the Registered Delaware of eastern Kansas that led them to enlist in the Union war effort. To a small, weak, and often removed Indian nation, the strategy of currying favor with the "Great Father" in Washington was the only survival option open to them. Tribal survival, not antislavery or other moral principles, made enlistment a necessity, even though they were joining in with local civilian and military personnel in Kansas who desired the Indians' removal. The "option" was also made more palatable when prominent Delaware were given commissions and/or were authorized to raise their own companies of Indian "volunteers."

In 1862, Frank Johnson, the Indian agent for the Delaware Agency, claimed that the Delaware's high enlistment rates were a direct result of "a patriotism unequaled in the history of the country." The culturally myopic agent called them "wild and untutored" people, but added that a Delaware "fully appreciates and understands the merits of the war, which are *alive to his own interest, the interests of his own tribe*, and the country. The Delaware volunteers are commanded by officers chosen by themselves of the tribe" (emphasis mine).[16]

The reasons for their involvement in the Union war effort are clearly evident in the lives of four famous Delaware. The most prominent Delaware Indian in North America in 1860 was Black Beaver [Suck-tum-mah-kway]. He was by far the most accomplished Indian scout before the Civil War. Black Beaver was born in Belleville, Illinois in 1806. From 1824 onward, his name appears frequently in the historical record. In 1834, he served as a guide and an interpreter for General Henry Leavenworth as well as an interpreter for Colonel Richard Dodge's councils with the Comanche, Kiowa, and Wichita Indians on the upper Red River. For ten years in the 1830s and 1840s, Black Beaver was an employee of the American Fur Company.[17] In the era of the mountain men, he "visited nearly every point of interest within the limits of our unsettled territory. He had set his traps and spread his blanket upon the headwaters of the Missouri and Columbia; and his wanderings had led him south of the Colorado and Gila and thence to the shores of the Pacific in Southern California."[18]

When the Rocky Mountain fur trade declined in the 1840s, Black Beaver turned to guiding wagon trains westward. He also guided the expeditions of the naturalist painter John Audubon. During the Mexican War at San Antonio, he raised a company of Delaware and Shawnee Indians, Beaver's Spy Company—Indian—Texas Mounted Volunteers. As the captain of the company, he served under General William S. Harney's command during the fighting. After the war, Black Beaver continued to serve the United States Army under contract as a scout.[19]

From the late 1840s through the mid 1860s, Randolph Marcy, the prominent explorer of the Southwest and Union general in the Civil War, publicized the exploits of Black Beaver as well as those of lesser known Delaware scouts. His frequent references to and praise of Black Beaver, whom he dubbed "the great Delaware," provide a valuable portrait of the Indian scout. According to Marcy's journals, the Delaware was a "meagre-looking man of middle size, and his long black hair framed in a face that was clever, but which bore a melancholy expression of sickness and sorrow. . . ." Marcy claimed that Black Beaver, his ideal of an Indian scout, spoke English, French, and eight separate Indian languages, had seen the Pacific Ocean seven times, and served the Americans in three wars "bringing back many a scalp."[20] In Marcy's writings, Black Beaver was described as a "cosmopolite," as a modest, "resolute, determined, and fearless warrior," and as a "competent" guide.[21]

Marcy frequently praised his famous scout and recommended that his readers planning overland travel "secure the services of the best guides and hunters, and I know of none who are superior to the Delawares and Shawnee Indians." He compared them favorably to the Khebirs, the guides who "escort the caravans across the great desert of Sahara."[22] Because of their skills, Marcy also insisted that they and other "civilized Indians" such as the Cherokee, Chickasaw, Choctaw, and Creek should be employed by American officials as "formidable partisan warriors against nomadic tribes of the Plains" since they were "intermediate social links in the chain of civilization."[23]

Despite this Anglo-Saxon supremacist tone, the explorer hit on a key, namely the niche that the Delaware used to survive on the frontier. They served as go-betweens—interpreters, guides, and allies of the United States—in the unstoppable push of a New World colossus to the Pacific slope. By the 1850s, Black Beaver and other Delaware were employed at Forts Arbuckle and Cobb as guides and interpreters by military officials as well as by the various Indian agents. They were employed in "pacifying" the frontier, hunting down Comanches and other Southern Plains raiders from northern Texas. Black Beaver was also used to convince other Indians such as the Caddo and Wichita to sign peace treaties and take up residence at Indian agencies rather than commit themselves to hopeless conflict against the omnipotent "Long Knives." Such was his role in the early spring of 1861 when the Civil War erupted.[24]

In need of troops in the East and realizing that Indian Territory was surrounded by secessionist states, federal officials ordered an evacuation of United States army personnel from Indian Territory in the spring of 1861. Many Indian departmental officials, agency employees, and traders in Indian Territory, including those at the Wichita Agency, were largely Confederate sympathizers from Arkansas and Texas. Moreover, a significant portion of the Five Civilized Tribes were slaveholders. Many Indians in the region also suspected, after the speech by Seward in the presidential campaign of 1860, that Lincoln was intent on opening up or reducing Indian Territory. Other Indians were annoyed at the evacuation and abandonment of American posts in Indian Territory because the action violated existing treaties with the newly resettled eastern Indian nations which guaranteed them military protection against Plains Indians, most notably the Comanches, and non-Indian marauders.[25]

In the winter of 1861, Black Beaver, well into his fifties, was leading a respected and comfortable life at Fort Washita in the Wichita Agency, after moving from the Brazos two years earlier. According to the local Indian agent, Black Beaver had the most substantial residence on the reservation, "a pretty good double log house, with two shed rooms in rear, a porch in front and two fireplaces, and a field of forty-one and a half acres inclosed with a good stake-and-rider fence, thirty-six and a half of which have been cultivated."[26] He was gainfully employed at the time as the interpreter for the Wichita, working for Matthew Leeper, the Indian agent.[27] With the Confederate firing on Fort Sumter, things changed swiftly, and Unionists in Indian Territory found themselves worrying about a Confederate invasion from secessionist Arkansas or Texas.

On April 16, the Union quickly abandoned Fort Washita and withdrew north under the command of Colonel William H. Emory. After concentrating his forces at nearby Fort Cobb, Emory then moved his troops against a Confederate advance guard of William W. Averell's Texas Mounted Rifles. According to Emory, Black Beaver warned him of the approaching Confederate column and "gave me the information by which I was enabled to capture the enemy's advance guard, the first prisoners captured in the war." The Delaware scout then guided Emory's forces and his Confederate prisoners northwest to Kansas. Black Beaver was the only Indian who "would consent to guide the column." The Union expedition, composed of the combined commands of Forts Arbuckle, Cobb, and Smith, the largest remaining concentration of federal troops in Indian Territory, arrived at Fort Leavenworth on May 31, after journeying through the Cherokee Strip north of present Hennessey, Oklahoma and passing through today's Bison, Waukomis, Enid, Medford, Caldwell, and Wellington. Despite this dangerous mission and the hardships of this five-hundred-mile expedition, the column arrived "without the loss of a man, horse, or wagon, although two men deserted on the journey."[28]

As a result of Black Beaver's support of the Union, Confederate officials later seized his cattle, horses, and crops and destroyed his ranch at the Wichita Agency; they also placed a contract on his head, making it impossible for him to return to the agency during the war. Until his death in 1880, Black Beaver attempted without success to secure compensation for his sizable loss, estimated at about $5,000, while in federal service as a scout.[29]

Soon after the Union abandonment of the Wichita Agency, Confederates moved in. They secured the services of Agent Leeper, an avowed secessionist and Texan who now became employed by the Confederacy in efforts to induce the Comanche, Tonkawa, Waco, and other Indians to come and settle on the reserve at Fort Washita. As early as the winter of 1861, Robert Toombs, secretary of state for the Confederacy, had proposed a resolution which was quickly submitted and passed in the Confederate Senate, authorizing President Jefferson Davis to appoint and send a special emissary to the Indian nations of Indian Territory. Albert Pike, a New Englander by birth, who had lived in Arkansas for many years, was selected to negotiate with the Indians. A military veteran of the Mexican War, Pike had served with Robert E. Lee in that conflict. He was well versed in Greek, Latin, French, Spanish, and Sanskrit, as well as several Indian languages. In Arkansas, he had become a well-known writer and attorney. Pike was soon given the title of commissioner of Indian affairs in the new Confederate Bureau of Indian Affairs. His primary responsibility was to negotiate treaties with the tribes west of Arkansas to keep them neutral and acquire their friendship for the Confederacy.[30]

Consequently, by the late spring of 1861, Pike began his efforts to negotiate with the Indians at the Wichita Agency, including a small number of Delaware, under Keh-ka-tus-tun's leadership, who remained behind after the federal evacuation of Indian Territory. By the end of May, working with Agent Leeper, Pike suggested that the Confederacy enlist the agency's Delaware, Kickapoo, and Shawnee Indians in a Confederate mounted battalion of three hundred fifty men; however, Pike and the much-despised Leeper were "playing a losing hand" since all three groups had long-standing grievances against Texans, now Confederates, and lived in mortal terror of their raids.[31] Although the Delaware and Shawnee at the agency signed a treaty of amity with the Confederacy drawn up by Pike and presented to them on August 12, few, if any, were going to serve as volunteers in the rebel army. Among those groups who signed the treaties were also the Caddo, Comanche, Tonkawa, Waco, and Wichita Indians. The Confederacy promised that the Indians were to be assured of maintaining their lands and to be provided with provisions as well as livestock and agricultural assistance. In return, the Indians pledged peaceful intentions toward the Confederacy and agreed, having little choice, to come "under the laws and protection of the Confederate States of America."[32]

Despite Pike's efforts, Black Beaver and most Delawares collaborated with the Union throughout the war both in Indian Territory and in Kansas. As early as September, 1861, Black Beaver's name was evoked by Union officials seeking to win support from Tusaqueh, the Wichita chief, as well as other leaders in the southern part of Indian Territory. Union Indian agent E. H. Carruth invited the Wichita chief and/or his delegates to come to Kansas to meet with him: "Your friend Black Beaver will meet you here and we will drive the bad men who entered your company last spring. The Texans have killed the Wichitas: we will punish the Texans."[33] Moreover, throughout the war, both Confederate and Union dispatches indicate Black Beaver's continuing role as a valuable Union scout.[34]

Neither the Indians' strategy nor their loyalty could save them or their lands in Kansas. Their fighting reveals the magnitude of this tragedy.

The Delaware troops were involved in one of the more controversial incidents of the Civil War, the sacking of the Wichita Agency on October 23 and 24, 1862. In Union reports, this episode was glowingly reported as a major Union victory, one that demonstrated Delaware "loyalty, daring and hardihood."[35] In Confederate reports, the attack was presented as nothing more than a vicious massacre of other Indians and Confederate Indian agency personnel, perpetrated by Indian marauders and deserters from the Union army.[36] To the historian Annie Abel, it was "one of the bloodiest scenes ever enacted on the western plains" carried out by "good-for-nothing or vicious" Indians.[37]

A Union cavalry of one hundred ninety-six men—one hundred Southern Kickapoo, seventy Delaware, and twenty-six Shawnee—left Fort Leavenworth in the first days of October, 1862, on a five-hundred-mile expedition to the Wichita Agency. Supplying their own horses and provisions, they had one objective: exact retribution upon Confederate officials and Confederate-allied Indians at the Wichita Indian agency.[38] Although each Indian contingent had its own leadership, the overall Union command of the expedition fell to Captain Ben Simon, a Delaware. A Rocky Mountain fur trapper by profession, Simon had long experience as a guide and scout and had even been employed by Brigham Young and the Mormon community while working in the Great Basin.[39] His leadership qualities were apparent since, as early as 1864, he was being referred to in Delaware Indian petitions as a "chief."[40]

Even before the attack, the Union force had employed scouts and spies who infiltrated the Wichita Agency. Through the cooperation of Indian friends there, they were able to take the agency back largely by surprise in the late evening of October 23. In the attack, they killed Agent Leeper and four other Confederate Indian agency personnel; one Delaware was killed and one Shawnee was wounded. They then proceeded to take booty—the rebel flag, $1,200 in Confederate money, one hundred ponies, and Confederate correspondence— original documents including Pike's treaties with the nations of Indian Territory.[41] Simon's force then burned the agency building along with the five dead agency personnel.

The next morning, the Union-allied Indians went after the Confederate-allied Tonkawa Indians at the agency. They relentlessly tracked them down and trapped them at noon in a blackjack thicket along the Washita River. Approximately half of the Tonkawa nation, one hundred thirty-seven people, were killed, including the Tonkawa chief, Placido, twenty-three warriors, and over a hundred women and children. The better-armed Southern Kickapoo, Delaware, and Shawnee suffered twenty-seven casualties. The official Confederate report of the massacre indicated that the "excuse" for this bloodletting was that the Tonkawa had "sided with whites against the Indians some time ago in Texas."[42] The Confederate report was an accurate one. The Southern Kickapoo had a deep-seated hatred for these Indians. Tonkawa scouts for the Texans, longtime enemies of the Kickapoo, had reported their movements in 1859 and 1860. Besides the Tonkawa's refusal to fight Texans, the Southern Kickapoo resented the "insolent behavior of the Wichitas, Caddoes and Tonkawas toward them" when the Kickapoo refused to sign a treaty of alliance with Pike and the Confederacy in August, 1861.[43]

Whether as comrades-in-arms or as witnesses to this massacre, the Delaware and Shawnee must take some of the blame for this Kickapoo-led atrocity. A sad irony is apparent. Although they frequently played the role of "civilized" Indians, worthy human beings who should be rewarded by the Great Father with permanent homes without the threat of further removal, they now sank to the depths of "barbarism" as allies of the North and with official Union sanction. Perhaps an even greater irony is apparent in the Civil War military career of Captain Falleaf, a third Delaware Indian scout. This famous traditionalist found himself in the uncomfortable position of fighting side by side in the Union army with the same Kansas politicians who were lusting over the Delaware tribal estate.

Captain Falleaf or Fall Leaf [Panipakuxwe or "he who walks when leaves fall"] was second only to Black Beaver in his fame in the Delaware community. A former scout, he was a major force in the Delaware community in Kansas. Unlike Black Beaver and many of the Delaware leaders in Kansas who were Baptists or his friend Ben Simon who was a Mormon, Falleaf clung to the traditional Native American religion, the Delaware Big House. More than any other Delaware in the period, he articulated the complaints about "government chiefs" and about the Delaware's precarious status. Falleaf was also responsible for raising Company D of the Second Kansas Indian Home Guard, a unit of eighty-six Delawares who served in the Union army in 1862 during the first federal attempt to capture the Indian Territory.[44]

As in Black Beaver's case, Falleaf's leadership skills were honed as a guide, interpreter, and trapper. For many years, he had faithfully served the white man in his quest for furs, gold, and land in the uncharted regions of the Trans-Mississippi West. He also served the interests of the frontier army from time to time. In 1858, Falleaf had been employed as guide for seven companies of soldiers under the command of Colonel Edwin V. Sumner in their military expedition against the Cheyenne. The next year, he once again served as a guide, this time for three companies of soldiers under the command of Major John Sedgwick. A longtime associate of the famous explorer, John C. Fremont, who frequently hired the Delaware for his major topographical surveys of the American West, Falleaf was instructed in the fall of 1861 by the "Great Pathfinder" to raise a company of Indians for the Union army and proceed on a special mission to Springfield, Missouri. The scout recruited fifty-four Delaware Indians and guided them from Sedalia to Springfield—without being spotted by Confederates.[45]

Falleaf's opposition to the Delaware leadership was manifest throughout the war. He and other Delaware of his faction petitioned the Interior Department, insisting they "want to live as before." He claimed that the "halfbreeds are ruining our people by making white man's law in our nation." Protesting the allotment and sale of Delaware lands under the treaties of 1860 and 1861, he urged that Washington officials allow his people to hold their "lands in common even if we move."[46] Three weeks later, Falleaf's faction once again petitioned: "We wish to live together as a Nation according to our former customs—we wish to have chiefs of our own selection—men who will take care of the poor people—of the women and children and of the interests of the whole tribe." He insisted that his Delaware community be allowed to act independently: "We want men who can act for themselves—now when the 'Braves' ask the Chiefs *'what did you do this for,'* they answer 'Government forced us to do so.'"[47]

After the defeat of Confederate forces at the Battle of Pea Ridge in early March, 1862, William P. Dole, commissioner of Indian affairs, recommended that the war department detail two regiments of volunteers and two thousand loyal Indians from Kansas to go with thousands of impoverished refugee Indians back to their homes in Indian Territory. Within a week, Dole's recommendation was accepted. Although some strongly opposed arming these Indians and there was turnover in command, plans for a federal invasion of Indian Territory, the "Indian Expedition," were now placed in motion. On May 2, 1862, General James G. Blunt was placed in command of the Department of Kansas. Blunt endorsed the plan to use two Indian regiments as guerrillas in the expedition, sped up the organization as well as the departure date for their invasion, and chose Colonel William Weer of the Tenth Kansas Infantry as the commander of the invasion.[48] The enrollment of the ten companies of the first regiment—the First Kansas Indian Home Guards—was rapidly filled with Creek and Seminole; however, the second regiment—Colonel John Ritchie's Second Kansas Indian Home Guards—was delayed. Ritchie had gone south to recruit Osage, and internal bureaucratic feuding of local Indian office personnel retarded efforts at recruitment. Part of the problem was also that the Second Kansas Indian Home Guard was more heterogenous in make-up, composed of Delaware, Kickapoo, Osage, Shawnee, Seneca, and members of some of the Five Civilized Tribes.[49]

Falleaf's Company D, Second Kansas Indian Home Guard, was an eighty-six-man mounted unit which employed their own steeds and which was a component of the Union Indian Brigade. With Falleaf's help, Ritchie recruited the Indians at Big Creek and Five Mile Creek, Kansas in June, 1862. These enlisted men had interesting names, including names such as Big Buffalo, Big Beaver, Young Bear, Black Horse, Broken Knife, Yellow Leaf, Big Moccasin, Moonshine, Johnny Raccoon, Little Shanghai, Bear Skin, Soldier, Black Stump, Jim Snake, Jim Smoke, Tea Nose, Black Wing, and Whippoorwill. The recruits ranged in age from seventeen to forty-two, with the average being 28.5 years. None were killed or wounded in action, although eleven died of disease. Nine were listed as deserters in the unit's regimental books.[50]

Besides Falleaf, Delaware officers in the Second Kansas Indian Home Guard included Lieutenant John Moses, a political ally of Falleaf, and Jim Ned, a forty-five-year-old Delaware who had been a leading scout in the Trans-Mississippi West.[51] Explorer Marcy had also written about the daring exploits of Ned. This Absentee Delaware was a "remarkable specimen of humanity," a Delaware "united with a slight admixture of the African. He had a Delaware wife and adopted the habits of that tribe, but at the same time he possessed all the social vivacity and garrulity of the negro." Ned was "exceedingly sensitive upon the subject of the African element in his composition, and resorted to a variety of expedients to conceal it from strangers. . . ." Marcy claimed that he shaved "off his kinky locks" or covered his head "a la Turk." The explorer also maintained that Ned had spent much time among the "wild tribes of the Plains," most notably the Comanches. He added that the Delaware scout was "one of the expert, daring and successful horse thieves among the southwestern tribes." Black Beaver had a long-standing dislike of Ned which Marcy intimated was based in part on racial prejudice.[52]

By the time Ned received a commission in Company C of the Second Indian Home Guard, he had earned a reputation as a spy for the Union. In the late summer of 1861, he was undermining the authority of Agent Leeper and encouraging Indians to flee the Confederate-held Wichita Agency. He eventually left. Leeper, referring to him as an "unmitigated scoundrel," indicated that Ned had "forfeited" his right to live at the agency and the protection which the Confederate States had guaranteed to him. In October, Leeper, as in Black Beaver's case, ordered the Confederate military "to kill Ned should they find him." Later, in January, 1862, the Confederate Indian agent explained the origins of his vendetta against Ned. He described Ned as a troublemaker who incited the Indians of the Wichita Agency, referring to him as an "evil-disposed" person, a tattler, and a tale bearer who instilled in the Indians a "high state of excitement and alarm."[53]

The free spirit Delaware scout, a man who dared challenge the turncoat Indian agent, soon found himself *persona non grata* in Confederate Indian Territory. Leeper actually placed a contract out on his head. Consequently, Ned viewed General Blunt's First Federal Indian Expedition as retribution. Later, in the war, Ned led "jayhawking" expeditions into Indian Territory, quickly striking Confederate positions and stealing cattle, ponies, and mules, until he was ordered to cease his operations by federal officials.[54]

The First Federal Indian Expedition composed of Delawares and other Unionist Indians moved south at dawn on June 28. On July 3, Colonel Benjamin Weer's two to three hundred Union troops surprised Colonel James J. Clarkson's Confederate Missouri forces at Locust Grove. Clarkson and one hundred ten Confederates were captured, one hundred were killed, and sixty ammunition wagons and a large amount of provisions were seized. Moreover, many Confederate Indian soldiers, especially Cherokee, deserted, soon enlisting in Colonel Ritchie's Second Kansas Indian Home Guards.[55]

In a two-pronged pursuit against Confederate forces led by the Sixth Kansas Cavalry, Captain H. S. Greene's Union troops captured Tahlequah, the capital of the Cherokee Nation, on July 16; Colonel Lewis Jewell seized Fort Gibson on July 18. The latter was the supreme objective of the First Expedition. Fort Gibson was a former United States army post which controlled the Three Forks, where the Verdigris and Grand (Neosho) Rivers fed into the Arkansas River. A strategic Indian trail, part of the Texas or Fort Scott–Fort Gibson Military Road, passed across the Grand River near Fort Scott. Jewell's taking of this important link was a major Union victory.

Although Falleaf's official report is difficult to decipher because of his broken English, his company of eighty-five Delaware apparently played a key role in the Union's advance guard on Fort Gibson. Falleaf insisted: "we saw the enemy, the Chocktaw Indians, the halfbreed, we play Ball with them, 50 we laid on the ground, 60 we took prisoners, even the Chocktaw General, him I took myself alone, he was a big seresh, 100 union men he had killed, I brought him to the [Unionist] Cherokees, they killed him."[56]

The Union expedition's fortunes, however, soon changed. Exhausted by the heat and running low on salt and other supplies, it ground to a halt at Fort Gibson. Colonel Frederick Salomon, the second officer of the expedition, arrested his commanding officer, Colonel Benjamin Weer. This mutinous act was spurred by charges of Weer's habitual drunkenness, his ignoring the advice of his subordinates, neglect of duty, his insanity, and his disloyalty. Later, because Blunt dissolved the court-martial proceedings, Weer was restored to the rank of colonel.

On July 19, Colonel Salomon decided to withdraw his Union regiments from Indian Territory, leaving Indian troops on the Verdigis

River as well as along the Grand River and the fords of the Arkansas River. Despite subsequent efforts by Union Colonel William A. Phillips to carry out this duty, he was unable to stop Stand Watie's Confederate forays and William C. Quantrill's plundering sweep into the Cherokee Nation. By the fall of 1862, the situation in Indian Territory was even more chaotic than before the First Federal Indian Expedition.

After this fiasco, the Second Indian Home Guard participated in Blunt's Union campaign in Missouri and Arkansas. Attached to the Department of Kansas, they engaged the enemy at Shirley's Ford, Spring River, Missouri on September 20. The regiment lost between twelve and twenty men and nine men were wounded. During and after the battle, Ritchie was unable to control his own men. For some unknown reason, the Indians in the Second Kansas Indian Home Guard began fighting with other Union troops in Colonel Weer's brigade. Later, Ritchie blamed the confusion on a "Bull Run retreat," caused by a stampede of fifteen hundred women and children who had crowded into camp for protection.[57] Ritchie was strongly reprimanded and "was reported upon for dismissal from service."[58]

Before his dismissal, Ritchie had given Falleaf a medical furlough to go home. When Falleaf left for Kansas, his men soon followed him. To these Delaware, war party leadership took precedence over any and all Union military regulations. The men were classified as deserters. For over a year after, Falleaf, aided by the Delaware Indian agent in Kansas, attempted to straighten out the mess. After being denied reentry in the Second Kansas Indian Home Guards by General Blunt, many of his same men were later accepted for service in the Sixth and Fourteenth Kansas Cavalry.[59]

Falleaf's and the Delaware Nation's involvement in the Civil War waned from late 1863 onward. In fact, he and the Delaware Nation as a whole by that time had more to worry about than fighting Confederates. Despite frequent promises by Sumner, Sedgwick, Fremont, and Ritchie about military bounties or other compensation for services, the Delaware, as late as December, 1863, insisted that they had not been paid. In eastern Kansas, Delaware had to contend with various pressures, including threats to their civilian population. At the end of 1863, Falleaf requested "about 200 guns, with powder and lead, so that we may be ready in case any danger arises at any time."[60]

Life for the Delawares in Kansas deteriorated during the war. Their lands, which prior to the conflict were subject to the invasion of whites—traders, squatters, land speculators, and railroadmen—were now being overrun by fifteen to seventeen thousand tribesmen fleeing Indian Territory. Ten percent of these refugees were to die as a result of unfit or inadequate food supplies as well as a lack of clothing and shelter. Besides frostbite, Indians suffered from measles, mumps, diphtheria, and pneumonia. Later, smallpox hit in fury.[61]

The situation was further exacerbated by the actions of Quantrill, the border ruffian who served himself as much if not more than the Confederacy. Quantrill trained and sent out bushwackers and guerrilla fighters, destroying property, stealing livestock, and butchering civilian populations until he was killed in 1865. As a nineteenth-century terrorist, Quantrill had few peers in spreading violence and destruction. Although commissioned by the Confederates to harass Union border settlements in Kansas and Missouri and to counter jayhawkers, Quantrill at times attacked Confederate settlements as well, and his operations ranged from northern Texas to Lawrence, Kansas. At times, Quantrill hid among the citizens of Lawrence under the alias "Charley Hart," claiming he had been hired by the Delaware Indians to recover their stolen horses, which only furthered resentment toward these Unionist Indians. According to one source, White Turkey, a Delaware scout and trapper, pursued Quantrill after his famous raid on Lawrence in August, 1863, picking off some of his men and bringing back their scalps.[62]

Writing in September, 1863, John G. Pratt, the Indian agent of the Central Superintendency, described the Delaware's plight as follows: "The Delawares are affected by the unsettled condition of the country. Many of them are in the army. Their families are consequently left without male assistance. The large children are withdrawn to labor at home."[63] In the same year, one hundred twenty-four

Delawares filed for compensation for property damage totaling $17,588.25—stolen cattle, horses, hogs, and hay—that were allegedly taken by white men.[64]

The Delaware's continued residence in Kansas became even more unsafe by 1864. In the summer of that year, a full-scale "Indian scare" soon spread through every white community in Kansas. Kiowa and Comanche began raiding Kansas along the Santa Fe Trail, while Cheyenne and Arapaho attacked from the north. These raids, mostly on stagecoaches and horse stations, crippled their operations well into 1865 and sent panic throughout the Sunflower State.[65]

It is little wonder that the young Delaware men in the Sixth Kansas Cavalry, many of whom had earlier served with Captain Falleaf in the Second Kansas Indian Home Guard during the First Federal Indian Expedition, deserted in droves in the last year of the war.[66] Serving the white man and the strategy of Delaware accommodation just went so far. Protecting one's home and family took precedence over hunting down the elusive Stand Watie, whose raids intensified by 1864.

At the end of the conflict, Interior Department officials advocated the immediate removal of the Delaware from the entire state of Kansas.[67] Long before Washington officials finalized these plans, the Delaware themselves came to the conclusion that their days in Kansas were numbered and they once again had to uproot themselves in order to survive. By the spring of 1864, different groups of Delaware requested meetings with the "Great Father" in Washington about the possibilities of purchase and resettlement of lands in Indian Territory, the Great Basin, or even in the Rockies.[68] Discussions also centered on the possibility of the Delawares moving to the Cherokee Nation in the northeastern part of Indian Territory.[69]

On July 4, 1866, the Delaware council, led by many of the same families who profited by signing the earlier three treaties, sold all their nation's remaining property in Kansas. Once again, the cozy relationship between "government chiefs," Kansas politicians and traders, railroad officials—now the Union Pacific Eastern Division and the Missouri River Railroad—and Washington policymakers and bureaucrats sealed the deal. Included in the profiteering were the Delaware's so-called "friend," General John C. Fremont, now a railroad magnate, and J. P. Usher, former commissioner of Indian affairs. The federal government agreed to pay the Delaware $2.50 an acre on behalf of the railroads. On April 8, 1867, the Delaware and Cherokee consummated an agreement in Washington, D.C. The Cherokee agreed to sell the Delaware a quantity of land east of the line of 96 degrees west longitude, equal in aggregate to one hundred sixty acres for every individual Delaware enrolled upon a register made by the Indian agent of those Indians who elected to be removed to "Indian country." Under the agreement, the Delaware paid $1 per acre for a total of 157,600 acres. They also paid the Cherokee $121,824.28 for the "privilege" of becoming full citizens of the Cherokee Nation with the same rights and immunities as native Cherokee. Nine hundred eighty-five Delaware "registered" on this enrollment list and left Kansas between 1867 and 1869 to live in the Cherokee Nation in Indian Territory.[70]

Falleaf and Ben Simon followed some of their Delaware political opponents into what is presently northeastern Oklahoma near Dewey. Falleaf clung tightly to his conservative values, maintaining the ceremonial cycle of the Big House, the Delaware traditional religion. Although no one knows if Black Beaver ever accepted Jim Ned as an equal, both men lived their lives out at Anandarko as Absentee Delawares, surrounded by Caddo in southwestern Indian Territory. In 1872, Black Beaver was the Absentee Delaware representative in an Indian delegation to Washington. He continued to play the role of the "good Indian." Visiting the Kiowa-Comanche Agency in 1874, he begged these southern Plains Indians "to stop raiding, to send their children to school, to settle down and do as their friends the Quakers wished them to do." The former rugged mountain man died in 1880, shortly after he had become a Baptist minister![71]

The strategy of accommodation had produced two communities of Delaware in Indian Territory; nevertheless, these peripatetic peoples had paid a dear price. They were now a half a continent away from their homeland. Although they had permanent residences by

Reconstruction, they had to contend with more powerful Indian nations who co-occupied the same lands. The Delaware at Dewey, in effect, were perceived by the more powerful Cherokee as anything but equals. The Delaware at Anandarko were now surrounded by more numerous communities of southern Plains Indians with distinct and sharply different languages and mores. Although they had survived their "continental drift" from the Middle Atlantic coast, they still had to depend on the "Great Father," continue to play at times the role of the "good Indian," and adjust to every new wind blowing from Washington.

The General

The Western Cherokee and the Lost Cause

ON JUNE 23, 1865, A BOWLEGGED MAN IN TATTERED CONFEDERATE gray, at the head of a small and ragged column of rebel cavalry, rode to a meeting place twelve miles west of the town of Doaksville in the Choctaw Nation in Indian Territory. This war-weary, aged soldier was Stand Watie, the legendary principal chief of the southern-allied branch of the Cherokee Nation and brigadier general of the Confederate States of America. He traveled the dusty road from Bloomdale to the environs of Doaksville that fateful day to meet with two Union officers, Lieutenant Asa C. Mathews and Adjutant William H. Vance, about the terms of Watie's surrender. The Cherokee chief handed his sword to the two officials and pledged to cease all hostilities against the United States. In addition, Watie agreed to use his influence to convince his Creek, Osage, and Seminole Indian allies to lay down their arms. This event came more than two months after Lee's surrender of his Army of Northern Virginia, and a month after E. Kirby Smith, commander of all Confederate troops west of the Mississippi, had capitulated. Indeed, Watie was one of the last Confederate generals to surrender and abandon the "lost cause."[1] His delay in ceasing hostilities was less related to his unswerving devotion to the Confederacy than to the nature of Cherokee politics.

From 1861 to 1865, the Cherokee Nation, which totaled around 21,000 members in Indian Territory, faced a civil war within the Civil War. During these years, there were two Cherokee nations in the West and each was intent on undermining and even destroying the other. Although there were significant numbers of Cherokee Unionists, especially in the Kansas Indian Home Guards, 3,000 Cherokee served in the Confederate army and anywhere between 8,500 and 13,500 sympathized with the South's war effort.[2] By 1863, Watie became principal chief of the pro-southern wing while John Ross, despite being in exile, continued to represent himself as "Principal Chief of the Cherokee Nation." Some of this internal power struggle was triggered by Confederate and Union pulls and the Civil War itself; much, however, had an older origin.

No other Native American community was more disastrously affected by the Civil War than the Cherokee Nation of Indian Territory. As a result of four years of desolation—Civil War fighting, economic displacement, refugee conditions, impoverishment, starvation, and smallpox and other epidemics—the Cherokee population in the West declined from 21,000 to 15,000 people. The war ravaged the Indian Territory with major battles fought within Cherokee Country—Caving Brooks in 1861; Cowskin Prairie, Old Fort Wayne, and Locust Grove in 1862; the First Battle of Cabin Creek and Webber's Falls in 1863; and the Second Battle of Cabin Creek in 1864. By the end of 1862, there were two thousand Cherokee refugees in the vicinity of Union-held Fort Scott, Kansas, and, by 1863, nearly seven thousand Cherokee refugees at Union-held Fort Gibson in Indian Territory. As early as 1863, one-third of married women were widows and one-fourth of the children in the nation were orphans. By the end of the war, 300,000 head of their cattle had been stolen in Civil War raids by Union and Confederate forces. In the six-month period after the war, nearly all of the surviving Cherokee were dependent on federal handouts at Fort Gibson, with $250,000 spent in relief efforts.[3]

The Civil War was the second ruination of the Cherokee Nation, the first being the removal era of the 1830s. To be sure, these two events were directly tied to each other. Importantly, Watie was directly involved in the politics of the nation during both of these critical periods in Cherokee history. Although Watie's fame rests largely with his Civil War military career—he was arguably the most successful field commander that the Confederacy had in the Trans-Mississippi West in the last year of the war—his early life in the Southeast is essential to understanding the man and the Cherokee political figure, as well as what transpired in Indian Territory from 1861 to 1865.

Watie was born on December 12, 1806 at the Cherokee town of Oothcaloga, near present day Rome, Georgia. His Indian name was Degadoga, "He Stands [on Two Feet]" and his Christian name was Isaac S. Watie. He later dropped his Christian first name and soon became known as "Stand Watie." Raised as a Moravian by his father David (Oo-wa-tie) and his mother Susanna Reese, both Cherokee, Watie, his older brother Buck, more well known as Elias Boudinot, and his younger brother Thomas were raised in comparatively well-off surroundings. They were also exposed to western ideas and educated in the white man's schools. The Watie family had large landholdings and ran a profitable ferry service on the Hightower River. Stand Watie was a member of the famous Ridge family that dominated Cherokee politics in the 1820s and early 1830s. As early as 1828, Watie, despite his youth, had already secured a position as clerk of the Cherokee Supreme Court. For more than forty years, he was to serve as a practicing attorney within the Cherokee Nation.[4]

Watie's life was soon shattered by the events that unfolded in Jacksonian America. In 1830, the Indian Removal Act authorized President Andrew Jackson to negotiate the removal of Indians to west of the Mississippi. The Cherokee Nation faced increasing pressures for removal to the West, failing in its attempt to gain enforceable protection and recognition of its lands from the federal courts in 1831 and 1832. Jackson then sent his nefarious missionary John C. Schermerhorn to negotiate a removal treaty with the Cherokee.[5]

By this time, a small group of Cherokee known as the Treaty Party had become advocates of removal, based on a variety of motives, some honest, others not. The Treaty Party was led by Major Ridge, his son John, and his nephew Elias Boudinot, who was the editor of the *Cherokee Phoenix*, the nation's newspaper. They were the counter-force to John Ross, the leading Cherokee opponent of all efforts at removal.[6] In December, 1835, about one hundred Treaty Party members and United States commissioners, including Schermerhorn, met at New Echota within the Cherokee Nation and negotiated a treaty. Despite the vast objections of the majority of the Cherokee, the Treaty of New Echota surrendered Cherokee ancestral lands in the Southeast. By agreeing to this treaty, the two Ridges as well as Thomas Watie and Elias Boudinot were also signing their death warrants since the Cherokee "law of blood" provided for the execution of officials who acceded to the unsanctioned sale of tribal lands. John and Major Ridge and Elias Boudinot were subsequently assassinated on June 22, 1839, by antiremoval forces in the Cherokee Nation's new lands in Indian Territory. In 1845, Stand Watie's brother Thomas and his friend James Starr were also assassinated in the continuing violence and retribution exacted under the Treaty of New Echota. The assassins in each instance were the son and followers of Ross, who remained Watie's major rivals right through Ross's death in 1866. Stand Watie, who was also marked for assassination since he too had signed the Treaty of New Echota, survived numerous attempts on his life. In order to survive, he organized his own military force at Beattie's Prairie and Old Fort Wayne in Indian Territory which protected him and his followers.[7]

Like the phoenix, the mythic bird in Cherokee cosmology that rises out of the ashes and is reborn every five hundred years, Stand Watie survived his death sentence. He subsequently emerged to prominence and respectability in Indian Territory. He and the surviving members of the Treaty Party allied themselves with the so-called "Old Settlers," a significant group of Cherokee who had moved from the East to Arkansas in the first decades of the nineteenth century. Although the Old Settlers had intended to settle in Arkansas permanently, they were displaced by white frontiersmen's pressures and reluctantly agreed, under a treaty of removal in 1828, to leave and settle in what is presently northeastern Oklahoma. This Old Settlers group thus preceded the arrival of Chief John Ross's antiremoval party, the so-called National Party.[8]

Arriving immediately after the Treaty of New Echota in December, 1835, Watie's Treaty Party cultivated their alliance with the Old Settlers. When the main body of the antiremoval party Cherokee arrived in 1838, the Treaty Party and its ally, the Old Settlers, resentful of being labeled "sell-outs" and considered Cherokee traitors by Ross's followers, opposed the newcomers' land rights as well as the installation of eastern Cherokee leaders, laws, and institutions. For the next seven years, the Cherokee in Indian Territory faced tribal vendettas and bloodletting that was resolved only when Watie and Ross "buried the hatchet" by shaking hands and signing the Treaty of 1846. The federal treaty recognized Ross's party's land rights in the Cherokee Nation. The treaty also pardoned all Cherokee who had committed crimes. In addition, it recognized the existence of one government and territory for the Cherokee Nation in the West.[9]

Under Ross's leadership—Ross became Principal Chief of the Cherokee Nation after the Treaty of 1846—the Cherokee in Indian Territory flourished. For the next fourteen years, during this economic revival, the Cherokee family feud subsided in efforts to rebuild the nation. By 1860, the Cherokee had 102,000 acres under cultivation, owned 240,000 cattle, 20,000 horses and mules, and 15,000 hogs. They also owned 4,000 slaves.[10]

The Civil War tore open the old wounds and revived the Ross-Watie family feud. The vendetta was revived as early as the spring of 1861, when General Albert Pike began his efforts to secure Indian allies for the Confederacy. Despite the fact that Ross, like Watie, was a major slaveholder—he owned approximately one hundred slaves—the majority of Cherokee under him owned no slaves. Some of his followers were Keetowahs, a secret organization whose roots may have been in an ancient Cherokee medicine society known as "Anikutani."[11] Ross was one-eight Cherokee by ancestry; however, the

Keetowah Society was organized for the "purpose of cultivating a national feeling among full-bloods, in opposition to the innovating tendencies of the mixed blood element."[12] This society, made up of Cherokee Christians, aimed to preserve the ancient tribal and religious rites which they feared were about to be lost. Evan Jones, a Baptist missionary with strong abolitionist sympathies, helped refound this society in 1859. From that date onward, the Keetowahs, and their associated Loyal League established during the secession crisis, were to maintain friendly relations with the United States, advocate the abolition of slavery, promote Cherokee treaty rights, and prevent any man suspected of treason against the Cherokee and the United States from gaining political office. These Indians, who numbered around five thousand [Cherokees], were also known as "Pin Cherokees" since they wore crossed pins on their coats or shirts as a sign of their membership in the Keetowah Society. Their goal was also to counter the efforts of Watie and his supporters. Despite Ross's ownership of numerous slaves on his Park Hill Plantation near Tahlequah, the Keetowahs, however strange as it may seem, remained loyal followers of their Principal Chief.[13]

Watie, on the other hand, was allied with another Cherokee secret society, the Knights of the Golden Circle, and their associated "Blue Lodge." This society, composed of many members of the pro-removal party, represented Cherokee slaveholding interests. Besides opposing Ross's group, their principal objective was assisting in capturing and punishing abolitionists who interfered with slavery in the Cherokee Nation.[14]

By 1861, Watie had a large two-story log house along Bush Creek. A slaveholder, Watie was a member of the Cherokee landed gentry, having a sizable amount of lands along the Grand and Arkansas Rivers, a general merchandise business at Millwood, and a successful law practice. By the early spring, Watie and his slaveholding followers were asked by Arkansas politicians to join the Confederacy in order to protect the region from abolitionism, especially from the "hordes of greedy Republicans" intent on the subjugation of the Cherokee and the imposition of their rule. By this time Albert Pike had begun his efforts to woo the Indian nations of Indian Territory to the Confederate side through treaties of alliance.[15]

Nearly three months before the Pike-Cherokee treaty of alliance was signed in October, 1861, Watie received a commission as a colonel in the army of the Confederacy. In July, he was authorized by General Ben McCulloch to raise a force to protect the Indian Territory from a federal invasion. Watie soon raised three hundred men to protect the northern borders of the Cherokee Nation from Kansas jayhawkers. McCulloch later informed Ross and John Drew, the chief's nephew by marriage, of Watie's mission. Knowing full well of the Watie-Ross split, McCulloch never fully trusted either Ross or Drew. In September, 1861, after writing of his suspicions to the Confederate secretary of war, McCulloch praised Watie as a "gallant man and a true friend of our country" and urged giving him a "battalion separate from the Cherokee regiment under Colonel Drew."[16]

Always wary of Watie's presence, Ross feared that Pike and his Confederate forces might remove him from his office as principal chief of the Cherokee and replace him with his enemy Watie. Yet Ross was in a bind since he was afraid of breaking Cherokee treaties with the United States, which would result in the loss of millions of dollars of Cherokee moneys held in trust by Washington. He also feared alienating the Pins who were his major supporters. While insisting on neutrality, Ross saw Watie rallying his followers for the Confederacy. By the fall of 1861, Confederates under the command of Colonel (later General) Douglas H. Cooper, the former Choctaw Indian agent from Mississippi, had assembled a formidable Indian force of 1,400 mounted men. This cavalry unit included six companies of Cooper's Choctaw and Chickasaw regiment, Colonel Daniel McIntosh's Creek regiment, and Lieutenant Chilly McIntosh's and Major John Jumper's mixed battalion of Creeks and Seminoles. These forces were supported by five hundred white soldiers of the Ninth Texas Cavalry.[17]

With Watie's actions in mind and because of the rising Confederate tide after major Union defeats in the summer of 1861 at Bull Run and Wilson's Creek, Ross, who had rebuffed Pike's efforts earlier, now signed a treaty with the rebel diplomat-general. Under the agreement signed on October 7, 1861, the Confederate States of America assumed all of the treaty obligations due the Cherokee from the government of the United States. The Confederates also guaranteed the Cherokee protection from invasion, respect for Cherokee title to their lands, payments of Indian annuities, and the recognition of the Cherokee right to maintain the institution of slavery. Ross pledged "perpetual peace and friendship, and an alliance, offensive and defensive, between the Confederate States of America, all of their states and the people, and the Cherokee Nation and all of the people thereof." The Cherokee agreed to furnish "a regiment of ten companies of mounted men, with two reserve companies" for the South and to allow the rebels to construct military posts and roads within the Cherokee Nation. No Indian regiment raised was to be called on to fight for the Confederacy outside of the Indian Territory. As a symbol of the Confederate commitment to the Indians, the treaty also provided that the Cherokee were to be allowed a delegate in the Confederate Congress at Richmond.[18]

Despite this treaty, Ross had little love for the Confederacy. The treaty formalized the Cherokee schism—separate regiments led by Watie and Drew symbolized the two sides. Although both mounted Cherokee regiments fought on the Confederate side through the Battle of Pea Ridge in early March 1862, Drew's forces were reluctant warriors. As early as December 1861, his regiment had been severely reduced as a result of desertions since some of the Cherokee refused to fight Creek Chief Opothleyahola's Union forces. In March, 1862, Pike and his Cherokee troops joined General Ben McCulloch's Texans in Arkansas. At the three-day battle of Pea Ridge, the Union forces won a major victory despite Watie's active leadership right to the end of the battle. After the defeat, Drew's Second Indian Mounted Rifles defected to the Union side while Watie and his forces made their way back toward the Cherokee Nation. Now the Cherokee schism was wider—between blue and gray as well as Indian and Indian. Besides joining Unionist Indian home guards in Kansas, Watie's Cherokee opponents later in 1863 abrogated the treaty of 1861 made with the Confederacy; they also abolished slavery.[19]

In contrast, Watie's leadership of the Confederate Cherokees was unswerving. As early as December 26, 1861, he met with success on the battlefield. Arriving immediately after the Battle of Chustenahlah, Watie's cavalrymen pursued the retreating Union force under Creek General Opothleyahola. Although outnumbered two to one and facing an enemy dug into their strongholds in the hill, Watie's forces routed the Unionist Indians, suffering few casualties, killing twenty or twenty-one federals, and capturing seventy-five others, twenty-five or thirty pack horses, 250 ponies, and eight to nine hundred head of cattle.[20]

As a consequence of the federal invasion of Indian Territory in the summer of 1862, the Union forces marched on the Cherokee capital of Tahlequah and captured Ross. The Cherokee's Principal Chief was soon paroled, spending the remainder of the war in Washington, D.C. and Philadelphia after a proclamation of Cherokee loyalty to the Union. Three of Ross's sons, three grandsons, and three nephews later served the Union during the Civil War.[21]

With Ross in exile, Watie's followers took over much of the operations of the Cherokee Nation. In March of 1863, at Cooley's Creek, Indian Territory, Watie was chosen as Principal Chief of the Cherokee Nation (South) by the Cherokee National Council. With his devoted son Saladin at his side and his able nephew Elias C. Boudinot as Cherokee delegate to Richmond, Watie consolidated his power. Thus, by the spring of 1863, when his wife Sarah was a war refugee in Confederate territory below the Red River near Rusk, Texas and his third son Cumiskey had died of disease, Watie was largely in control of the affairs of the Cherokee Nation. His followers soon passed a conscription bill drafting all Cherokee men between the ages of eighteen and forty-five, later amended to fifty, into Confederate military service. A significant number of Pins continued their Union activities, but Watie and his Cherokee supporters never accepted the existence of two Cherokee Nations in Indian Territory and frequently attacked their Cherokee opponents.[22]

Besides his numerous hit-and-run attacks on Union supply lines along the vital link, the Fort Scott–Fort Gibson military trail, Watie's forces often raided within the Cherokee Nation, carrying off horses, cattle, hogs, wagons, farm utensils, beds, bedding, and clothing, while at times capturing and killing Pins. Sometimes atrocities were committed by his men. In the late winter of 1862, Watie's nephew Charles Webber killed and scalped Chunestootie, one of Drew's men. At another time in 1863, Watie's son Saladin, much to the regret of his mother, murdered a prisoner of war. Watie personally took part in at least one act of retribution against Ross and his followers. On October 29, 1863, he led a scouting party northwestward to the Cherokee capital at Tahlequah. After killing a few Pins and burning the Cherokee Council House, Watie's cavalry captured several Northern-allied Cherokee, including John Ross's son William; Watie spared Ross's life. He then moved his force to Park Hill where he set fire to Rose Cottage, John Ross's home, and destroyed the plantation. In the assault, Watie's men also killed four Union soldiers, including two blacks, and captured a number of Chief Ross's slaves; they also killed Andrew Nave, a Cherokee Unionist and friend of Watie, who had stubbornly refused to surrender the plantation to the Confederate force.[23]

Watie was ruthless, a negrophobe, and no saint, but his reputation has been unfairly sullied further by historians and contemporaries who often associated him with the terrorist Quantrill. Yet unlike Quantrill, Watie was no bushwacker with little loyalty to either side.[24] Unlike Quantrill's band, Watie's activities were focused on military objectives and/or his Cherokee Pin opponents. Watie's men destroyed dwellings and barns when used by the enemy for headquarters, for barracks, or for supply storage. His frequently undersupplied forces preyed on the lifeline between Fort Scott and Fort Gibson. Union mule trains which were militarily significant were easy targets. The booty could supply Confederate Indians as well as their families, scattered throughout the Indian Territory and north Texas. Watie, in ruthless fashion, could also disrupt the massive Union efforts at feeding sixteen thousand loyalist Indian refugees who depended on these supplies. Yet Watie constantly distanced himself from the marauding terrorist actions of Quantrill. In a letter to his wife in 1863, Watie wrote that he had been unfairly accused of heinous crimes and that he was hardened to it. Insisting he was "not a murderer," Watie suggested that if he erred, he did so "without bad intention" and that his "great crime in the world is blunder[.] I will get into scrapes without intention or any bad motive."[25]

Upon his ascension to Principal Chief, Watie addressed the Cherokee National Council. On March 24, 1863, speaking "with a heavy heart, for evil times have come upon our country," he insisted that "disaster upon disaster has followed the Confederate arms in the Cherokee country."[26] Despite his trusted son Saladin's presence at his side and his able nephew Elias C. Boudinot as the Cherokee representative at the Confederate Congress in Richmond, Watie was unable to secure either victories in the field nor a firm Southern commitment to supply his forces.[27]

By August 8, 1863, he was pinning the blame in his typical race-conscious fashion on Confederate military and civilian officials and on the "mongrel force" of "hostile Indians, negroes and one battalion of Kansas troops" numbering two thousand who had possession of Fort Gibson in the heart of the Cherokee Country. Writing to S. S. Scott, Confederate commissioner of Indian affairs, Watie accused the South of "no vigorous efforts" at dislodging the Union force which has "laid waste our country, driven the women and children from their homes, and kept the other Nations, which have yet escaped invasion, in a continual state of alarm." He also accused the South of prejudice towards his Indian troops since they were not "paid as promptly nor as equipped as thoroughly as other soldiers." Despite their utmost fidelity, money and clothing allowances due them had been "appropriated to the use of other commands."[28]

On the following day, Watie appealed directly to Jefferson Davis about the failure of Confederate officers to recapture Fort Gibson and the rest of Indian Territory, asserting that the Confederate-allied Five Civilized Tribes were "victims of incapable and slothful" Southern leaders. While complaining to the Confederate leadership, Watie, in a letter on the same day, wrote to his allies within the Choctaw and Creek Nations that the North was intent on conquering Indian Territory through the "traitors that have deserted us, the negroes they have stolen from us and a few Kansas jayhawkers they can spare from that detestable region." Watie vowed to his Indian allies that he did not intend "to be subjugated and enslaved by such a class."[29]

Although Watie had no intention of abandoning the struggle, he had begun to realize that his cause was a markedly different one from that of the Confederacy. By the summer of 1863, he was comparing his troops' deplorable conditions to those of the Russian tsar's Siberian exiles.[30] By November, Watie also realized that the Confederate cause was lost. Fearing reprisals if he abandoned the South and wanting to insure the continuing leadership of his family in Cherokee tribal affairs in any future peace, Watie urged his followers at a council at Camp Creek to press on "for the preservation of the Indian country." If the South continued their present inability to aid their Indian allies, Watie "proposed that the Indians carry on the war alone," expressing "full confidence in their success." Urging the council to unite to save Cherokee lands and homes, Watie appealed to their sense of nationalism: "Will it be a history which will cause your children to be ashamed, or will it be one which will cause their eyes to lighten with joyous pride."[31] Right through the end of the war, Watie defined his objectives quite differently from his southern allies. Despite President Davis's assurances of better treatment of his allied Indians and Watie's promotion to the rank of brigadier general in the spring of 1864, the Cherokee leader's fervor in the later campaigns of the war was largely motivated by factors other than the preservation of the Confederacy or slavery. At all times, Watie continued his commitment to the South with one eye on his longer-standing enemies, namely the followers of John Ross.

In 1864, Watie was placed in command of the Indian Cavalry Brigade, which was composed of the First and Second Cherokee Cavalry, the Creek Squadron, the Osage Battalion, and the Seminole Battalion. From his headquarters south of the Canadian River, he sent squads of mounted raiders to attack federal details sent out to cut hay to feed their cavalry mounts at Fort Gibson or to graze their starving horses on the prairie flats outside of the post. During this time period, Watie achieved his greatest successes on the field of battle: the capture of the Union ferry steamboat *J. R. Williams* on June 10 and especially his capture of a major Union supply train at Cabin Creek on September 19.

The *J. R. Williams* was loaded with a cargo of commissary stores intended to resupply the Union garrison at Fort Gibson. In its manifest, the ferryboat had 150 barrels of flour and sixteen thousand pounds of bacon. Making its way along the Arkansas River from Fort Smith, the boat had an escort of only twenty-six Union soldiers and had no federal cavalrymen on shore to reconnoiter. Knowing that the boat had left Fort Smith and that it would come into shallow water close to the southern bank of the river near Pleasant Bluff, Watie prepared his ambush. He placed artillery in bushes on a bluff overlooking the river at intervals of one hundred yards.

In total surprise, the Confederates opened fire, hitting the ferryboat's smokestack, pilot house, boiler, and pipes, causing a release of steam which blinded the small military force on board. The boat drifted helplessly and ran aground on a nearby sandbar. When the hopelessly outnumbered crew of the *J. R. Williams* deserted, the small federal detachment on board then assumed defensive positions on the sandbar. After overrunning this force, many of the Confederate-allied Indians, especially the Creek and Seminole cavalrymen under Watie's command, plundered the ferryboat of its supplies. Watie was largely unable to control the Indians, many of whom were motivated by their destitute conditions, desperately in need of food for themselves and their families scattered throughout the Indian Territory. Since the Confederates had not provided Watie with wagons, the supplies not taken by individual Indians could not be evacuated. When the Union command at Fort Smith was alerted to Watie's action, a force of seven hundred men was sent to retake the boat. Despite the boldness of Watie's operation, he and his forces were compelled to burn the remaining supplies and retreat from the advancing Union forces.[32]

The attack on the *J. R. Williams* occurred only three months before Watie's legendary fifteen-day expedition through Indian Territory which caused a major blow to Union efforts. Subsequently, the Confederate high command in the Trans-Mississippi West had the highest praise for Watie's efforts: "There has not been a more daring or successful raid according to size during the whole war, and the officers and men engaged are entitled to the thanks of the country."[33] His troops, in action culminating with the Second Battle of Cabin Creek on September 19, traversed four hundred miles of Indian Territory, inflicted more than three hundred casualties on Union forces, burned five thousand tons of hay needed for Union steeds, captured or destroyed the largest wagon train ever to leave Fort Scott, seized hundreds of mules and horses, captured sizable quantities of quartermaster, commissary, and sutler supplies—ammunition, army boots, clothing and shoes, food and medical supplies, mowing machines, as well as cannon and other weapons—and inflicted what has been estimated as $1.5 million worth of damage on Union forces.[34]

In August of 1864, Watie asked General E. Kirby Smith, the commander of the Trans-Mississippi Department, for permission to begin raiding southeastern Kansas. The Confederate plan was two-pronged: While Watie went into Kansas, General Sterling Price would initiate a Confederate campaign into Missouri. Before the plan was put into effect, Watie learned from Union prisoners of war about a large federal supply train scheduled to travel the Fort Scott–Fort Gibson military trail in mid-September. In desperate need of supplies, the Confederates changed their original strategy. Watie and General Richard Gano came together in an extraordinary move and worked out a brilliant stroke, even though Gano, a white man, was senior to the Cherokee chief in Confederate service. Gano's Texas Brigade of 1,200 mostly white soldiers was to combine with Watie's own brigade, the 350 Indians of the First and Second Cherokee Cavalry, 325 Indians of Chilly McIntosh's First and Second Creek Cavalry, now assigned to Watie, and the 130 men of John Jumper's Seminole Battalion.[35]

Watie's forces were composed of Indian cavalrymen who had decrepit animals, antique firearms, and wore shredded rags. Yet they had advantages: (1) they were all veterans who were loyal to their trusted commanders, especially to Watie; (2) they were extremely mobile, traveling without much baggage, foraging provisions from the land, striking hard and disengaging quickly; and (3) they had defined attainable objectives with no grandiose goals about occupying ground or liberating territory. Thus, they were a model cavalry operation that was also aided by the unusual interracial cooperation of Gano and Watie.[36]

The two commanders met on September 12 to work out the details of the raid on the Union wagon train. On the following day, they assembled and organized the expeditionary force. On September 14, they moved their cavalry across the Canadian River and galloped northward into the Creek Nation. The next day, they forded the Arkansas River. After bearing northeastward and reaching Sand Town on the Verdigris River on September 16, the Confederates came upon 185 Union troops composed of two companies of the Second Kansas Cavalry and troops of the First Kansas Colored Infantry Regiment, who were busy cutting hay for the livestock needs at Fort Gibson twelve to fifteen miles away. Watie's and Gano's forces sprayed the mowers with canister and grapeshot and scattered the Union troops. In all, they slaughtered the Union force, killing one hundred and taking the remainder as prisoners. They also shot down every African American they could apprehend. They subsequently burned one hundred tons of hay and destroyed the mowing equipment. The Confederate expedition pressed on towards Fort Scott, bivouacking at Wolf Creek on September 17. The following day, Gano's reconnaissance patrols spotted the prize, the Union wagon train.[37]

On the evening of September 18, the Indians prepared for battle. Gano formed his line on the right while Watie's brigade, the First and Second Cherokee Cavalry, the 1st and 2nd Creek Cavalry, and the Seminole Battalion formed their line on the left. The Confederates held the position on the elevated prairie that descended to the enemy's position on Cabin Creek. Well after midnight in the early morning hours of September 19, the Indians and their Texan allies could hear the Union teamsters carousing in their camp along the creek, totally unaware that their encampment was slowly being surrounded and that the enemy was hiding in the nearby grasslands. Just before the battle commenced, some of the Indians, including First Lieutenant Tsup-ofe Fix-ico—Thomas Benton as he was called in English—passed around an Indian herbal concoction of what they deemed war medicine "which they proceeded to use by rubbing it on and about the clothing of the body and limbs as thoroughly as they could within the limited time they had for taking the treatment," since they believed it protected them from danger.[38]

At 3:00 A.M. under a bright moonlight, the Indians and the Texans struck, swooping down on the Union wagon train, composed of 250 armed teamsters, 300 Indian Home Guards, including some Cherokee Pins, and 430 troops from Fort Scott and Fort Gibson. Watie later reflected on the six-hour battle that followed: ". . . For a considerable length of time the firing was heavy and incessant. Our forces steadily advanced, driving the enemy to his cover. During the night our left drove the enemy from his position, leaving in our possession a part of his train, around which a guard was immediately thrown and most of the wagons moved to our rear." At daybreak the Union wagon train tried to escape from the Confederate trap and retreat over the creek in the direction of Fort Scott. Watie "sent Lieutenant Colonel Vann with two Cherokee regiments across the creek on the left to gain the enemy's rear and intercept the trains." Vann captured eighteen prisoners. After daylight, Gano and Watie moved up a battery on the left, supported by the First and Second Creek. They "opened a vigorous fire from this advantageous position on his encampment and fortifications." The Seminole Battalion and Twenty-ninth Texas Regiment then moved on the left of the battery, driving "the enemy from his cover and through the encampment. Soon the confusion became great in his ranks and a general stampede ensued, leaving in our possession his train, stockade, hay, camp and garrison equipage."[39]

The Confederates won a total victory at the Second Battle of Cabin Creek. They captured 129 of the wagons loaded with supplies as well as 740 mules. The rest of the wagons were burned as were the ricks of hay and the mowing machines. By a skillful decoy, Watie's and Gano's forces eluded a Union brigade attempting to come to the relief of the wagon train. In order to do so and make their escape, the Confederates marched three days and nights with little sleep, and graded banks and cleared trees to make passage for wagons, cannon, mules, and horses. In all, the Confederates inflicted more than 200 casualties and captured 120 Union soldiers; in contrast, the two Confederate brigades suffered few casualties, seven Texas and one Seminole officer being killed in the action.[40] Later, the Confederate forces were accused of massacring and mutilating a number of wounded prisoners belonging to the Second Indian Home Guard, which was composed of numerous Cherokee Unionist Pins.[41]

Their victory in September had greatly encouraged the Confederates and sent terror into the hearts of Union supporters; nevertheless, in the month that followed, the Confederates were busier raising troops and reorganizing their brigades and commands than threatening Union-held Indian Territory and Kansas. And with Sterling Price's failures in Missouri in the early fall, the Confederate dream of ultimate victory in the Trans-Mississippi West was virtually shattered. From November to the end of the war, the major fighting of the Civil War shifted to the East, and more specifically to General Sherman's Grand Army of the West's devastating march through the Carolinas. When General Cooper took overall command of all Confederate troops in Indian Territory on March 1, 1865, the final bell had begun to ring for the South's war effort. Six weeks later, news of Lee's surrender filtered to Indian Territory, where at first Confederate officers refused to believe its veracity. In the following month, General Smith's command virtually disintegrated. On May 26, 1865, Smith's chief of staff, Lieutenant General Simon Bolivar Buckner, formally surrendered the Army of the Trans-Mississippi and the public property under his control to Union General Edwin R. S. Canby at New Orleans.[42]

When Watie met Mathews and Vance near Doaksville on June 23, he agreed to end his hostilities. Importantly for him, the United

States also agreed that his Confederate-allied Cherokee "be protected by the United States authorities in their person and property not only from encroachments on the part of whites, but also from the Indians who have been engaged in the service of the United States."[43] To someone who had watched over his shoulder since 1839 for fear of assassination attempts by his Cherokee enemies, the wording of the surrender was not simply American official rhetoric. He *needed* assurance of protection for himself, his family, and his supporters. The surrendering Confederate-allied Cherokee were committed to this binding agreement until a new Cherokee grand council convened in September. The site selected was important. It was a neutral site in the Choctaw Nation. For a man who hunted down Pins during the Civil War, there was danger to return too soon to the Cherokee capital at Tahlequah, although Watie had earlier allowed most of his men to take their remaining Confederate supplies and firearms and go home. Historian Kenny A. Franks, Watie's best biographer, has observed that the "peace" was "in name only, as both the Northern and Southern Cherokees continued to contest for control of the tribe."[44]

On July 13, 1865, the Northern Cherokee National Council passed an act of amnesty and pardon for those who fought against Cherokee members loyal to the United States. All those seeking the restoration of Cherokee citizenship had to swear an oath to God and to agree to abide by the Constitution and Laws of the Cherokee Nation; Watie, however, along with a coterie of his most trusted supporters, were subsequently denied a pardon.[45]

When the grand council of Cherokee leadership met at the Armstrong Academy in the Choctaw Nation on September 1, the federal commissioners failed to attend. Instead, the commissioners met with representatives of the Cherokee, mostly pro-northern Indians, at Fort Smith on September 8. Because of the sudden change of venue, most of the pro-Southern representatives arrived late. In the end, both groups were forced to agree to terms imposed by the United States government. The United States was represented at the historic meeting by Dennis N. Cooley, Commissioner of Indian Affairs, and his assistant Charles Mix; General William S. Harney; Elijah Sells,

Superintendent for Southern Indians; and General Ely S. Parker, the prominent Seneca sachem and General Grant's military secretary during the Civil War. Thomas Wistar of the Society of Friends was also in attendance. The Northern-allied Cherokee were represented by Smith Christie, Thomas Pegg, White Catcher, H.D. Reese, and Lewis Downing; while Watie, Elias C. Boudinot, Richard Fields, William Penn Adair, and James M. Bell were the major delegates of the Southern Cherokee faction.[46]

At the Fort Smith conference, the Cherokee were treated as one people, as if they had *all* supported the Confederacy. Since the Cherokee Nation had signed a treaty with the Confederacy, Cooley insisted that it had forfeited all rights of every kind, character, and description—annuities, lands, and protection—which had been promised and guaranteed to them by the United States. The United States officials required the Cherokee to agree to a permanent peace; the abolition of slavery (the Cherokee Nation [North] had done so as early as February 1863); a cession of their lands in Indian Territory; and a readjustment of their treaties to arrange and settle all questions relating to or growing out of former treaties as affected by any treaty made by the Cherokee with the Confederate States of America.[47] Thus, in effect, the entire Cherokee Nation was considered disloyal and punished for its transgressions. Both Ross and Watie as well as their followers protested this treatment, although differences over equal distribution of annuities, railroad rights, and the wording of a reconstruction treaty still separated them. Some of Watie's southern-allied Cherokee also clung to the belief that the United States would cede them a separate territory apart from their northern-allied opponents.[48]

On August 11, 1866, ten days after Ross's death in Washington, a new Cherokee federal treaty was ratified by the United States Senate. Under its terms, the Cherokee-Confederate treaty of October 8, 1861 was declared void. All Cherokee as well as their former slaves were allowed to reside wherever they wished. The Southern Cherokee were permitted to remain in the Canadian District, and if sufficient land was needed, additional territory between the Grand River and the Creek Nation would be provided in the Cherokee Nation. Once again, slavery was prohibited with no compensation for emancipation of slaves. Railroad rights-of-way were established. The United States had the right to settle other non-Cherokee Indians, such as the Delaware, in the Cherokee Nation. Cherokee neutral lands in Kansas and the Cherokee Strip were ceded to the United States; Cherokee lands remaining in Arkansas or any state east of the Mississippi could be sold by the tribe as their council prescribed, but only after approval of the Secretary of the Interior. Cherokee Nation lands could be surveyed and allotted to individual tribal members. The abolitionist missionary Evan Jones was given $3,000 for his forty years of arduous service. Cherokees in the Union Army were to receive bounties for service. The United States was also given the right to establish military posts or stations in the Cherokee Nation. The United States agreed to pay for the provisions and clothing furnished to the pro-Northern Indians during the winters of 1861 and 1862 and for the expenses of the Cherokee delegates to Washington.[49]

The Southern Cherokee delegation refused to sign the treaty. This faction soon split into competing factions, with Watie turning away from tribal politics in order to overcome his destitution and rebuild his family's livelihood. By November, 1867, he moved his family to Breebs Town near Webber's Falls on the Canadian River where his son Saladin had land.[50]

Watie then formed a tobacco company with his nephew Elias C. Boudinot, soon becoming a successful businessman again. His company processed tobacco in a manufacturing plant and then shipped and sold the product throughout the Trans-Mississippi West. In 1868, the United States Congress passed the Internal Revenue Act which put a federal excise on tobacco and distilled spirits and did not exempt the Indian Territory. Watie and Boudinot refused to pay this tax, arguing that their enterprise was operating within the Cherokee Nation and their tobacco enterprise was tax exempted under the Cherokee Treaty of 1866 made with the federal government. The old Cherokee warrior and his nephew then brought suit in federal court. Eventually, in 1871, well after their business had fallen into bankruptcy when their plant was impounded for tax foreclosure, the United States Supreme Court decided against the two Cherokee on the grounds that a law of Congress could supersede the provisions of a treaty. This landmark decision was the harbinger of the congressional doctrine of "plenary power" later set forth by the court in the more famous case, *Lonewolf v. Hitchcock*, in 1903.[51]

This defeat was one of several that Watie faced in the last years of his life. In 1868, his son Saladin, who had so faithfully served his father's side during the Civil War, suddenly died. Watica, Watie's last surviving son, died the following year. In 1870, Watie, both emotionally and financially bankrupt, returned to his prewar home along Honey Creek in the Spavinaw area of the Grand River. A year later, on September 9, Watie died. The former Confederate general and Cherokee chief appropriately was buried in the Old Ridge Family Cemetery, later named Polson's Cemetery, in today's Delaware County, Oklahoma, near the home of his assassinated cousin, John Ridge.[52]

To be sure, Watie's life was filled with blunders and wrong paths. Yet no one questioned his bravery. Moreover, he had few equals as a cavalry officer and military tactician for the Confederate States of America; however, by joining the South's cause, he had committed the second major blunder of his life. In hindsight, his first major political error was his signing of the Treaty of New Echota in 1835. The second one, his joining the Confederacy, contributed to his people's ruination and an almost equal number of deaths as the Cherokee Trail of Tears of 1838! Although Ross must bear some of the blame for the failure to hold the Cherokee together in the Civil War, Watie's personal ambitions did outweigh his personal judgment and attempts at the national betterment of his people. As a result of the lingering Ross-Watie family feud, Cherokee fought Cherokee. It is only one of the ironies of the Civil War that it provided a bloody stage on which Indian vendettas could be played out to their utterly destructive ends.[53]

Part Two

The South

4

River Pilots and Swamp Guerrillas

Pamunkey and Lumbee Unionists

OUTSIDE OF THE AMERICAN INDIANS OF CALIFORNIA IN THE YEARS approaching the Civil War, no Indians had a more uncertain position in the American polity than did the Indians of the Southeast. Although at one time this region had one of the largest and diverse groups of Algonkian, Iroquoian, Muskogean, and Siouan Indians, the native population had shrunk considerably and numbered less than 25,000 people by 1860. From the Carolinas to the Mississippi Delta, Indian communities had been ravaged by disease, wars of conquest, and removal to the West. The Creek and Seminole alone fought a total of five wars between 1812 and 1858 against the "Long Knives." Although its origins were rooted well back in American history, Andrew Jackson's policy of forced removal was largely "perfected" and implemented on members of the Five Civilized Tribes of the Southeast. All southeastern Indians had to contend with the growing states' rights tone that was a feature of Southern nationalism in the antebellum period. Most Indians in the South were faced with increased efforts in Dixie to extend state jurisdiction and control over their communities and were increasingly resentful of racist treatment toward them. They objected strongly to being legally defined out of existence by state legislation. By the time of the Civil War, overwhelmed by gigantic armies fighting each other on their turf, some southeastern Indians had become Unionists in a determined effort to preserve their lives and the cohesion of their communities.

The Pamunkey Indians of Virginia and Lumbees of North Carolina served the Union, playing less official but nonetheless major roles in the North's war effort. The Pamunkey were mostly employed by the Union as civilian and naval pilots for federal warships and transports. The Lumbee, who were coerced into Confederate labor service, operated as guerrillas for the Union, sabotaging Rebel efforts. Both of these Indian communities were motivated to join the Union side because of their intense dislike for the South's subservient treatment of their communities. They especially resented the increasing white supremacist tone and repressive legislation affecting Indians in the Southeast since the presidency of Andrew Jackson. Both communities sought retribution against their intolerant white supremacist neighbors. In each instance, the Indians' involvement was directly affected by their location. Both communities were in the path of a major Union advance: the Powhatan's Pamunkey and Mattaponi reservations were in the route of General George McClellan's Army of the Potomac troop movements during the Peninsula Campaign of March to July 1862; and the Lumbee in the route of General William Tecumseh Sherman's Grand Army of the West's devastating march through the Carolinas in January through April 1865.

The Pamunkey Indians were the descendants of the powerful Powhatan empire. At the time of European contact, these Algonkian-speaking peoples occupied the entire coastal plain of modern Virginia, about one hundred miles from east to west. Their lands stretched from the Atlantic Ocean in the east to the Appalachian fall line—the land of the Siouan-speaking Monacans—in the west. In disastrous wars in 1622 and 1644, they were defeated by the English and made "tributary Indians" to the Virginia royal governor. Because of these conflicts and numerous epidemics, their population, estimated to be between thirteen and fourteen thousand people at the time of European contact, was reduced to less than seven hundred by

1712. By the end of the nineteenth century, there were fewer than one hundred twenty Pamunkeys left.[1]

The Powhatans—the Chickahominy, Gingaskin, Mattaponi, Nansemond, Pamunkey, and Rappahannock Indians—faced a perilous existence, and their lives were increasingly circumscribed by the white power structure of Virginia in the years before the Civil War. As early as 1802, free nonwhites were required by Virginia state law to carry certificates of manumission or free birth. If they did not have these county-issued certificates, they could be arrested and even sold into slavery. In 1813, the state assembly passed a law forcing the Gingaskin Indians to abandon their communal landholding patterns on the eastern shore of Virginia; twenty years later, after repeated interference and coercion by state and local authorities, these Indians "sold off" almost all of their remaining 370 acres of tribal lands.[2]

Conditions worsened as a result of white reaction to the Nat Turner slave insurrection of 1831. In August of that year, Turner, a Southampton County, Virginia black slave preacher with a reputation for visions and prophecy, set out with a handful of slaves. Armed with clubs and axes, Turner's force soon gained recruits. During their revolt, they killed fifty-five white men, women, and children. Soon, however, Turner's forces were overwhelmed by the Virginia militia. Turner and about twenty of his comrades were hanged. In addition, angry whites "retaliated," killing about one hundred innocent slaves.

This major slave insurrection led to a backlash of immense proportions throughout Virginia and well into the other southern states. Because of white supremacists' exaggerated fears that all persons of color planned to ally themselves against white authority, each of these states enacted strict laws for the control of slaves as well as "free persons of color." In Virginia, Pamunkey, who had owned slaves in the colonial period, now were directly affected by a wave of repressive laws. In the next three decades conditions for all nonwhites worsened as the Civil War drew closer. Whites perceived Indians, rightly or wrongly, as being in sympathy with free Negroes and their fears for the preservation of their racist social system escalated. Thus, in

1832, the state assembly enacted a law making it illegal for all non-Indians—blacks, mulattoes, Indians—to preach even if they were already ordained ministers. Nonwhites were allowed to attend church as long as the services were conducted by whites. No free nonwhite could purchase a slave for declared manumission purposes unless the slave was a spouse or a child. A nonwhite assaulting a white person was to be charged with a capital offense, as was anyone writing, printing, or calling for insurrection; those nonwhites receiving stolen property would be prosecuted as if they were thieves. Free nonwhites accused of a crime were also denied a jury trial.[3]

In 1843, the so-called Gregory Petition was drawn up by local whites in the vicinity of their reservation. The petition, designed to get at the Indian's protected landbase, claimed that the Pamunkey had intermarried with free blacks who lived on their reservation "until their Indian character had vanished." Although no evidence was provided, this petition gave impetus to a movement to dispossess these Indians.[4] The Pamunkey in particular faced increasing pressures. In the mid 1850s, they were dispossessed without compensation of twenty-two acres on the northern part of the reservation as a result of the Richmond and York River Railroad's laying of track.

In 1857, local whites tried to disarm the tribe, leading to a Pamunkey protest. The Virginia governor's response was to allow the Indians to have their guns since their "mode of living is by hunting, and to deprive them of their firearms is in effect to drive them away from their tribal lands which the laws most emphatically forbid." However, he added that an annual census of these "Indians" should be required "to ascertain their blood" in order to identify the "Tributary Indians" among them; "if any become one-fourth mixed with the Negro race then they may be treated as free negroes or mulattoes."[4] Thus, state officials of Virginia set their own racist criteria for Indian survival which they could employ in the future to terminate Pamunkey existence and/or get at the tribal landbase of twelve hundred acres. Despite the governor's "recognition" of the Indians' right to bear arms, when the abolitionist John Brown raided Harper's Ferry in 1859, the Indians "again fell under suspicion, and the Pamunkey, in spite of state recognition as Indians, were temporarily disarmed, while the unorganized bands [of Powhatan Indian descendants] were subject to worse treatment."[5]

By the time of Virginia's secession from the Union on April 4, 1861, the descendants of the mighty Powhatan Empire had little love for the commonwealth. Categorized as "free persons of color," they had deep-seated feelings of hatred for the state's oligarchy, whose ancestors had vanquished the Indians in the first half of the seventeenth century. By the Civil War, these officials had circumscribed the Indian's world, economically, politically, and socially. As proud people surrounded by a threatening white world, the Pamunkey and other Virginia Indians rankled with the intensification of white supremacist legislation and, with it, the grouping of their existence with slaves or "free Negroes."

In November 1861, after the Union's disastrous loss at the First Battle of Bull Run, President Lincoln appointed General George McClellan commander of the Union army, to replace the aged General Winfield Scott. The thirty-five-year-old McClellan, a brilliant administrator but a military enigma, organized and reorganized, gathered supplies and equipment, drilled and disciplined what would become the Army of the Potomac from November 1861 to March 1862. Refusing to engage the enemy even though he outnumbered their forces three to one, he frequently covered up his lack of will and other insecurities by his arrogant behavior or by blaming others. Finally, on March 17, 1862, McClellan moved twelve divisions—seventy thousand soldiers, horses, wagons, supplies, as well as three hundred cannon—in three hundred vessels from Alexandria to Fortress Monroe.[6]

The federal advance up the peninsula of the Tidewater began on April 4. Despite his sizable military advantage, the "Young Napoleon" constantly delayed, allowing the Confederates to move most of the troops from the Department of Virginia. Instead of waiting for McClellan's siege guns to tear their undersized army apart, the Confederates evacuated their trenches on May 3 and pulled back their forces from the York River toward Richmond. The Union forces attacked the retreating rebels and won a rearguard victory at Williamsburg on May 5. The Confederates soon evacuated Norfolk, resulting in the rebels' scuttling of the *Merrimac* since the ironclad was now deprived of its base. The abandonment of Norfolk allowed the Union navy to sail up the James River, known to the Indians as "Powhatan's River." Five Union gunboats, including the ironclad *Monitor*, steamed up the river toward the Confederate fort at Drewry's Bluff, south of Richmond; however, rebel sharpshooters picked off Yankee sailors and Confederate artillery inflicted heavy damage on the gunboats, resulting in a Union setback.

After the Battle of Williamsburg, the Army of the Potomac seized three Confederate supply depots at Eltham's Landing, Cumberland Landing, and White House Landing. These actions specifically affected the Pamunkey and Mattaponi Indians by invading their territories. On May 6, General William B. Franklin, a clone of McClellan in every way, proceeded with a Union division up the York River. A West Point graduate who was highly skilled in military administration but not in combat strategy, Franklin had trained and equipped his division for an amphibious landing. His objective was to capture the terminus of the Richmond and York Railroad at West Point, Virginia and to put his division ashore at the Eltham plantation on the south bank across the York River. Through the use of light pontoon boats under the guard of five Union gunboats, Franklin landed his advance troops. The Union force then assembled a four-hundred-foot-long floating wharf from pontoons, canal boats, and planking, making it possible to land its soldiers, artillery pieces, and supplies.

On May 7, the Union force came head-to-head with General John Bell Hood's legendary Texas Brigade, a formidable Confederate unit of three regiments from Texas and one from Georgia. According to one soldier from Maine, the ensuing battle was fought in "one of the closest growths of pine trees and underbrush I ever saw." Franklin's force took one hundred eighty-six casualties compared to Hood's forty-eight; however, at the end of the battle, the Union held the strategic position—the railroad terminus and the northern end of the York River where it splits into the Pamunkey and Mattaponi rivers.[7]

The capture of Eltham's Landing and West Point, Virginia was soon followed by the Army of the Potomac's seizure of both Cumberland Landing and White House Landing after the Confederate forces pulled back to the perimeter of Richmond's defenses. White House Landing, which lies just outside the bounds of the Pamunkey Indian Reservation, was the plantation of William H. F. "Rooney" Lee, General Robert E. Lee's son, and had been a residence of Martha Washington. By the middle of May, 1862, this area became the base of McClellan's operations in the Peninsula Campaign. This location was a strategic one since it was the point at which the Richmond and York Railroad from West Point crossed the Pamunkey River. Richmond, the "Holy Grail," lay twenty-three miles of track eastward in a direct line. This generally isolated area was now transformed into a Union arsenal. The landscape was dotted with sails, smokestacks, and masts, flatboats, and sloops; floating docks made from barges and canal boats; massive artillery pieces and acres of supplies and equipment; and locomotives, boxcars, and flatcars.[8]

From May to early July, 1862, at the end of the Seven Days Battles, Union and Confederate forces hammered each other in and around "Indian Country." The Mattaponi have preserved oral traditions of "gunboats going past their reservation and of a ship containing slaves being sunk nearby."[9] Moreover, a strategic rail link, the Richmond and York Railroad, crosses the Pamunkey Reservation; after McClellan's capture of White House, it became an important supply line for Union forces. Many of the Indians became war refugees in order to avoid the ravages of war and/or forced Confederate work details in North Carolina. Many other Virginia Indians, especially Chickahominy and Rappahannock, fled northward. Some of the Indians made it to the eastern shore of Maryland, Delaware, and southern New Jersey, while others reached as far north as Ojibway country in southern Ontario; these refugees intermarried with the Great Lakes Indians, some later returning to Virginia.[10]

George Alfred Townsend, the famous journalist, was sent by James Gordon Bennett to cover the Peninsula campaign for the *New York Herald*. Despite his overt racism and inability to differentiate between blacks and American Indians, his writings reveal something about Pamunkey-Mattaponi life during the Civil War. As was their custom, the Indians ferried him over to their community. According to Townsend, they were all concerned to find out whether "they were to be protected" by the massive Union army in their midst.[11]

Townsend came upon fifty Indians, whom he derogatorily referred to as "half-breeds" and "mixed Indians and Negroes from Indiantown Island." These Indians included a medicine woman named "Mag," of "great repute at medicines, powwows and divination," who smoked tobacco in "a stump of clay pipe" in front of her dilapidated cabin. The loquacious Indian woman, pictured as a drunken charlatan and as a beggar by Townsend, "brought from the house a cup of painted earthenware" and "pretended to read the arrangement of the grains within the cup." To this day, Pamunkey women are famous for making earthenware. Almost as quickly as he arrived, Townsend departed, noting the glare of Union army campfires and ship lights on the river and nostalgically bemoaning the fate of the "vanishing race."[12]

One of the Union regiments fighting its way up the Peninsula contained American Indian troops. Company K of the 57th Pennsylvania Volunteer Infantry included twelve Iroquois (mostly Seneca) soldiers, who described their experiences in the Peninsula vividly in letters home to relatives at the Allegany Indian Reservation in New York.[13] They wrote about how the retreating rebels had dumped fifteen artillery pieces in the Potomac River. During lulls in work details and in the fighting, the Iroquois delighted in "oystering," taking advantage of every culinary opportunity that came their way.[14] Yet disaster soon awaited them at places they had never heard of before: Fair Oaks (Seven Pines) on May 31 and June 1, 1862; and at Charles City Crossroads during the Seven Days Battles, from June 25 to July 1, 1862. The horror of the action at Fair Oaks was described by Levi Turkey Williams, an Onondaga Indian who was killed a month later at Charles City Crossroads. Writing to the father of an Indian comrade killed in action, Williams sorrowfully recounted that "my friend your son Cornelius Plummer" was "now dead." After being shot while "marching upon the rebels," he was struck "in his mouth" and the ball "came out near his ear [and] he fell sudden and died in an instant."[15]

In a subsequent letter to his father, Willet Pierce, a Seneca Indian in the company, went into further detail about the same battle, remarking that another Indian, Wooster King, had been badly wounded, shot through both legs, and that his major and one Henry Kerr, a white man from nearby Titusville, Pennsylvania, had been killed. He then assured his father that the "rest of our Indian soldiers are all well. . . ." The Seneca private, however, added: "[T]he bodies of the rebels dead was lying thick on the ground more than a man can count or to say innumerable." Only seven miles from Richmond with cannonade around him, Pierce nevertheless continued resolute, since he soon expected "another battle to be fought . . . and we are all prepared to fight for our country to the last extremity."[16] In the end, of the twelve Iroquois soldiers in Company K, two were killed in action, one died of tuberculosis, four were discharged for disabilities incurred in service, and at least two were classified as deserters.[17]

Although McClellan often lacked the will to pursue the Rebels, he did, to some degree, take into account the complex terrain he had chosen as a field of battle. Because of their special knowledge of this intricate ecosystem, the Powhatan Indians were utilized by the Army of the Potomac as land guides, river pilots, and spies. Navigating the four major rivers of the Peninsula—the James, the Potomac, the Rappahannock, and the York—and their tributaries such as the York's Pamunkey and Mattaponi rivers or the James' Chickahominy River—required experienced river pilots. Large Union warships and supply ships could be piloted more than one hundred miles inland in the navigable waters of eastern Virginia.

The Virginia Indians' role as land or river guides was hardly a new one. From the seventeenth century onward, they had served as guides. They were employed by the noted explorer John Lederer in that capacity in 1669–1670. Powhatans had been utilized as "trackers of fugitive servants." During Bacon's Rebellion in 1675–1676, they had also been used by English colonial authorities to hunt down and pursue other Indians. Even as late as the twentieth century, Pamunkey served as professional hunters, trappers, and guides for white visitors who came to hunt on the reservation which they kept in part as a game preserve.[18]

Terrill Bradby, a Pamunkey man of Chickahominy ancestry, was the most documented of the fourteen Virginia Powhatans who served as Union guides and pilots during the Civil War. Others included Thornton Allmond, Sterling Bradby, John Langston, William Sampson, and Powhatan Weisiger. Those who served the Yankees were immediately thrown off the church rolls of the Colosse Baptist Church, the local congregation whose members prior to the Civil War contained whites as well as some Indians.[19]

One of those who lost membership was Terrill Bradby. Born William Terrill Bradby in 1833, he received no formal education. Before and after his Civil War involvement, he lived on the Pamunkey reservation. Between five feet six and five feet eight inches in height and weighing between 150 and 170 pounds, he was described as of "copper color" with a visible scar over his left eye.[20] Like other Pamunkey men of the era, he wore his hair long in the traditional manner.[21] He married in the 1850s, and his wife Elizabeth bore him four children. She died in May, 1884; four years later, Bradby married Catherine Sampson. Because he was largely illiterate prior to the Civil War, his recruiting officer wrote his name down for him when he enlisted in May of 1862.[22]

Bradby's Civil War service was both on land and sea. During the Peninsula Campaign, he served as a land guide and scout for the Army of the Potomac. He also was employed by Allan Pinkerton's Secret Service as a spy, gathering intelligence on Confederate positions and movements. Later, in 1863, he was transferred to "water duty," serving as a pilot second class on the James River until May, 1864. While serving on board the U.S.S. *Schockon* in the Union flotilla along the James, Bradby was shot in the leg by a piece of a Confederate shell at the Dutch Gap Canal. Although it was only a flesh wound, the rheumatism that developed as a result troubled him for the rest of his life.[23]

Bradby became a pilot in the North Atlantic Blockading Squadron, the Union attempt to strangle the Confederacy's war effort, and served until May 29, 1865. Besides the U.S.S. *Schockon*, Bradby served on the U.S.S. *Onondaga* and *Huron*, gunboats named after two prominent North American nations of the Northeast; he also served on the picket tugboat *Epsilon*, the chartered steamer *Daylight*, and the torpedo boat *Spuyten Duyvil*.[24]

Toward the end of his military service, Bradby was involved in what appears to be an accidental killing. He was accused of murdering his brother Sterling, another Union pilot who had been the Pamunkey chief since 1859.[25] Bradby was brought to trial, but his brother's death remains a mystery to this day since no record of the proceedings has survived. We do know that Ulysses S. Grant was the presiding judge.[26] Terrill Bradby's pension record does not indicate a conviction and suggests that he was honorably discharged. The record also indicates he was worthy enough to receive a pension for his war service, at least until a bureaucratic foul-up in the early 1890s. Terrill Bradby was a well-respected member of his Pamunkey community after the Civil War and remained a prominent resident of the community until his death in the first years of the twentieth century.[27]

In the last years of his life, Bradby became a "show Indian" entertainer and a major informant to anthropologists James Mooney and Albert Gatschet about Powhatan traditional culture and history.[28] As an "Associate" of the Smithsonian Institution, he was given letters of introduction and sent by this great mecca of knowledge to Chicago, to the Columbian Exposition at the World's Fair of 1893, as "one of the very few remaining descendants of the Pamunkey Indians of Virginia."[29] Unfortunately, Bradby and other Indians at this remarkable event were little other than exotic curiosities to a Victorian America, treated as symbols of a "vanishing race." Instead of educating Americans about the great contributions of Indians, including their valuable Civil War service, the Pamunkey were relegated to serve as mild diversions, relics of a world that was rapidly disappearing. The Anglo-Saxon idea of progress had no place for the weak, the impoverished, the culturally distinct.[30]

Unlike the Pamunkey, the Civil War was a defining experience for the Indians in the environs of the Lumber River in Robeson County, North Carolina.[31] For a decade starting in December 1864, many of these Indians waged a guerrilla war against white supremacists, the North Carolina Home Guard, the Ku Klux Klan, and their supporters. This band of guerrillas was led by the teenaged Henry Berry Lowry, who became a legendary figure in the Indian history of North Carolina. Besides his family, who were at the nucleus of his band, Lowry's comrades-in-arms included other Indians, poor and aggrieved blacks and whites, as well as Union soldiers who had escaped from a nearby Confederate prison in Florence, South Carolina. In the eyes of most Indians, Lowry was the Robin Hood of Robeson County—a man of mystery, a person of many disguises who quickly appeared, disappeared, and reappeared on numerous occasions to foil his pursuers; to most whites, he was a common outlaw, a bushwacker in the manner of Jesse James.

The Lowry Band was the classic example of what historian Eric Hobsbawm would label social bandits, "peasant outlaws whom the lord and state regard as criminals, but who remain within peasant society, and are considered by their people as heroes, as champions, avengers, fighters for justice, perhaps even leaders of liberation, and in any case as men to be admired, helped, and supported."[32] Adolph Dial, the noted educator and Lumbee, has written about Lowry's significance to his people: "While the name [Henry Berry Lowry] meant lawlessness and terror to the white community, it meant more truly a man who fought oppression to the Indians." Lowry, known as the "King of Scuffletown," soon "became a folk hero to his people, a symbol of pride and manhood."[33]

The Indians of the Lumber River, known in history as Cheraw, Croatan, Cherokee of Robeson County, Lumbee, Scuffletonian, Siouan, Tuscarora, as well as by other designations, suffered many of the same indignities that affected their Virginia neighbors. Although they owned no tribal reservation land by the time of the Civil War, most lived in the extensive but impoverished hardscrabble Robeson

County, a 949-square-mile rural region in the south central part of North Carolina. The vast lowlands and dense and tangled swamps of this county were to provide protection for the Lowry Band in their decade-long war.

The status of American Indians in North Carolina had declined sharply since the late eighteenth century and more acutely after the Nat Turner Rebellion. Before 1800, they were already designated as "free persons of color" and denied the right to testify against whites in legal proceedings. In 1835, faced with increasing racial paranoia following the Nat Turner Rebellion, the North Carolina Constitutional Convention stripped "free persons of colors" of most of their rights, including the right to vote, to serve on juries, and to learn to read or write. In this setting, Indians were and all nonwhites were seen as dangerous and potential rioters.[34] Only after the Civil War did state officials recognize the continued tribal existence of an American Indian nation—the Eastern Band of Cherokee in North Carolina—but only after the Thomas Legion, four companies of Cherokee, served the Confederacy with distinction.[35]

In certain ways, the Lumbee were treated worse than the Cherokee. Unlike the Cherokee, they were never designated as part of the Five Civilized Tribes. Their Indian ancestry was always questioned and they were more often than not grouped by the white Carolina world with African Americans, especially in the fifty years before the Civil War. The North Carolina State legislature and state courts circumscribed much of their existence. In a law passed in 1840, free nonwhites were prohibited from owning or carrying weapons.[36] Moreover, in the years preceding the Civil War, the Lumbee faced what they describe in their own traditions as "tied mule incidents." According to Dial:

> Such an incident occurred when a white farmer tied his mule on an Indian's land, freed several cows in the Indian's pasture, and put a hog or two in his pen. Then, the white farmer would arrive with the authorities and claim that the Indian had stolen his animals. Knowing he had little chance for justice in the courts, the Indian would agree to provide free

labor for a period of time, so that charges would not be pressed, or to give up a portion of his land as a settlement. This was, of course, only one way in which the Indians were deprived of their labor and property; other, more "sophisticated" quasi-legal means were also used.[37]

The Indians of Robeson County, who had owned all of the territory within the region at one time, were gradually dispossessed of their lands, as a result of legal proceedings which attached their property for the recovery of debts. In the white supremacist world, few Indians, especially the Lowry family, believed they had been given equitable treatment by the local courts and for years they looked upon the local power structure as having robbed them.[38]

The Civil War brought a continued deterioration of Lumbee existence. According to historian W. McKee Evans, the Lumbee "had the misfortune to live near the lower Cape Fear River, where, at the outbreak of the war, the Confederate government undertook what would be its greatest enterprise of military engineering."[39] After a major yellow fever epidemic in 1862 in which 10 percent of the population of the Cape Fear region died and free labor fled, Indians, along with African slaves, were conscripted against their will to build a system of forts which were intended to defend Wilmington, North Carolina. This major port was Confederate naval headquarters and served as the home port of most of the South's destroyers and blockade runners. Wilmington, about seventy miles east of the center of Robeson County, was also a major city port, shipping cotton and naval stores, timber, turpentine, hemp, and pitch. It was tied to Robeson County by a Confederate railroad line, the Wilmington, Charlotte and Rutherford Railroad.[40]

The most important of these Confederate forts was Fort Fisher, known as the Gibraltar of the Confederacy. This huge earthenwork with seventy-five guns, including two 150-pounders, was built between 1861 and 1864 and was one of the "strongest installations in the world" by the time of its completion. It was L-shaped, with the angle pointing to the sea in a northeasterly direction. The massive installation had a horizontal arm extending nearly seven hundred yards across a peninsula. With its superior mound battery with long-range guns and the treacherous currents around it, the fort seemed secure. Fort Fisher remained a major cog in the Confederate wheel until a Union combined military operation seized it on January 15, 1865.[41]

The Confederacy first conscripted slaves, then free blacks, then "Scuffletownian" Indians. According to a later report on the "Lowry gang" by John C. Gorman, North Carolina's adjutant general, "Scuffletown was included in the impressment and almost every able-bodied male in the settlements was dragged from home and railroaded to the coast." Indians with the family names Lowry, Oxendine, and Strong found themselves conscripted against their will from a five-square-mile area from Pembroke to Prospect, North Carolina.[42] The Indians had now been reduced to slave status. Their labor battalions were underfed, inadequately clad, given unheated and crowded living quarters, denied proper medical attention, and subjected to work in water during the winter. Now, after a century of degradation, they had fallen to rock bottom in the South's racial hierarchy. Historian Evans has observed that they "had lost their lands, their civil rights, and their social status. Now at last the line that separated the brown-skinned Indian labor conscript from the black-skinned Negro slave must have seemed a subtle legal distinction indeed."[43]

The forced conscription of Lumbee added to their growing resentment toward white local, county, and state officials. Nor did they feel any allegiance to the Confederate "stars and bars" for sending them to die in the inhumane conditions of the lower Cape Fear. Despite laws taking away their right to bear arms, Lumbee squirreled their rifles and ammunition away. Although they used these firearms to put food on their tables, some Lumbee began to consider using them against the local white establishment of Robeson County, since more and more young Indian men were being "requisitioned" as laborers. These young men often fled into the surrounding swamps. This only added to the burden on the rest of the Lumbee community, old men, women, and children; nevertheless, it was there in the swamps that these young Lumbee met up with Yankee soldiers who had escaped from the Confederate prison at Florence, South Carolina. These encounters and an approaching Union tornado—General William Tecumseh Sherman's Grand Army of the West—were to set in motion the creation and legendary operation of the Lowry Band of guerrillas.

Sherman, the most successful of all Union generals, had captured Atlanta in September and Savannah in December 1864, marching his magnificent army with devastating results. (American Indians were with him in his operations. Oneida Indians, in Company F of the Fourteenth Wisconsin Volunteer Infantry, were frequently cited for their sharpshooting abilities and took casualties during the campaign. Indians were also present at Sherman's sacking and burning of Columbia, South Carolina in December 1864.[44]) Although Sherman is best known for the Atlanta Campaign and his "March to the Sea," his Carolinas campaign from January 1865 to war's end in April may have been even more outstanding than his previous victories.[45]

The Carolinas Campaign lasted fifty days. From Savannah, Georgia to Goldsboro, North Carolina, the Grand Army of the West covered 425 miles, despite continuous fighting and only ten days rest. The relentless Sherman stretched his troops to the limits of their physical endurance, pushing them even more than in his famous march through Georgia. However real or imagined, his dreaded reputation preceded his famous campaign in the Carolinas. After his army sacked and burned Columbia on February 17, 1865, Sherman's image as a modern-day Genghiz Khan reverberated through Dixie. Long before he crossed into North Carolina, his forces had sent shock waves into Robeson and other counties in the southern part of the state.

While Sherman's army was planning to move north, the Lowrys were striking hard at their enemies. On December 21, 1864, the band attacked the plantation of James P. Barnes, with Henry Berry Lowry killing the wealthy slaveholder and minor official of the Confederacy in execution style. Barnes had aided in Robeson County's conscription of Indian labor, including several of the Lowrys, for the breastworks in the Wilmington area. Earlier, the planter had also made accusations of thievery against the family after searching the Lowry farmstead and finding the ears of two of his recently slaughtered hogs there.[46]

While American Indians were serving in the Union and Confederate armies, the frontier army of the United States was waging relentless warfare against the Indians of the Trans-Mississippi West. "Pacification" campaigns against the Santee in Minnesota, Cheyenne in Colorado, and Navajo and Apache in Arizona and New Mexico all occurred during the Civil War. Efforts to recruit a frontier army, as shown in this recruitment poster, continued despite manpower needs for federal troops in the East in 1864. (Courtesy Colorado Historical Society)

ATTENTION!
INDIAN
FIGHTERS

Having been authorized by the Governor to raise a Company of 100 day

U. S. VOL CAVALRY!

For immediate service against hostile Indians. I call upon all who wish to engage in such service to call at my office and enroll their names immediately.

Pay and Rations the same as other U. S. Volunteer Cavalry.

Parties furnishing their own horses will receive 40c per day, and rations for the same, while in the service.
The Company will also be entitled to all horses and other plunder taken from the Indians.

Office first door East of Recorder's Office.

HAL. SAYR.

Central City, Aug. 13, '64.

Previous to the Civil War, Delaware Indians were highly acclaimed guides and scouts for the wagon trains westward, for scientific explorations of the West, and for the Rocky Mountain fur trade. During the Civil War, Delaware continued to serve in this role for the Union army in the Trans-Mississippi West. Here they are shown as "Scouts for the National Army in the West." Sketch by Henry Lovie in *Frank Leslie's Illustrated*, December 6, 1862. (Courtesy New York State Library and New York State Museum)

While General Grant's Army of the Potomac was besieging Petersburg, the frontier army was busy "pacifying" Indians. Colonel John M. Chivington, Colorado's "Fighting Parson," shown here, led a force of 700 men that massacred approximately 200 Cheyenne Indians—men, women, and children—at Sand Creek on November 29, 1864. (Courtesy Colorado Historical Society)

General James G. Blunt (1826–1881), a Kansas physician and politician, was commander of the Department of Kansas for the Union army in 1862. He endorsed the plan to organize regiments of Kansas Indian Home Guards and a federal invasion of Indian Territory, the "First Indian Expedition," which ended largely in failure because of inadequate supplies and internecine bickering among the commanders. (Courtesy Oklahoma Historical Society)

Black Beaver (1806–1880), *Suck-tum-mah-kway,* has been credited with facilitating and guiding Union forces out of Indian Territory in April–May, 1861, and transporting them through Confederate-infested lands to Fort Leavenworth, Kansas. A leading scout in the Trans-Mississippi West, and a captain in the United States Army in the Mexican War, Black Beaver was the most famous Absentee Delaware of the nineteenth century. (Courtesy National Archives)

After the Civil War, Black Beaver and his Absentee Delaware people returned to the southwestern part of Indian Territory. Black Beaver served as a delegate to Washington in the late 1860s and 1870s and remained active in tribal affairs until his death in 1880. His tombstone, shown here, has the peace medal motif symbolizing the historic friendship and alliance of the Delaware with the United States which dates from 1778, the date of the first federal treaty with an American Indian nation. (Courtesy National Anthropological Archives)

The Creek Indian Nation in Indian Territory splintered down the middle into pro-Confederate and pro-Union camps during the Civil War. The pro-Union Creeks, the Upper Town, mostly full-blood Indians, were led by Opothleyaholo (shown here as a young man). This McKenney-Hall lithograph of 1837 was based on an 1825 painting by Charles Bird King. (Courtesy Oklahoma Historical Society)

General Stand Watie (1806–1871), *Degadoga*, who had become Principal Chief of the Cherokee Nation (South) in 1863, was the most successful Confederate commander in the Trans-Mississippi West in the last year of the Civil War. His capture of the Union ferry steamboat *J.R. Williams*, and his decisive victory at the Second Battle of Cabin Creek in 1864, were acts of military daring. Watie was one of the last Confederate generals to surrender his forces (June 23, 1865). (Courtesy Oklahoma Historical Society)

John Ross (1790–1866) was the Principal Chief of the Cherokee Nation from 1846 to 1866. Although he signed a treaty with the Confederacy, he and his supporters later gave their allegiance to the Union and served in the federal army. A bitter political opponent of Stand Watie, Ross remained in exile in Philadelphia and Washington from 1862 to the end of the Civil War. (Courtesy National Anthropological Archives)

Saladin Watie was the son of Stand Watie who served at his father's side as a Confederate officer during the Civil War. After the war, he represented the Cherokee Nation (South) faction in meetings with federal officials. Photograph by Brady's National Portrait Gallery, c. 1865. (Courtesy Oklahoma Historical Society)

Colonel John Jumper, a chief of the Seminole in Indian Territory, commanded the Seminole Battalion in the Confederate army in Indian Territory. In 1864, it was part of General Stand Watie's Indian Cavalry Brigade that captured the Union ferry steamboat *J.R. Williams* and successfully achieved a Confederate victory at the Second Battle of Cabin Creek. (Courtesy Oklahoma Historical Society)

William Terrill Bradby (b. 1833), shown here, and other adult men of the Pamunkey and Mattaponi Indian nations, served as Union river pilots, land guides, and spies for the Union army during the Peninsula Campaign of the spring and early summer of 1862. Indeed, General McClellan's headquarters at White House, Virginia, was just off of the Pamunkey Indian Reservation. Later in the 1890s, Bradby became associated with James Mooney and the Smithsonian Institution in efforts to document and preserve the culture of Virginia's Indians. (Courtesy Smithsonian Institution)

Henry Berry Lowry, shown here, is a folk hero to his people, the Lumbee Indians of North Carolina. Seen by local whites as a common outlaw and even a murderer, American Indians saw him as a leader against the enslavement and murder of Indians during and after the Civil War by the North Carolina Home Guards and the Ku Klux Klan. Lowry's guerrilla band's efforts in late 1864 and early 1865 aided the Union and facilitated General Sherman's Carolinas Campaign. (Courtesy North Carolina Department of Archives and History)

After the war, the controversial activities of Henry Berry Lowry and his famous band received national attention in an article, "The North Carolina Bandits," in *Harper's Weekly*, March 30, 1872. (Courtesy North Carolina Department of Archives and History)

General William Tecumseh Sherman (1820–1891). Sherman's Atlanta and Carolinas Campaigns were aided by Indian troops in the "Grand Army of the West." These troops included Oneida and Stockbridge Indians in the 14th Wisconsin Volunteer Infantry. Sherman's efforts were also helped by the activities of Indian guerrillas such as the Lowry Band who opposed the Confederacy. (Courtesy National Archives)

The Catawba Indians of South Carolina served as loyal allies of American colonists and the United States prior to the Civil War. In 1861 they, like their white neighbors, supported secession and the Confederate cause. Nineteen of their men served in the Confederate army, most of them becoming casualties of war. In 1900, Fort Mill, South Carolina, honored their extraordinary service by dedicating the Catawba Military Monument, inscribing it with the names of seventeen Indian soldiers in Confederate Park. (Photograph by author)

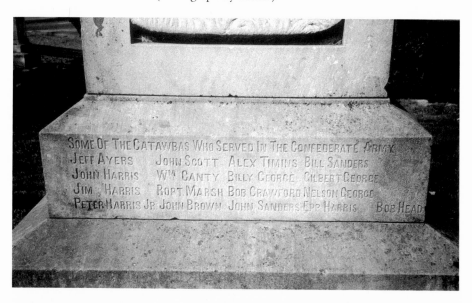

Although atrocities were common during the Civil War, Unionists were quick to stereotype Indian "savagery," especially by the Cherokee. Shown here are "Thomas' Rebel Indians Murdering Union Men" as depicted in Daniel Ellis, *Thrilling Adventures of Daniel Ellis* (1867).

Colonel William Holland Thomas (1805–1893) was a white trader, a North Carolina legislator, and an officer of the Confederate States of America. In his youth, he was adopted into the Cherokee by Chief Yonaguska. Thomas later served as attorney and spokesman for the Eastern Band of Cherokee. He was responsible for raising over 400 Cherokee troops for the Confederacy. These famous troops of the Thomas Legion became mountain rangers in western North Carolina and eastern Tennessee, guarding the passes as well as enforcing Confederate conscription. (Courtesy National Anthropological Archives, Smithsonian Institution)

The officers of the Thomas Legion (William Holland Thomas in the center) loyally served the Confederacy until Thomas's surrender at Waynesville, North Carolina, on May 9, 1865. (Courtesy North Carolina Department of Archives and History)

Like other Civil War veterans, Cherokee Confederate veterans of the Thomas Legion held annual reunions. They are shown here in 1901. (Courtesy North Carolina Department of Archives and History)

One of the reunions of Cherokee Confederate veterans of the Civil War was held in New Orleans in 1903. (Courtesy Museum of the Cherokee Indian)

General Ambrose Burnside (1824–1881) commanded the Union forces that captured New Bern, North Carolina, in March 1862. Later that year, he commanded the Army of the Potomac until he was relieved of command after admitting blame for the fiasco at the Battle of Fredericksburg. In subordinate positions of command in 1863 and 1864, he nevertheless urged Generals Grant and Meade to train and use the United States Colored Troops in the assault on Petersburg on July 30, 1864 (Battle of the Crater). Among these troops were American Indians. (Courtesy National Archives)

Ely S. Parker (1828–1895), *Do-ne-ho-ga-wa*, was a Seneca Indian sachem, engineer, and Union officer who served on General Grant's staff from 1864 onward. He served as Grant's military secretary and, on Grant's orders, transcribed the official surrender that General Robert E. Lee signed at Appomattox. He later became a brigadier general and the first American Indian to serve as United States Commissioner of Indian affairs, 1869–1871. Parker is seated in the far right of the photograph of General Grant and his staff, late spring, 1864. (Courtesy Buffalo and Erie County Historical Society)

Colonel, later General, Ely S. Parker, Seneca Indian sachem, General Grant's military secretary, and first American Indian to be United States Commissioner of Indian Affairs. (Courtesy National Archives)

Isaac Newton Parker (b. 1833), the brother of Ely S. Parker, was a Seneca Indian farmer, teacher, and entertainer who served as 3rd Sergeant of Company D of the 132nd New York State Volunteers, which was stationed in North Carolina for much of the war. His letters home to the Tonawanda Indian Reservation are one of the greatest portraits of American Indian life in the Union army. Although in this photograph he appears in a stereotypic, staged pose, he is wearing traditional Seneca garb of the early 1850s. (Courtesy Missouri Historical Society)

Opposite page: After the Confederate disaster at Gettysburg, (top) General George Pickett (1825–1875) was sent to recuperate and recruit in the Confederate Department of Virginia and North Carolina. In late January and early February 1864, he, as departmental commander, attempted along with his subordinates, (middle) General Seth M. Barton (1829–1900) and (bottom) Robert F. Hoke (1837–1912), to recapture New Bern, North Carolina, and seize Union supplies and railroad operations. His attack failed, in part because the Indians of Company D, 132nd New York State Volunteers, held a vital bridge and repulsed their advance.

Lieutenant Cornelius C. Cusick (1835–1904), a Tuscarora Indian, was a hero of the Civil War. As a member of D Company of the 132nd New York State Volunteer Infantry, he was cited for heroism twice in the Official Record. Cusick later became a captain in the regular army on the frontier, serving with distinction until his retirement in 1891. (Courtesy National Archives)

General John Henry Martindale (1815–1881) commanded the defenses of Washington in the first year of the Civil War and later led the XVIII Corps during the Petersburg Campaign in 1864. A prominent western New York attorney, Martindale was employed by the Tonawanda Seneca Indians and helped restore their lands prior to the Civil War. (Courtesy National Archives)

The band then struck by killing James Brantley Harris, a merchant and liquor dealer, who had led local white efforts to hunt down Indians in the swamps. Harris, a brutish man weighing two hundred thirty pounds, had been in charge of conscripting Indians into Confederate work gangs. Hated by all the Indians and even by many whites because of his rough, overbearing qualities, he had organized the Home Guard effort to capture the Indians fleeing work duty. Part of the problem in Harris's eyes was that these "lawless" Indians hid out in the junglelike swamps of Robeson County and survived by raiding wealthy white-owned plantations, stealing hogs and other livestock for food provisions.[47]

The Lowrys had a deep-seated resentment toward Harris. Henry Berry's young cousin Jarman had been ambushed and killed by the white bully, who had never been charged with the murder. Among the many Lumbee Harris had conscripted into service were Henry Berry's first cousins, Wesley and Allen Lowry, Jarman's older brothers. Later, after being arrested on the pretext of being absent without leave from Confederate labor service by Harris's Home Guard, both men were mysteriously found dead. In retaliation, Henry Berry executed Harris on January 15, 1865, in a barrage of gunfire while the white bully was riding in his buggy. Soon after, the Band raided the Robeson County Courthouse in Lumberton where they seized arms and ammunition, and stepped up their raids on local plantations for needed provisions.[48]

The diary of Washington Sandford Chaffin, a prominent Methodist minister in Lumberton, provides insights into what was transpiring in Robeson County during the winter of 1865. Chaffin constantly referred to rumors of approaching Yankees and General Sherman's progress; simultaneously, he mentioned the increasing local chaos within the region caused by alleged "deserters." On February 25, he insisted that these deserters "are doing much mischief in this country" and that they had "torn up and destroyed" much of the McKenzie homestead. Three days later, he claimed that the "deserters are committing numerous depredations in the country around Lumberton. People from this and other counties are running to and from and know not what to do." Chaffin's so-called "deserters" were undoubtedly members of the Lowry Band.[49]

The Lowry's raid on the Argyle plantation on February 27, 1865 set in motion a series of events that was to permanently affect the Indians of Robeson County. In the assault, a band member, Owen T. Wright, an escaped Union prisoner, was wounded. Soon Captain Hugh McGregor, along with the reorganized Home Guard, went in pursuit of the wounded Yankee and the rest of the band.

In retaliation for the Argyle plantation raid, paranoid about Sherman's imminent approach, and fearful of Yankees within their midst, one hundred officers and men of the North Carolina Home Guard began rounding up Indians and suspected white sympathizers. The Home Guard force, which included county magistrates, clergymen, and a lawyer, largely represented the interests of the planter class. On March 3, under McGregor's command, they raided the farm of Allen Lowry, Henry Berry's well-respected father, in their search for the wounded Yankee soldier, Yankee collaborators, and stolen property from the Argyle and other plantations. They found rifles, ammunition, blankets, clothing, and an inscribed golden head of a cane previously taken from a white squire during one of the Lowry Band's raids. The Home Guard then arrested Allen and his wife Mary Cumba, their children Calvin, Purline, Sally, and Sinclair, Allen's brother William, as well as a visiting friend, Anne Locklear. After plundering the Lowry farmstead, they bound their prisoners and carted them away to the smokehouse of Robert McKenzie, a member of the Home Guard. Allen Lowry was accused of housing one Union soldier in his home on one occasion, while William was charged by an eyewitness with being a member of the "outlaw" band who had rifled a nearby plantation. After William's failed attempt to escape, the Home Guard carted Allen and William back to the Lowry farmstead, blindfolded them, and then executed them with a twelve-man firing squad. They then stuffed the two bodies in a shallow makeshift grave. Henry Berry's father and uncle were thus added to the list of family members killed by the Home Guard.[50]

The Home Guard captured Owen Wright at the home of a local white schoolmistress sympathetic to the Lowrys and gained information from George Dial, one of their Lumbee captives, about a small cave hideout used to house arms and provisions.[51] On March 5, the Reverend John H. Coble, a member of the Home Guard, was ordered to read the letter of the law to the prisoners who were subsequently freed: ". . . if they fed or harbored any more Union soldiers or gave a deserter a meal [or] victuals, or if there was any more mischief through that neighborhood, they would have to suffer for it."[52] The next day, the Indians gathered at Allen and William Lowry's graves, reburied them in respectful fashion, and then pledged themselves to an all-out commitment to the Union effort, seeking retribution against the Home Guard for the Lowry murders.[53]

The Lumbee soon had a chance to pay back their local Robeson County enemies. On March 8, two days after Lowry's funeral, Sherman's army crossed into North Carolina. In torrential rains, the mighty force had to cross the Lumber River and its adjacent swamps with thousands of troops, wagons, and artillery pieces. In Sherman's own words: "It was the damnest marching I ever saw."[54]

Local Indians volunteered to guide Sherman and his army through the swamps.[55] Recalling this treacherous country, one Union general, John Logan, reflected on the difficulty of passage into southern North Carolina. Because of the heavy rains, Sherman's second division, after crossing the Lumber River, found that the bottom of the roads had been washed out. Logan claimed that the "roads were so bad that in places no ground could be found solid enough for the animals to stand upon, and wagons had to be pulled out of the mire by relays of men. . . ."[56]

Sherman's forces foraged and forcibly requisitioned in order to push forward at amazing speed. Ironically, the local Indians, who had cooperated with the Union at every turn in 1864 and early in 1865, soon found themselves worse off. Solomon Oxendine, a Lumbee who had been forced against his will to serve the Confederate labor needs at Fort Fisher, now saw his farm plundered in Sherman's whirlwind.[57] Later, in a petition for compensation that was granted a decade after the Civil War, Oxendine described how he and his wife had begged the Yankees to let him keep his mule, his only draft animal, but the soldiers insisted that, since they "were in this low country," they were "obliged to have good teams to get out."[58]

On March 9, General Francis Preston Blair sent a Union mounted force to Lumberton, the heart of Robeson County, thirty miles to the east, to burn all bridges and railroad property in the area.[59] To the white Confederate sympathizers, Mephistopheles had now made his appearance; their living hell was about to begin. Minister Chaffin reported in his diary that he heard two riders on the street shout, "The Yankees are coming, the Yankees are coming." Soon three to five hundred Union men descended on the town. They stole the minister's horse, destroyed his wagon, fired upon his neighbor, and obliterated the railroad bridges over the Lumber River, the rail depot, six boxcars, and approximately one mile of track. After entering many houses and committing "many depredations," they departed as quickly as they had entered the town.[60]

Despite the impending collapse of the Confederacy, the Home Guard continued to operate through the end of the war. On April 1, 1865, these white supremacist ruffians raided the residence of Sinclair Lowry. In a state of panic, Mary Cumba Lowry, who had been living there since the murder of her husband and her brother-in-law, ran off. She was subsequently captured, tied to a stake, and blindfolded. After Mary refused to reveal the whereabouts of her son Henry Berry, the commander, Neathan Thompson, in a mock execution, attempted to terrorize the woman into submission. Instead, she fainted. The Home Guard left without gaining any information about Henry Berry's hiding place.[61]

These guerrillas operated with abandon for the next decade until the death of Steve Lowry, the band's last active member. From 1865 to 1874, they sacked courthouses, robbed banks, plundered plantations, and attacked the new racist organization of Reconstruction, the Ku Klux Klan. The Lowry Band was often protected by local black and Indian communities terrorized by the resurgence of racial repression, after the pullout of Union troops from the region.

Despite his probable death in 1872, Henry Berry Lowry "reappeared" in alleged sightings as far away as California in the years that followed. Much like Emiliano Zapata and his devoted followers in Mexican Indian history, Lowry and his Band remain heroes, well ensconced in the minds and souls of North Carolina Indians. He, his band, and their legend helped define Indian existence even now at the end of the twentieth century. The legacy of the Lowry Band is clear to anyone who spends any time with Lumbee or in Robeson County. To anthropologist Gerald M. Sider, Lowry was "a hero who could not only change his own shape, as legends and contemporary accounts illustrate, but who changed the shape of a whole people."[62]

Today, Henry Berry Lowry, the "King of Scuffletown," is honored by Lumbee with plays and pageants recounting his famous story and by an annual award, the "Henry Berry Lowrie [Lowry] Award," given to a citizen who best exemplifies the highest standard of service to the community.[63]

To be good citizens of their Indian nation and help it survive, the Lowrys had to become "outlaws" in the eyes of the North Carolinian establishment. To present-day Lumbee this "outlaw" role is most fitting considering the desperate conditions that their ancestors faced. Unlike their Indian neighbors the Catawba of South Carolina, they chose to fight back against a Southern white supremacist order that surrounded and enslaved them. Indeed, their stance as guerrillas in the Civil War era separates them from most other southeastern Indians.

5

Infantrymen in the Army of Northern Virginia

The Catawba

ALTHOUGH SOME OF THE INDIANS OF THE SOUTH WERE UNIONISTS, greater numbers served in Confederate military service. The vast majority of southern Indians were nonconscripted recruits, although some eastern Choctaw in the First Choctaw Battalion, Mississippi Cavalry, were forced against their will to serve the Confederacy until their mass desertion and capture by Union forces during the onset of the Vicksburg Campaign in the spring of 1863.[1]

In stark contrast with the Pamunkey and Lumbee experiences, the Catawba Indians of South Carolina loyally served the Confederacy. Despite repeated efforts by South Carolina politicians to rid the "Magnolia State" of its American Indian populations by removing them westward and/or amalgamating them with other Indian nations, the Catawba participated in the heaviest fighting of the war as soldiers in the Army of Northern Virginia. Even before the Confederate assault on Fort Sumter, these Indians had thrown in their lot with the South.

In this specific instance, as in the other cases described previously, the Indians' choice of sides in the conflict was based on their precarious existence. By 1860, the Catawba had become almost totally dependent peoples whose tenuous economic, legal, and political status led them to choose the Confederacy. These Indians were historically tied as military allies, as slave catchers and/or day laborers to the planters of the piedmont. The Catawba chose an "accommodationist" strategy of survival, surrounded by perhaps the most loyal Confederate populace, the state that initiated the rebellion.

From well before the American Revolution through the early national period, white South Carolinians believed that "of all the Southeastern Indians, the Catawba were the best friends the colonists had."[2] Only once in the colonial period, during the Yamassee War of 1715, did they ever attack Americans. In this era, because of their legendary skills as warriors, they were indispensable allies of the Colony of South Carolina against the French and the Cherokee Indians. Edmond Atkin, a South Carolinian politician and British superintendent of Indian affairs for the southern colonies, insisted during the 1740s that "in War, they [Catawba] are inferior [to] no Indians whatever."[3] Later, historian James Adair, in his classic study of American Indians written in 1775, concurred, ranking Catawba warriors on an equal plain with the Chickasaw for their aggressive disposition.[4]

The Catawba also served white South Carolinians in other ways. The planters used them to terrorize their black slaves to prevent this labor force from running away and fleeing into the interior. In the event the slaves escaped, Catawba were hired to track them down. Because of fears of slave insurrection after the Stono Insurrection of 1739 and the demographic reality that blacks outnumbered white South Carolinians—African American slaves comprised more than two-thirds of the colony's population in the first half of the eighteenth century—Catawba warriors were considered lifesavers in this role.[5]

Catawba service was noted by Governor Charles Greville Montagu in 1769. Montagu wrote about the apprehension of black runaways who fled into the swamps about Christmastime of 1765. Fearing a major conspiracy, the governor of South Carolina sent his militia along with a "number of Catawba Indians" to "hunt out the fugitive slaves in their different recesses almost impervious to White

Men at that Season of the Year." The Indians "partly by the Terror of their name, their diligence and singular sagacity in pursuing Enemies through such Thickets soon dispersed the runaway Negroes." The Indians caught some of the slaves while "most of the rest of them chose to surrender themselves to their Masters, & return to their duty rather than Expose themselves to the attack of an Enemy so dreaded and so difficult to be resisted or evaded, for which good service the Indians were very amply rewarded."[6]

Despite their friendly service, however, the Catawba world was turned upside down by the whites. Between 1759 and 1760, a small-pox epidemic killed one-half to three-quarters of their population, leaving only three hundred or so alive. They had over three hundred warriors at the onset of the French and Indian War, but war with the Cherokee in the 1750s and early 1760s also substantially reduced Catawba population. Moreover, in retaliation for their loyal service to the Americans in the Revolutionary War, the British burned the Catawba's major village to the ground.[7]

After the American Revolution, the small Catawba community could not avoid the increased numbers of white settlers, mostly Scots-Irish, seeking lands in the piedmont. These intruders began to settle on tribal territory, a fifteen-square-mile, 144,000-acre estate which the Colony of South Carolina had recognized as the Catawba Reservation in 1763. By the first three decades of the nineteenth century, white South Carolinians' quest for cotton lands put a pre-mium on the best of the Catawba's land base. Instead of using the Catawba as allies and/or as employees in holding the slave system together, the white South Carolinians now desired the Indians' land. They encouraged the underpopulated Catawba to lease their vast tribal estate. By the mid-1820s, the Indians had leased out almost all of their prime lands. By that time, they had become weak and im-poverished, overdependent on the white man and largely dissipated on his alcohol.[8]

In order to survive, the Catawba became "show Indians," putting on archery exhibitions for the locals in Camden or Charleston, South Carolina or at Fayetteville, North Carolina. They also performed their songs and dances in theaters as far away as Great Britain. Those that stayed behind became day laborers for whites in the piedmont.[9] By the late 1830s, some had migrated to live among their former enemies, the Cherokee in western North Carolina.

In 1840, as a result of pressures from these lessees, South Carolina largely imposed a "solution" to their "Indian Problem." Hoping to secure title to their leased lands, the white settlers convinced state officials to negotiate a land purchase from the Indians. In clear violation of the federal Trade and Intercourse Act of 1790 which prohibited acquisition of Indian lands without Washington's permission, South Carolina negotiated the so-called "Treaty" of Nations Ford with the Catawba, taking advantage of the Indians' leaderless state after the deaths of their principal chief, General Jacob Ayers in 1837, and Ayers's successor, "Acting Chief" William Harris. James Kegg, a Pamunkey-Catawba and the oldest man in the nation—he was fifty-five—signed the agreement. Kegg, lacking the necessary leadership requirement of having been a Catawba warrior, was "ready to sell out and join the Cherokees, where prospects seemed brighter." It is important to note that some of the major leaders opposed to land sales had died in the late 1830s and that Catawba cohesion had been weakened by tribal outmigration.[10]

By the Treaty of Nations Ford, the Catawba Indians agreed "to cede, sell, transfer and convey" their entire territory to South Carolina, namely fifteen square miles, "all their right, title, and interest to their boundary of land lying on both sides of the Catawba River, situated in the Districts of York and Lancaster." In return, the state agreed to furnish the Catawba "a tract of land valued at $5,000," three hundred acres "to be good arable lands fit for cultivation" in Haywood County, North Carolina "or in some other mountainous or thinly populated region." The state also agreed to pay the Catawba $2,500 "at or immediately after their removal," and $1,500 each year for nine subsequent years.[11] The agreement was farcical. Not only did South Carolina have no federal authority to make a "treaty" with the Catawba, state officials did not even secure permission from neighboring North Carolina to relocate the Catawba there.

Despite these failures, the Cherokee council approved the idea, and, by 1847, nearly one hundred Catawba had left for the North Carolina mountains; there, however, the Catawba found Cherokee Country largely unfriendly. Past conflict between the two groups and Cherokee insistence that the refugees become tributary Indians and give up their language and identity led many Catawba to leave, some returning to become squatters on their lost homeland.[12]

Approximately half of the Catawba had remained behind in their South Carolina homeland in spite of the treaty. Because they had not been removed, the Indians were not "entitled" to collect the $2,500 or their nine-year annuity payment. Now, the impoverished Catawba had to deal with the State of South Carolina that no longer recognized Indian title to their fifteen-square-mile territory. When efforts to remove all the Catawba to North Carolina failed, South Carolina officials reluctantly "rectified" the situation until they could find a way to amalgamate the Catawba with other Indians as far west as Indian Territory. In 1842, state officials "temporarily" set aside an infertile, hilly, 630-acre tract of land, nine miles from Rock Hill, South Carolina, near the eighteenth-century Catawba village of Newtown. The largely destitute Indians were allowed to remain and subsist as best they could, the agent being instructed to draw a sum of about $1,000 a year to purchase supplies for them. Except for a grist mill and a ferry service at Land Ford (Landsford), the Indians depended on day labor, often wandering far and wide to secure their economic survival.[13]

South Carolina officials continued to urge wholesale Indian removal from the state. Some of the Catawba actually went west. Throughout the 1840s and 1850s, plans at both the state and national levels were floated, with at least some Catawba support, to merge the remaining Indians with the Choctaw and Chickasaw of Indian Territory. Although some Catawba remained in the West, both of these efforts were subsequently rejected by the respective Indian councils.[14]

By 1850, there were only a little over one hundred Catawba Indians left, with an approximately equal number living in North and South Carolina. This number included at least twenty adult men, forty-three adult women, and twenty male and female children under ten years of age. These numbers changed little in the ten years remaining before the war. In 1856, still only fifty Catawba lived in South Carolina; by the outbreak of the Civil War, their number had only risen to fifty-five.[15] Far from the proud and brave Indian warriors who were an essential part of South Carolina's frontier defense and slave system in the colonial era, the Catawba had become a splintered nation, a vanishing people whose survival was tenuous at best.

Yet despite this tragic sequence, and despite their deplorable, splintered, alcohol-encumbered condition, after South Carolina seceded in December 1860 and Fort Sumter was attacked in April 1861, nearly all of the adult male population of the Catawba enlisted in Confederate military service, serving in the Fifth, Twelfth, and Seventeenth South Carolina Volunteer Infantry regiments. Perhaps a few other Catawba were represented in the ranks of the Cherokee Indian companies of the Thomas Legion of Indians and Highlanders, which operated as units in the Confederate army in the mountainous country of western North Carolina and eastern Tennessee.[16]

Undoubtedly, the Confederate bounty for enlistment—up to $50 in 1861—was an enticement for all impoverished Indian enlistees in the South. More importantly to the Catawba, to prove oneself in war was the highest manly virtue and a requirement for political leadership. Memories of the glory years of the first half of the eighteenth century were well etched in their folk traditions. They had not shirked from combat with their powerful Iroquois and Cherokee enemies.[17] As historian James Merrell has written, their warfare was not based on "mere protection or simple survival." Merrell added: "Warfare was part of life, and Catawbas shared with Indians throughout eastern North America a culture of conflict, with its own rules and symbols, sorrows and satisfactions."[18] From their high enlistments, Catawba a century later still saw battle as an arena for securing their full manhood. Thus, for Catawba, as well as for many white southerners, combat was a proving ground for manliness.[19]

Decades after the Civil War era, Catawba told anthropologist Frank Speck that the Indians were threatened by Ferguson Barber, a white man who lived near their South Carolina homeland. According to this tradition, Barber demanded that the Indians "would have to enlist or the whites would come down and kill them."[20] Although South Carolina–Catawba relations were often tense and the state frequently attempted to remove the Indians, the explanation given to Speck appears to be a concocted postwar rationale for Catawba involvement in the Confederate cause. The Catawba had an outstanding military record, one that cannot be simply rationalized by their "impressment" into the South's military service.

But there was more behind their enlistment than mere Confederate conscription, money, or their general attitude toward war. Anthropologist Charles Hudson provides the best explanation for Catawba Confederate military service. According to Hudson, as "the Civil War approached, the Catawbas were an obscure enclave in a social system [southern plantation slavery] that was beginning to break down." Hudson added: "When the Civil War came, a few Catawbas served in the Confederate Army, thus indicating their agreement with white ideology."[21] Their slave catching in the eighteenth and nineteenth centuries signaled something deeper than mere convenience. The Catawba had not only become economically dependent on the white power structure of South Carolina, but also had become psychologically dependent peoples as well. In effect, the Southern way of life was meaningful to them, and worth fighting for.[22]

In this respect, they had much in common with poor Confederate recruits, who owned no slaves but nevertheless identified with the "Stars and Bars." The Catawba could not match the power of the planter class. Although they were considered to be on a lower plain in the social hierarchy of the South than their poor white neighbors, both groups saw themselves as distinct, more powerful, and superior to local blacks, slave or free. As "good neighbors," each deferred to the leadership of the planter class, their so-called "betters" on whom they were dependent.

Some Catawba had already signed up for military service even before the first shots on Fort Sumter. In January 1861, an editorial writer in *The New York Times* reported that these Indians "had offered themselves to Governor Perkins, to serve in a military capacity, and that the offer had been accepted by the Governor." The Northern editorial writer dismissed as outlandish the gloomy thought of "myriads of scowling Catawba" who "should bend their bows against New-York, or sharpen their tomahawks on the steps of St. Nicholas." Describing the Catawba as "utterly degenerated and degraded" and living in a state of abject poverty, indolence, and alcoholism, the writer implied the Catawba commitment was hardly a deep one.[23] He was wrong. In all, nineteen Catawba served in the Confederate army: Jeff Ayres, John Brown, Frank Canty, William Canty, Bob Crawford, Billy George, Gilbert George, Nelson George, Allen Harris, Epps Harris, Jim Harris, John Harris, Peter Harris, Jr., Bob Head, James Kegg, Robert Marsh, John Sanders, John Scott, and Alexander Timms. They comprised nearly all the able-bodied tribesmen.[24]

Right through Appomattox, Catawba remained loyal to the South. They fought in the Peninsula Campaign, the Second Battle of Bull Run, Antietam, and in the trenches before Petersburg. At least seven died.[25] According to one scholar, "only three returned home whole in body. Others died in battle, died in Northern prison camps, died as a result of health problems aggravated by field life or came home hopelessly crippled."[26]

Catawba were part of Captain, later Colonel, Cadwalader Jones's famed Company H of the Twelfth South Carolina Volunteer Infantry.[27] Jones's unit was part of the First Corps of the Army of Northern Virginia, General Ambrose P. Hill's Light Division, General David McMurtrie Maxcy Gregg's Second Brigade. Frequently mentioned in the official war record, in the first year of the war, the regiment, largely served in providing coastal defense of North and South Carolina ports bombarded by the Union navy.[28] Their first true test by fire came in the Peninsula Campaign, especially at the Seven Days Battles in the early summer of 1862.[29] It was in August and September of 1862, at the Second Battle of Bull Run and at Antietam that the Twelfth South Carolina made its mark.

These two battles have been well chronicled elsewhere, and some readers may not need to be reminded of the extraordinary carnage, close-range destruction, and battlefield chaos that ensued. But since an appreciation of Catawba loyalty and commitment to the South is meaningless absent the awful context of these engagements, I will give a brief recap. At sunset on August 28, at the Battle of Groveton, General Thomas Stonewall Jackson's three Confederate divisions pounced on one of General John Pope's Union divisions in the wooded ridge along the Warrenton turnpike just west of where the First Battle of Bull Run had been fought a year earlier. Pope hoped to destroy Jackson's army, stationed in a railroad cut, the next morning before it could be reinforced by General James Longstreet's forces since the Union general had more than three times the Confederate force of twenty thousand men with him.[30]

At around ten o'clock on the morning of August 29, despite Jackson's orders not to engage the enemy, General Gregg sent Colonel Dixon Barnes and the Twelfth South Carolina down the slope of a rocky knoll. His troops and the 1st South Carolina struck the federal troops of the Fifty-fourth and Fifty-eighth New York who were charging up the hill. After inflicting heavy casualties, the South Carolinians advanced on the open fields and then into the woods, where they met up with the Seventy-fifth Pennsylvania. The Confederate movement forward came to an abrupt halt after taking heavy fire from the Pennsylvanians. Gregg called up the Thirteenth South Carolina and soon the "strip of woods in front of Gregg's rocky knoll filled with smoke from the fire of fifteen hundred men."[31] Gregg's regiments actually lost contact with each other in the brutal fire-fight.

By eleven o'clock, after an hour of this fighting, Gregg's men faced a new onslaught of Union forces: the Eighth West Virginia, the 1st New York, the Sixty-first Ohio, and the Seventy-fifth Pennsylvania. Barnes' regiment attempted to hold back the tide since his forces were now badly outnumbered. He decided on a bold move: He sent his three-hundred-twenty-man regiment forward through the forest and ordered them to charge. The South Carolinians broke through the federal lines, overwhelming the forces of the First New York. Soon, both the Fifty-fourth New York and the Eighth West Virginia collapsed. The center of the Union line in the woods "cracked like an old pane on a winter morning."[32]

Unable to move forward without reinforcements, the South Carolinians now had to contend with five field pieces of Yankee artillery. Gregg's exhausted men regrouped atop the knoll once again. The battle soon drew to a stalemate. The calm proved temporary; it abruptly ended between two and three in the afternoon when General Pope decided to test Jackson's line. He ordered General Joseph Hooker to move forward into the woods and attack. Around three o'clock, Hooker sent General Cuvier Grover with his New England troops, which included the First and Eleventh Massachusetts and the Second New Hampshire, to carry out a frontal attack. Grover had his men fix bayonets and then charge forward; by accident, they found a 125-yard gap in the Confederate lines. Grover's regiments rushed up the railroad cut. The Union forces threatened to cut off Gregg's men from the rest of the Confederate army; however, the federal unit's heavy casualties and the absence of Union reinforcements slowed his progress, giving the Confederates time to respond.[33]

Gregg reshuffled his lines, once more ordering Colonel Barnes and the Twelfth South Carolina into the fray. Employing their bayonets, the Twelfth advanced "with a rush and a shout, and with cold steel and nothing more."[34] The South Carolinians challenged Grover's advance, pounding them and trapping them in deadly fire.

With the ebb and flow of the battle, the South Carolina units again found themselves on the defensive around five o'clock that same day. General Phil Kearney's Union forces—the Third Michigan, 105th Pennsylvania, Fortieth and 101st New York, and the Fourth Maine—encircled them and then poured on their rifle fire at a stone's-throw range. Gregg responded. He drew out his grandfather's revolutionary sword and boldly strode down the lines, shouting: "Let us die here, my men, let us die here."[35] Teetering on the edge of defeat, the South Carolinians re-formed their crumbled lines. The heavy fire of the South Carolinian rifles pushed the Union force back three hundred yards in close, hand-to-hand combat. They held the line until they were reinforced by General Jubal Early's 2,500 Confederates a half hour later, an action that isolated and devastated Kearney's tired federals who were forced to retreat.[36]

In his official report, Colonel Cadwalader Jones of the Twelfth South Carolina described his men's rout of Kearney's men at the Second Battle of Bull Run:

> Very soon the enemy, in numbers considerably exceeding our own, were seen advancing through the woods on our left. It became necessary immediately to charge front, which being done we exchanged several rounds with the enemy, when the Twelfth advanced and the enemy retreated. They soon reformed with the assistance of fresh troops, who endeavored to flank us on the left. Here one or two of our companies on the left were caused to change front and fire on the flanking column. A single well-directed volley put them to flight. Wheeling these companies again into line, the Twelfth charged in the most gallant manner, firing as it advanced, and putting the enemy completely to rout, pursued them with heavy slaughter through the woods and until they crossed the field beyond and ran out of sight. Being now about half a mile from our starting point, we fell back into the woods a short distance. Very soon a fresh column of the enemy, probably three regiments, were seen advancing. Just at this time the First Rifles, most opportunely, were also seen advancing through the woods to our support. Forming a line with and on the left of this regiment, together we gave them battle, and without much difficulty or loss again drove back the enemy.[37]

Pope's dispirited army fled across Bull Run via the Stone Bridge and the neighboring fords to Centreville. On August 31, in a torrential downpour at Chantilly, Virginia, Jackson once again clashed with Pope. The Union force soon after pulled back to the security of the District of Columbia defense perimeter. In all, the Army of Northern Virginia had inflicted 16,000 casualties on Union forces during the Second Bull Run Campaign; Union forces were responsible for inflicting 9,200 Confederate casualties.

Less than three weeks later, on September 17, 1862, the Twelfth South Carolina fought at Sharpsburg, Maryland, in the Battle of Antietam, the bloodiest single day of fighting of the Civil War. After

Pope's defeat at the Second Battle of Bull Run, Lee undertook his first invasion of the North. Lee was intent on retaining the initiative, winning the border state of Maryland to his side, fomenting an anti-war movement in the North, and drawing Union troops away from his beloved Virginia, especially Richmond.

On September 15, Jackson captured Harper's Ferry. Keyed by Jackson's success, Lee, with only 19,000 men and standing with his back to the Potomac River, decided to take a stand at Sharpsburg, Maryland, even before Jackson could arrive with his additional 21,000 men. Knowing of Lee's plan in advance from captured orders and realizing he had the overwhelming numerical advantage, McClellan was ready, but unable to win the day. The Union general launched a series of uncoordinated attacks, first on the north flank, then on the center, and next on the right. His underling, General Ambrose Burnside, delayed his Union attack on his right, allowing Lee to shift forces from one area to another to oppose the repeated Northern assaults. The most intense fighting of the war subsequently occurred at the Corn Field, the West Woods, the East Woods, Dunkard Church, the Roulette House, Bloody Lane, and at the stone river crossing dubbed "Burnside Bridge," because of the Union general's repetitive but foolhardy suicidal attempts to cross it under crushing fire.

Although the Confederates had secured their left and center flanks, the Union forces began to penetrate the Confederate right. Suddenly General A. P. Hill's Confederate division, as a result of a forced march, arrived from Harper's Ferry. Hill's forces delivered a crushing counterattack which saved Lee's right. Hill's contingent contained the 12th South Carolina Volunteers, Jones' company. Much of their fighting ironically centered on combat in the "Forty-Acre Cornfield," full of Indian corn. General Maxcy Gregg's brigade, which included the Twelfth South Carolina, arrived around four in the afternoon along the Harper's Ferry Road and the Miller's Saw Mill Road.[38] As the battlefield darkened in the late afternoon and early evening, Gregg's men moved directly into the fields south of the advancing federal line.[39]

Gregg's men took the federals by surprise. The two hundred fifty men of the Twelfth South Carolina, now behind a stone wall, fired directly into the Union forces only about ten feet away. Colonel Dixon Barnes' Confederates unloaded directly into the Sixteenth Connecticut Volunteer Infantry. The South Carolinians fooled the Union force by waving captured Northern colors and "shouting not to shoot at 'friends.' Too many of the startled Yankees complied." In the slaughter that immediately followed, the Connecticut regiment took more than three hundred casualties in a matter of minutes. They fled in panic to Antietam Creek.[40] The Union forces, which totaled 75,000 men, took 12,000 casualties, 2,108 killed. Despite the incompetence of their command, the Union army inflicted 13,724 casualties, 2,700 killed, on the Confederate forces; however, the Union's real chance of ending the war by trapping Lee at Sharpsburg was lost in McClellan's inaction and delay, allowing the Army of Northern Virginia to escape across the Potomac to safety and regroup for another two and a half years of resistance.[41]

The story of two of the nineteen Catawba in gray is particularly drenched in the irony of the tribe's experience as a whole. Prior to the fighting, John Harris and his brother James, both in the Twelfth South Carolina Regiment, were serving as cooks for their comrades-in-arms; as foot soldiers at the Battle of Antietam, they were both wounded and taken as Union prisoners of war. John Harris was shot with a Union musket ball in the left leg and led away to Fort Monroe. He was later freed in a prisoner exchange in May, 1863, and sent back to Confederate military service. In September, 1864, he was discharged because of a disability of his left leg. After the Civil War he served as the Catawba chief. James, also wounded at the Battle of Antietam, remained incarcerated as a Union prisoner of war for the remainder of the Civil War.[42]

In 1885, the *Rock Hill Herald* reflected on the Harris brothers' service and suggested that their white neighbors honor these loyal Confederate soldiers "with suitable headstones" at their Indian reservation gravesite. The editorial writer of this South Carolina newspaper indicated that "their conduct throughout that bloody conflict was marked with great conduct and fidelity." As a result of the war, they suffered immensely and died soon after the conflict. John Harris "was a cripple through life from a wound received at the battle of Sharpsburg." After being shot and fearing that he "might fall into the hands of the enemy," John "begged his comrades to kill him rather than permit this [to] happen." The editorial concluded that the two Harris brothers were "both good soldiers under all circumstances and it is suggested that Company H take steps to preserve the memory of their gallantry and fidelity in some suitable way."[43]

After more than a decade of planning, the white people of York County eventually honored their Indian neighbors by erecting a statue for Catawba veterans of the American Revolution and Civil War in Confederate Park at Fort Mill, South Carolina. At its base are the names of seventeen of the nineteen Catawba who fought as "good neighbors" side by side with the white folk of York County. The statue, which is ten and a half feet high on a four-foot foundation, is surrounded by other monuments to the "lost cause," and is the most impressive statue in the park. It was erected by Samuel Eliot White and Thomas McKee Spratt, the latter a descendant of frontier settlers of the piedmont of the 1750s. In its cornerstone were placed Confederate relics as well as Indian "arrowheads and pots."[44]

Fifty Indians from the Catawba Reservation attended the ceremonies and dinner that followed the monument's dedication on August 3, 1900. One local reporter covering the events considered John Harris to have been "one of the bravest members of the Twelfth South Carolina," and so it was only fitting that a highlight of that summer day was the speech of Ben Harris, the son of John. Playing the role of "good Indian" neighbor, Ben claimed that love makes the Indian a friend of the white man. Of his white neighbors, he added: "The Catawbas never took part against him [the white man]. . . ." in any war.[45]

We know something of the other Catawba Confederates. George Nelson, also in Jones's H Company, was captured and remained a prisoner of war until May 1865. Just prior to his capture, Nelson and his Catawba friend William Canty, who had previously served in the

Seventeenth South Carolina, had reenlisted for Confederate service in the Twelfth. Even at the bitter end, the Indians continued to commit themselves to the "Stars and Bars." This fact is even more surprising in Canty's case. While serving in the Seventeenth South Carolina in his first year of Confederate service, he was wounded three times—at the Second Battle of Bull Run, Antietam, and Boonesboro. He also suffered from jaundice, undoubtedly caused by infection from his wounds.[46]

Catawba also served in the Lacy Guards, Company K of the Seventeenth South Carolina Volunteer Infantry. Much like the early involvement of the Twelfth, the Seventeenth largely served initially on coastal duty protecting the ports of the Carolinas from Union bombardment and invasion. They provided valuable service at the Second Battle of Bull Run, taking heavy casualties when they broke through a federal line of batteries in the late afternoon on August 30, 1862. Also with the 12th Regiment, they participated in the bloodbath at Sharpsburg, Maryland on September 17. Soon after, they were sent to North Carolina to ward off a federal attempt to block the Confederate rail link between Wilmington, North Carolina and Richmond and to build coastal defenses.[47]

From May 1864 to April 1865, the Seventeenth served in the Army of Northern Virginia in the Confederate trenches before Petersburg. They were involved in repulsing each of the six assaults on the city, holding off the Union forces until a few days before spring in 1865. They played a key role in preventing the Union forces, some of whom were themselves American Indians, from penetrating the city's defenses in the Battle of the Crater on July 30, 1864. Elliott's Brigade held their hilltop position from early morning until the end of the day. Despite heavy losses, they prevented the Federals from breaking through, mowing down the Union troops "like wheat in a harvest field," until General Mahone saved the day. In the regimental history of the unit, Captain W. H. Edwards wrote: "No command during the Confederate war or any other war of modern times ever opposed successfully greater odds or fought with more distinguished gallantry than did Elliott's Brigade at the

Battle of the Crater." Indeed, they continued to hold their line until March 15, 1865.[48]

One Catawba, Jefferson Ayers, was shot in the head at Hatcher's Run during the Petersburg Campaign. After his capture, he was sent to Hammond General Hospital, a Union medical facility at Lookout, Maryland, where he died in July 1865. Ayers had reenlisted in November 1863, even though he had earlier been wounded at the Battle of Boonesboro.[49]

Almost all Catawba who fought became casualties. Alexander Timms was wounded at the Second Battle of Bull Run while Robert Marsh was in and out of Confederate military hospitals throughout the war, dying on the Old Reservation on August 28, 1864.[50] Of the Catawba in the Seventeenth, only John Scott, who became a chief in the post–Civil War era, appears to have survived Confederate military service unscathed, and was mustered out on February 3, 1863, at Charleston.[51]

Although Catawba served in other units, most notably Company G of the Fifth South Carolina Infantry, their involvement in this regiment is harder to piece together. At least three served in this unit—Robert Crawford, Peter Harris, and Robert Head—all enlisting on May 13, 1862. Head died of wounds or disease, and Harris was captured after the fall of Petersburg on April 2, 1865; he was also imprisoned for a short tenure at Hart's Island, in New York harbor.[52]

The Catawba were not the largest Indian group to join the Confederates, nor were they the most significant in military terms. But they were far and away the most committed to the Confederate cause. Brave and loyal to the bitter end, they were exposed to the very worst of the war, and though nearly utterly destroyed, they fought as a matter of course, with deep commitment and as a matter of pride. Unlike the Lumbee less than two hundred miles to the east who frequently and aggressively challenged their domination by the surrounding white power structure, the Catawba always attempted to adjust themselves and accommodate. Although they had already been decimated by contact with whites, they nevertheless perceived themselves as Indians as well as Southerners, always ready to take to the warpath in their role of "good neighbors."

6

Confederate Rangers of the Smokies

Wil-Usdi's Eastern Band of Cherokee

BY FAR THE MOST IMPORTANT INDIAN CONTRIBUTION TO THE Confederate war effort in the East occurred in the mountains of western North Carolina and eastern Tennessee. Over four hundred Indians, a vital part of William Holland Thomas's famed Confederate Legion of Cherokee Indians and Highlanders, served the South from early 1862 to May 1865. Frequently mentioned in the official records of the Civil War, they enforced the Confederate Conscription Act of 1862, helped weed out Unionist efforts at spying and recruiting in the region, served as valuable sentinels in the high-pass country, and attempted to block Union incursions through the mountains.[1] Holding strategic positions in one of the more impenetrable regions of the Southeast, these Indian rangers stymied Union efforts to dislodge them throughout the war.

Any discussion of these noted warriors must begin by focusing on the extraordinary life of Colonel William Holland Thomas, their commander. Thomas was born on February 5, 1805, at Waynesville (Mount Prospect) in the rugged mountain world of western North Carolina. He was the son of Richard Thomas, of Welsh descent, who had fought on the American side in the War for Independence, and

Temperance Calvert Strother of Newcastle, England. Just prior to his son's birth, Richard Thomas drowned. The fatherless boy was raised by his devoutly religious mother. In his youth, he became fascinated with the nearby Cherokee Indians who lived near his home along Raccoon Creek, two miles east.

At the age of twelve, William Holland Thomas was adopted by Cherokee chief Yonaguska (Drowning Bear). Through this physically and intellectually imposing Indian leader, who was well respected by his people, Thomas learned the language and customs of the Cherokee. He was bestowed with the name Wil-Usdi, "Little Will." Yonaguska in many ways became his surrogate father. More precisely, in the context of Cherokee culture, Yonaguska assumed the role of Little Will's maternal uncle since Cherokee uncles served as role models for their nephews.[2] It should be noted that Yonaguska, as a result of pressures of white frontier settlement, eventually moved his people near the confluence of the Soco Creek and Oconaluftee River. Often referred to as "Oconaluftee" or "Lufty" Indians, Yonaguska's Cherokee became the core community of Cherokee Indians who today occupy the Qualla Boundary Reservation in western North Carolina.[3]

By the age of thirteen, Thomas was already working at Felix Walker's Trading Post along the Soco Creek. The majority of his customers were Cherokee who bartered furs, hides, and herbs for general merchandise. By 1822, Thomas established his own store at Indiantown (Quallatown) at the Cherokee crossroads. Within the next fifteen years, years of crisis in Cherokee history caused by pressures for removal, Thomas became a leading entrepreneur in western North Carolina. By 1837, he was the owner of seven trading post/general merchandise stores and had acquired grist mills, saw mills, and tanneries. Within the next twenty years, he acquired thousands of acres of lands. From 1848 to the Civil War, as an elected North Carolina legislator, he also pushed for railroad and other major economic development in western North Carolina.[4]

Despite his growing acquisitiveness and fondness for new capitalist ventures, Thomas served as an advocate for Cherokee treaty rights and played the role of Indian benefactor through the Civil War. It is clear that he also went beyond this, seeing himself as a Cherokee, a transculturated person, in the classic "white Indian" syndrome found in captivity narratives.[5]

In the 1820s, Thomas had read law, a background that served him in his efforts to secure Cherokee Indian rights. In 1830, he was appointed attorney for the Cherokee, representing many Indians for the next forty years. During the removal crisis of the 1830s, he served as the Cherokee agent. Thomas worked with Yonaguska drafting a new governmental structure, laying out towns—Bird Town, Wolf Town, Yellow Hill, Big Cove, Pretty Woman Town—and developing a strategy to ward off removal to the West.[6]

At that time the Appalachian Cherokee were a diverse and disunited people. Political struggles between the forces of John Ross and the Watie-Ridge family led to violent blood feuds. Yonaguska, with Thomas's help, presented his people at Quallatown as law-abiding and peaceful Indians outside the bounds of the discordant elements of the Cherokee Nation. These approximately 330 Oconoluftee Indians were pictured by Yonaguska and Thomas as desirous of being American citizens and citizens of the state of North Carolina. As so-called "Citizen" Cherokee, they saw their best hope in Article 12 of the New Echota Treaty of 1835. This nefarious treaty of removal provided annuities to any Cherokee individual or family who did not want to move provided they became citizens of the state in which they resided.[7] For the next thirty years, Thomas attempted to obtain annuities for his destitute charges, gain a firm assurance that the Indians at Quallatown could remain in North Carolina permanently, and secure constitutional protections for these Citizen Cherokee and their lands.[8]

Not all Cherokee resisted removal and fled into the mountains in the 1830s. Some actually cooperated with American military personnel and even served in tracking down other bands of Appalachian Cherokee. One scholar has insisted that, despite the universal image of Cherokee resistance to removal in 1838, Yonaguska's "Oconaluftee Citizen Indians" actually gave United States military personnel assistance in bringing so-called fugitive Cherokee to Fort Cass at the Calhoun agency. In return, General Winfield Scott "made it clear that these Indians were not to be disturbed." These "Citizen Indians, comprised of approximately seventy households, formed the nucleus of what became the Eastern Band of Cherokee Indians."[9] This core group was later joined by Euchella's band of Cherokee, some of whom had also been associated with rounding up Indians during the removal.[10]

Quallatown Cherokee cooperation with the white power structure continued to be a feature of Indian life in the antebellum period after the 1830s. Unlike Pamunkey and especially Lumbee who were avenging past wrongs in 1860, the Oconaluftee had survived by playing the role of "good Indian." With their white benefactor Wil-Usdi, they attempted to improve their anomalous position by repeated petitioning, sending delegations to Washington, and insisting that they were American citizens.

At the death of Yonaguska in 1839, Flying Squirrel of Paint Town at first succeeded to office; however, because of Thomas's abilities and ties to Yonaguska, Wil-Usdi soon became de facto chief. Although not trusted and even resented by many, Thomas had the backing of the core group at Quallatown and became their voice in their appeals to Washington and to Raleigh. More than ever, the Oconoluftee attempted accommodation with the whites. From 1839 onward, Thomas frequently urged federal and state officials to allow the remaining Cherokee to stay in their North Carolina homeland. He also appealed for annuity payments for his impoverished charges, and bought land in his name in order to skirt state legal restriction about Indian land purchases. He allowed Indians to buy on credit at his stores, promoted Indian conversion by importing Bibles and hymnals in the Cherokee language and giving land to the Methodist Church, encouraged Indian efforts at temperance, and urged the Cherokee to shun imitation of the lawless elements in the mountains.[11]

While Thomas was emerging as a spokesman for the Indians of Quallatown, he was also becoming a major figure in regional economic and political circles. He became a leading voice of states' rights, internal improvements, and public education in Cherokee, Haywood, Jackson, and Macon Counties in Western Carolina. As an aspiring Democrat politician, he supported the views of John C. Calhoun, the leading voice of the South in the period before 1850, and stood firm with President James K. Polk in advocating expansion and war with Mexico. In 1848, his fellow mountaineers elected him to the North Carolina Senate, and he served for fourteen years in that position. Thomas also prospered financially and socially. By the late 1850s, although he had only three slaves, he had acquired 34,000 acres for his own use and had become an advocate of railroad development in the region. Through his business assistant and friend, James W. Terrell, Wil-Usdi managed his seven stores and tannery within the Indian country. In 1857, Thomas married Sarah [Sallie] Love, a white woman whose cousin James later served with distinction as a lieutenant colonel in the Thomas Legion. The couple had three children, the eldest being William Holland Thomas, Jr., affectionately named "Junaluska" after the famous Cherokee chief.[12]

Despite some historians' writings to the contrary, Thomas was an avowed Southern nationalist and advocate of secession.[13] He railed at Hinton Rowan Helper, a fellow North Carolinian, who opposed slavery in his book *The Impending Crisis* and who also believed that the peculiar institution was harmful to the well-being of poor whites of the South. Thomas condemned abolitionists and charged that both Seward and Lincoln were traitors and that they were responsible for the nation's economic downturn of 1860–1861.[14] As early as January 1861, Thomas enunciated the hope that "the mountains of western North Carolina would be in the center of the [not as yet formed] Confederacy where the Southern people would congregate during the summer, and spend their money instead of spending it in the North."[15] Throughout the spring, he continued to charge that Lincoln had "usurped all the powers not only of Congress but also of some of the states." He pondered that "western North Carolina, one of the most prosperous country [sic] in the world" and the rest of the South would soon have the North quaking in its boots.[16]

He fervently advocated the inclusion of state legislators, most of whom were secessionist, in any North Carolina convention deciding secession, and was himself elected to represent Jackson County at the secessionist convention, one of only four North Carolina state legislators chosen. On May 20, 1861, he and his colleagues at a convention at Raleigh unanimously ratified North Carolina's ordinance of secession.[17] Thomas also attempted, without success, to secure concessions for the Cherokee from President Jefferson Davis and Governor William T. Clark throughout 1861 and 1862 in return for Indian service on the Confederate side.[18]

Besides Thomas's real concern for the Cherokee, the Indians' precarious status contributed to their involvement in the war effort. The Cherokee had an anomalous legal and political status, claiming to be Citizen Indians, yet not having their person or lands protected under state and federal laws. Moreover, their desperate economic condition and their inability to purchase land for themselves because of racial restrictions made them overly dependent on Wil-Usdi, their patron and benefactor.

In May of 1861, immediately after North Carolina voted to secede, Thomas returned to Quallatown and mustered two hundred Cherokee as home guards into state service as the "Junaluska Zoaves." Most of the Confederate Cherokee, especially those at Quallatown, were more loyal to Thomas than to the South. During the war, Wil-Usdi lobbied for their interests and even attempted to divert Confederate supplies to support their families in Quallatown.[19]

Even before he failed in his quest to be elected to the Confederate Congress at Richmond in the fall of 1861, Thomas prepared an alternative career move, becoming a commissioned officer and commander of a contingent of Indian and white mountaineer troops, which he designated as highland rangers. His force later became widely known as "Thomas's Legion of Indians and Highlanders." By 1862, he was commissioned a colonel. With the assistance of Lieutenant Colonel James R. Love II, his wife's cousin, Major William W. Stringfield, and Lieutenant James W. Terrell, Thomas raised a formidable force. At its height, the Thomas Legion was composed of 2,800 men, one infantry regiment of ten companies, an infantry battalion of six companies, a cavalry battalion of eight companies, a light field battery, and a company of engineers.[20]

Through Wil-Usdi's efforts, nearly "every able-bodied man in the tribe" sought service in the Confederate militia.[21] Only about thirty Eastern Cherokee in all served the Union. Through the encouragement of Diganeski, a few Cherokee were induced to desert from Confederate ranks. Moreover, a dozen Cherokee Confederates were captured near Charlotte, North Carolina, now Bryson City in Swain County, in 1862, and taken to Knoxville, eventually switching sides and ending up serving the Union forces as members of the Third North Carolina Mounted Volunteer Infantry until the close of the Civil War. Their Union service, according to anthropologist James Mooney, led them to be ostracized on their return home. One source claims that Cherokee Unionists also were later blamed for bringing smallpox to the community, which ravaged Quallatown and took over one hundred lives in 1865–1866.[22] The remaining Cherokee who deserted "went over the hill" at the end of February, 1864. According to Vernon Crow, in his standard history of the Thomas Legion published by the Cherokee: "Tradition maintains that after the war, several of these disloyal Indians were murdered by their brothers for betraying Thomas."[23] If a total of thirty went over to the Union ranks during the Civil War, the Cherokee desertion rate—approximately 7.5 percent—was substantially less than the overall Confederate desertion rate of 13 percent. This would confirm the writings of Major W. W. Stringfield, who frequently praised the Indians' loyalty, and insisted that their presence "in these mountains [of western North Carolina and eastern Tennessee] were a great protection to the country."[24]

Despite having no military training, Thomas's hand was everywhere in the recruitment of Indians for the Confederacy. On October 8, 1861, he requisitioned clothing for his Indian volunteers and suggested to Governor Henry Clark of North Carolina that his Cherokee and other highlanders then stationed in Virginia be transferred back to be used as a home guard in the mountains of the state.[25] Nine days later, Thomas complained to Governor Clark about Captain George W. Hayes's mistreatment of two Cherokee, Jonathan Welch and F. M. Taylor, in Hayes's cavalry, and insisted that the governor advise Hayes not to recruit any more Indians into his company.[26]

At the beginning, state and Confederate officials placated his frequent demands. After his unsuccessful bid for the Confederate Congress in November 1861, Thomas turned his full attention to organizing his command. He jotted town in his notebook in early January 1862 that he "went back to Qualla Town to try to raise my company" which he commenced on January 3 "for local defence of western North Carolina."[27] In March of 1862, Thomas wrote Governor Clark describing his plans to hold the mountain passes, insisting that he "never had any doubts as to our mountain boys proving true to our southern cause."[28] On April 15, James G. Martin, the adjutant general of North Carolina, gave Thomas some flexibility in command since his company was so distant from Raleigh, but warned him to use "sound judgment and discretion in every case" and to seek direction when "a case arises which you cannot dispose of."[29]

Late into the war, Thomas continued to interject himself and his ideas, but with less success. He wrote Davis in November 1862, recommending that the Confederacy establish a line of posts fifteen miles apart and protected by guardposts and Indian sentinels to secure a communication and transportation link between East Tennessee, Virginia, and Kentucky. Thomas argued that if the Confederacy lost these valuable passes, "we sink under a despotism."[30] In the same month, Thomas urged Governor Zebulon Vance of North Carolina to extend Confederate rail links by employing slave labor.[31]

On April 9, 1862, Major George Washington Morgan, himself of Cherokee descent, formally mustered Cherokee Indians into three-year Confederate military service as part of North Carolina's commitment to Richmond. This initial recruitment of two companies included perhaps as many as two hundred Indians, including major figures in Cherokee history—commissioned lieutenants Peter Greybeard and Astoogatogeh, and noncommissioned sergeants Enola and Swimmer.[32]

Before setting out for war, the Confederate recruits underwent the ancient war rituals of their culture. According to Mooney:

> Before starting to the front every man consulted an oracle stone to learn whether or not he might hope to return in safety. The start was celebrated with a grand old-time war dance at the townhouse on Soco, and the same dance was repeated at frequent intervals thereafter, the Indians being "painted and feathered in good old style," Thomas himself frequently assisting as master of ceremonies.

Mooney also maintained that Cherokee soldiers continued to play their ball game (lacrosse) during the war, and, on one occasion while playing, were almost overrun by federal troops.[33]

Cherokee language documents reveal much about Indian soldiers during the war. They indicate the hopes of the Indian soldiers for a speedy end to the conflict and a quick return to Quallatown. They also show the variety of military assignments given the soldiers and their attempts to retain their Indian lifeways during the war. In a letter dated July 20, 1862, one soldier, Tseigh(I)sini, writing from Strawberry Plains, Tennessee to Wolftown, the easternmost township of the present-day Qualla Boundary Cherokee Reservation, noted that he had no hope of getting a furlough to visit home; nevertheless, he assured his family that Colonel Thomas had told his men that he intended to move close to home in the Smoky Mountains in the near future. Like many other Indian and non-Indian troops, the Cherokee recruit overestimated the Confederate success rate: "Our ranks were decreased by 10,000; we decreased the Yankees by 30,000." Tseigh(I)sini insisted: "One would think that he [Union forces] would be more than ready to give up."[34] On August 3, 1863, Iinoili, another Cherokee Confederate, wrote that in North Carolina his legion had captured "29 Yankee pretenders," possibly referring to Union collaborators or spies. Iinoili added that he and his troops had searched a house and found a cache of weapons. The residents of the house turned out to be a family sympathetic to the Confederacy; however, before that fact was determined, shooting broke out and one of the occupants of the house was wounded in the incident. At the end of his letter, Iinoili, a medicine man in training, reflected that he feared sickness but realized that he could always obtain a "root" from home if needed. In a subsequent letter in the winter of 1864–1865, Iinoili indicated that while nine Cherokee were killed in action in the war, at least nineteen others had died of disease.[35]

From the latter part of 1862, the Thomas Legion's duty was largely to enforce Confederate conscription, "tiresome, thankless, disagreeable, galling and verging on the *unmanly*," and "always a disagreeable duty to a soldier and gentleman." From their base high in the Smokies, 6,700 feet above sea level at Clingman's Dome, the Indians held a strategic position for the Confederacy. Captain R. A. Aiken of W. C. Walker's regiment of the Thomas Legion maintained that the Indians "were loyal to us to an intense degree" and provided immense service to the South.[36] Aiken specifically hailed Cherokee Captains Cami Taylor of Company I and Sou-ate-Owle of Company A for their service. Although perhaps too defensive in tone, Aiken insisted that the Indians "were never cruel to prisoners or anyone else." He praised Cherokee steadfastness, citing the case of one Indian who as a sentinel in an isolated outpost "stood at his post *all night, or near fourteen hours*, in one of the fiercest and most terrific snowstorms in the history of the country."[37]

In late April, 1862, Thomas's Legion was sent to Strawberry Plains or Zollicoffee in upper East Tennessee, fourteen miles from Knoxville, to guard the Tennessee and Virginia Railroad bridge over the Holston River. On April 27, they arrived with great fanfare at Knoxville, a major transport link connecting Bristow, Chattanooga, and Knoxville, vital in maintaining the Confederate supply line. Their camp, known as "Junaluska," at Strawberry Plains was seventy miles south of the Virginia state line between the Cumberland and Smoky Mountains. This region was seen by Union officials as the gateway to the heartland of the South. Among Thomas's officers at Camp Oconostota were Lieutenants William W. Terrell and Astoogatogeh [Unaguskie], the grandson of Yonaguska and translator of the New Testament into Cherokee.[38]

From May through the summer of 1862, Thomas's forces saw little action; however, in June, while at Chattanooga, Thomas captured a Michigan soldier. In a letter to his wife, he wrote: "The Indians say as I took the first prisoner each of them must take one to be even."[39] Meanwhile, his Indian troops, with their archaic squirrel guns, drilled on the parade grounds of Strawberry Plains throughout the summer. By mid-July, Thomas's forces had increased in size, reaching battalion strength with two full companies of Indians and six companies of whites. By the late summer, the Indians were better armed and well drilled, and had become a vital part of the Confederate Army of East Tennessee. Besides the monotony and homesickness of camp life, the first months at Strawberry Plains brought several problems. A rail accident occurred and diseases such as measles and mumps ravaged the camp, claiming four lives despite the treatment by Oosawih, a Cherokee herbal doctor who relied on his traditional charms and medicines for relief.[40]

The Thomas Legion's first major engagement with federal forces occurred at Rogersville, Tennessee on September 13–15, 1862, near the Virginia border. Union forces attempted to pass through gaps south of the Cumberland Mountains and enter into eastern Tennessee. Commanded by Lieutenant Terrell, the Indians at this skirmish at Baptist Gap routed the Union soldiers and drove them from the valley. Terrell ordered Second Lieutenant Astoogatogeh to lead the charge against the Union force of Indiana troops. Before their reinforcements arrived, the federal soldiers panicked. Astoogatogeh was killed in the ensuing charge. His fellow Cherokee, reacting to their leader's death, scalped several of the fallen Union troops in retaliation.[41]

This confirmed incident of scalping as well as other alleged atrocities were highlighted by Unionist Governor Andrew Johnson, federal military personnel, and the Northern news media for war propaganda purposes; there is some evidence to suggest that Cherokee in the Thomas Legion did indeed scalp federal troops on other occasions and that Thomas could not or did not want to control this practice.[42] Later, in his reminiscences, Lieutenant Terrell admitted this, claiming that "throughout the war they did scalp every man killed if they could get to him, which they generally managed to do."[43] One historian has suggested that Thomas himself cultivated the image of Indians' ferocity and invincibility, although he did not sanction or approve of scalping. The more powerful his Indian force appeared, the more his role as their commanding officer rose in importance.[44]

From September 1862 to September 1863, Cherokee military service was largely focused on pacifying East Tennessee. Much of the region is mountainous and not fit for cotton agriculture. This region, then one of the poorest areas of the United States, had the fewest slaves in the state and many of its residents were lukewarm to the "peculiar institution." East Tennessee was geographically a state unto itself, separated from the other areas of the state by the Cumberland Plateau. Substantial Unionist sentiment and strong opposition to Confederate conscription flourished in the region.[45]

The Cherokee, who knew the terrain of the high mountain country of western North Carolina and eastern Tennessee better than any other people, were logical choices for the Confederacy to employ in this area. Besides mountain pass duty, Cherokee rangers hunted down the ubiquitous spies and recruiting officers from the Union army, disarmed citizens, enforced conscription, tracked down deserters, impressed crops and livestock, and obtained loyalty oaths from fiercely independent locals. Few residents took kindly to authoritarian measures and some even viewed the Cherokee as Confederate "bloodhounds." Others in this war-devastated country fled behind Union lines for protection or became bushwackers intent on taking advantage of the chaos.[46]

After the skirmish at Baptist Gap, their job was mainly, in the words of General W. G. M. Davis, "to arrest all deserters and recusant conscripts and all tories who have been engaged in unlawful practices on the Tennessee line of the mountains."[47] Throughout much of 1863, the Thomas Legion instilled fear in the populace of mountain country. Their image as Confederate intimidators was brought home by an incident in October, 1863. Goldman Bryson, a white man who had robbed and murdered John Timson, a prominent Indian of Cherokee County, was a captain of a North Carolina Unionist regiment. From late 1861 onward, Bryson was involved in terrorizing and recruiting for the federal army. The Cherokee in the Thomas Legion, with long and bitter memories of the Timson robbery and murder, used the war to seek revenge against Bryson. Captain C. H. Taylor, a Cherokee, led a detachment of twenty-five Indians from the Thomas Legion that hunted down and killed him. The Cherokee also dispersed the captain's Unionist forces. After the execution, some of the Indians paraded down the streets of Murphy, North Carolina with "portions of Bryson's bloody and bullet-pierced uniform."[48]

On September 1, 1863, General Ambrose Burnside's federal army captured Knoxville, forcing Thomas to withdraw his command from Strawberry Plains eastward to the North Carolina side of the mountains, around Clingman's Dome, in what is today's Great Smoky National Park. Because of their significance to the Confederate cause, Burnside's men were ordered to pursue Thomas's retreating forces. Yet Thomas's men continued their hit-and-run attacks on Union soldiers and pro-Unionist civilians throughout the fall of 1863. After several of the Indians were captured and jailed, Thomas sent two hundred men to break into the jail near Sevierville and free them. His forces captured six federal soldiers as well as sixty Unionists in the raid; federal authorities retaliated by sending a Union contingent after Thomas's Legion.[49]

On December 10, 1863, Colonel William Jackson Palmer and his Fifteenth Pennsylvania Cavalry attacked Cherokee soldiers along a ridge near Gatlinsburg, Tennessee. Palmer, later a general and after the war a builder of western railroads, caught the Cherokee by surprise, capturing one Indian, wounding three others, and driving Thomas's retreating forces through the rugged mountains. Colonel Thomas's hat was seized as a federal trophy. The Pennsylvanians were aided in their pursuit by East Tennessee Unionist Charles H. Kirk, first lieutenant in the Fifteenth Pennsylvania Cavalry, who described the federal victory at Gatlinsburg:

> There were the blazing fires and the corn cakes baking, just ready to eat; so we gobbled them from out the frying pan, and finding no Indians in the huts, we started out and fought them until we had driven

them away into the dense forest and we could no longer hear their war whoop.

After about four hours' fighting we returned and went into their tents. We found bags of dried apples, salt, blankets and sheepskins. John Benner, of our company, beat the tattoo on their drums, then took out his camp knife and cut out the heads. In their surprise and hurry they left behind about fifteen horses tied to the stakes. I destroyed, by striking against the trees, twenty rifles, as they were of no possible use to us, and then we set fire to the Indian camp and left the place with the boys shouting the war whoop.[50]

From the skirmish at Gatlinsburg onward, Thomas's force was on the defensive. By February 1864, the war reached the center of the Cherokee territory. On February 2, Major Francis M. Davidson's Fourteenth Illinois Cavalry attacked at Deep Creek, near Quallatown. Davidson was under orders from General S. D. Sturgis to pursue the "rebel Thomas" and his Indians "who had become a terror" to the Union people of East Tennessee and western Tennessee because of the "atrocities they were daily perpetrating."[51]

Davidson's force of six hundred men was guided by forty to fifty Tennessee Unionists who surprised Thomas' men. For over an hour, the Battle of Deep Creek raged.[52] According to the standard regimental history of the Thomas Legion: "If Davidson's objective was to eliminate Thomas' force, he failed; if he intended to harass the Confederates, he succeeded."[53] Estimates of casualties at the Battle of Deep Creek vary substantially. Sturgis later claimed in a greatly exaggerated report that Davidson's forces met an enemy of 250 men on his quick-strike raid, that twenty-two Indians and thirty-two whites were captured in the assault, and that nearly two hundred were killed. In sharp contrast, Thomas indicated that the Union captured twenty to thirty Indians and whites, total, and that two Indians were killed. Colonel Thomas also later claimed that his men killed eight Union soldiers and took one prisoner.[54]

Both the Cherokee and their commander faced declining fortunes after the Battle of Deep Creek. During the winter of 1864, the

Cherokee at home in Quallatown faced starving conditions and were forced, according to Thomas's wife, to survive on weeds or gnawing on bark. Others fled southward while Thomas attempted to divert Confederate supplies to Quallatown. By the spring of 1864, Thomas's frustrations with the Confederate war effort were apparent, especially with his commander, the ill-tempered and incompetent General Alfred E. "Mudwall" Jackson. Thomas recruited one hundred much-needed miners and sappers to Confederate service, but soon they nearly all deserted when Jackson insisted that they bear arms.[55] Thomas also complained that he was responsible for an area of one hundred miles but did not have "troops sufficient to defend it." Yet throughout this period and into July, Thomas remained loyal to the Confederate cause, insisting that he was firmly committed to holding the mountains "and never surrendering to the enemy."[56]

Well into the summer of 1864, he continued to requisition cattle from locals for the war effort, recruited the citizenry of the mountains for Confederate service, and made detailed reports about East Tennessee and its chaotic conditions. Yet a crisis was brewing in Confederate ranks in the mountains. The poorly led western army of the Confederacy was beset by internal fighting and Thomas frequently made his disgust with the situation public. He also did not get along with Governor Zebulon Vance, who unfairly blamed Thomas for the Union's capture of his brother.[57] On July 8, 1864, Thomas complained about the incompetence of the Confederate leadership in East Tennessee and North Carolina and criticized the military order that had divided his legion, which he insisted demoralized his troops.[58] Not surprisingly, he was court-martialed. In October 1864, Thomas was convicted of receiving twenty-one deserters, for conduct unbecoming an officer and a gentleman, for making a false statement to his superiors, for disobeying orders, and for disloyalty. After being convicted, Thomas was "saved" by the efforts of his new superior officer, Brigadier General James G. Martin, the former adjutant general of North Carolina. Martin, a West Point graduate, hero of the Mexican War, and veteran of Confederate campaigns in Virginia, wrote to General Robert E. Lee, minimizing Thomas's offenses, stating that the white chief, the head of a small command, was not a military man by background and that allowances should be made. President Jefferson Davis and Secretary of War James A. Seddon eventually overturned the decision of the military tribunal, undoubtedly influenced by the severity of the crisis facing the Confederacy in late 1864.[59]

Because of Thomas's problems, the Indians of the Thomas Legion remained leaderless and scattered in western Carolina throughout much of 1864. Federal forces under Colonel George W. Kirk, a Confederate deserter who effectively organized pro-Union men of the mountains, took advantage of Confederate weakness and successfully raided rebel strongholds. Undersupplied and with Union forces converging on them, the Confederates' prospects were dim indeed. Only in January 1865 was Thomas reinstated and he once again began reorganizing, by recruiting men.[60]

Colonel Kirk returned in February 1865 with his six hundred men. After raiding and burning Waynesville, en route to Quallatown, his Union force was repulsed by detachments of the Legion, including Indians, at Soco Creek, "on almost the same spot where Tecumseh had exhorted the Cherokees during the War of 1812."[61] Nevertheless, the Confederate end was at hand. General George Stoneman's troops captured Salisbury on April 17, and, by that date, Colonel Isaac M. Kirby's brigade had surrounded Asheville.

The Thomas Legion was the last Confederate unit to surrender east of the Mississippi River. This surrender took place in the town of Waynesville, North Carolina, Thomas's birthplace. On May 6, 1865, Lieutenant Colonel W. C. Bartlett, commanding the North Carolina Mounted Infantry, a unit of Unionist troops, skirmished with units of the Legion totaling six hundred men under the command of Thomas and Colonel James R. Love near Waynesville. In the skirmish, one federal troop was killed and Bartlett's force was driven into the hamlet of fifteen to twenty dwellings and surrounded. Despite Lee's surrender a month earlier, Thomas continued to challenge and intimidate the federal forces. Throughout the night of May 6, his men held fast to their mountain positions above the town.

Their numerous campfires lit up the region, giving Bartlett the impression of thousands of Confederates in the vicinity. Indian war whoops and rebel yells also helped create an uneasy feeling among the Union forces.[62]

On the next morning, Bartlett, a New Yorker by birth, sent out a flag of truce and asked for a conference in the Battle House, Waynesville's hotel, with the Confederate commanders. One of Thomas's closest aides gives us insights into what followed. Belligerent to the end, Thomas was accompanied by twenty imposing Cherokee bodyguards, nonenlisted men. According to Major W. W. Stringfield, Thomas atypically became "quite boisterous." He and his bodyguards were also "stripped to the waist and feathered off in fine style," in the manner of warriors prepared for battle. Stringfield added that Thomas and the Indians in attendance made "the welkin ring with their war whoops."[63] Thomas, according to another account, "told Bartlett if he did not immediately surrender and make haste to get away from Waynesville, he would turn his Indians upon the Yankee regiment and have them all scalped."[64] After two days of talks, attended by Thomas and Confederate General Martin, the exhausted conferees on May 9 agreed to terms. Realizing that his cause was lost despite Thomas's apparent victory at Waynesville, General Martin agreed to abandon his continuing resistance. In return, the Indians and whites of the Thomas Legion were allowed to keep their firearms and ammunition and return home. The war in the mountains was over.

Thomas's bizarre actions have been interpreted as being caused by the onset of mental illness, perhaps resulting from a case of untreated syphilis.[65] But Bartlett's occupation of Waynesville had triggered something deeper in Thomas's psyche. Waynesville was no mere western Carolina mountain crossroads. It was there that his mother, a single parent, had raised him. It was there that he had met Yonaguska, had learned Indian ways, and had been adopted as a Cherokee by that extraordinary chief.

In many ways Thomas had become Cherokee. Although he rose to prominence in the white world, he identified with and was more comfortable in western Carolina frontier society than with the state's power structure at Raleigh. As a child, he had been imbued with the lifeways of the Indian and knew the mountains as they did. This knowledge contributed to his Civil War success, despite his lack of formal military training.[66] As historian John Finger has written: "So important were these [Smoky] mountains as hunting grounds, so central to Cherokee identity that Thomas often alluded to them in his legal treatises."[67]

Even in May 1865, Thomas saw himself as Wil-Usdi, the boy who had been privileged to be adopted by the great founder of the Eastern Band of Cherokee, Yonaguska. His decision to "go native" was no act of a madman. At Waynesville, he consciously presented himself as a proud Indian warrior reliving the stories of the ancient grandeur of the warpath told to him by Yonaguska, the most important figure in his life, rather than as a defeated rebel officer whose Confederate nation no longer existed.

Memories of the Civil War faded slowly in western Carolina. The Cherokee themselves were active in postwar reunions and were extremely proud of their military service. In 1900, Indian veterans founded the United Confederate Veterans, an organization later renamed for Sou-noo-kee, a Cherokee hero of the Civil War who was killed in a skirmish at the Cumberland Gap.[68]

Despite the commemorations and reunions, the Civil War had largely been a disaster for these Indians. A devastating epidemic of measles immediately followed the return of troops to Quallatown. Tribal political factionalism intensified after the war as well, with acculturated Cherokee spokesmen such as George W. Bushyhead and James W. Taylor attempting to fill the role that Thomas had played since 1839. Alcoholism and extreme poverty further weakened the community.[69]

The Cherokee did get one immediate postwar benefit as a result of their Confederate service. On February 19, 1866, the North Carolina General Assembly granted a specific affirmation of the Cherokee's right to residency in the state. Perhaps as recognition of their loyalty to the South, the act provided: "That the Cherokee Indians who are now residents of the State of North Carolina, shall have the authority and permission to remain in the several counties of the state where they now reside." It added that the Cherokee "shall be permitted to remain permanently therein so long as they may see proper to do so, any thing in the treaty of eighteen hundred and thirty-five to the contrary notwithstanding."[70] Yet their existence remained precarious despite congressional federal recognition of their distinct tribal status in 1868 and the drawing up of a new constitution and tribal roll the following year.[71] The Cherokee were unable to vote in North Carolina until 1930, and their claims for protection as citizens were ignored right through the late nineteenth century. The common tribal lands around Quallatown became the Qualla Boundary Reservation, but the Cherokee lacked standing as a group in state and federal courts to protect their privately owned tracts outside the Boundary from squatters and timber strippers.[72]

Thomas's personal fortunes declined rapidly after the Civil War. The war had bankrupted him. Through the rest of his life, he fought off creditors and contended with terrible mental illness. As early as 1867, he was declared insane and was sent for a time to an asylum in Raleigh. On May 15, 1877, Thomas's wife died. After this he was periodically committed to mental asylums where he drifted into a world of fantasy. His body was eventually riddled with sores, his ankles nearly crippled. In his mental delusions, he would sometimes become agitated and violent. At the end of his life, he had become a pathetic maniac who had to be chained to the asylum floor. Wil-Usdi died at the age of eighty-eight on May 10, 1893. He was buried in Waynesville.[73]

In assessing Wil-Usdi, historian John R. Finger has concluded: "Without his assistance they [Cherokee] would never have remained in North Carolina. Without his constant support they would never have acquired the lands they were still fighting to retain." Finger concluded: "Despite a normal measure of human shortcomings, he was the best friend the Indians ever had."[74] In North Carolina and East

Tennessee, the Cherokee followed a white man into the ferocious meat grinder of the Civil War, just as other Indians had done on all fronts of the war. Thomas's ultimate fate was far worse than that of his fellow white men as a whole; for the Indian, the results were distressingly the same.

Part Three

The North

7

Sharpshooters in the Army of the Potomac

The Ottawa

IN 1860, FEWER THAN THIRTY THOUSAND AMERICAN INDIANS STILL resided in the North. Approximately two-thirds of this population was concentrated in three states—Michigan, New York, and Wisconsin. From the War of 1812 onward, the United States government considered removal of the Indians from the North. Whether the Indians had fought the Long Knives, such as the Shawnee, or had allied themselves with the Americans, such as the Oneida and Stockbridge, they faced removal far from their homeland.

Unbridled American expansion had brought hundreds of thousands of non-Indian settlers westward. The pressures for Indian lands intensified, leading to renewed fighting in the Old Northwest—the Winnebago War in Wisconsin Territory in the 1820s and the Black Hawk War in Illinois, Iowa, and Wisconsin in the 1830s. The industrial revolution transformed transportation after 1815. Canals that had transported population and resources in the 1820s and 1830s faced stiff competition from railroads by the 1840s and 1850s. Chicago, a small Indian village in the early 1800s, had become a major American city of well over 100,000 people by 1860.

While the burgeoning American nation was debating the merits of free soil, the Dred Scott decision, and the "saneness" of John Brown's actions, American Indian independence and strength were being sapped by epidemics, alcohol, and the rush of white settlement. Surely, of all Northerners, American Indians cared the least about slavery. Unlike many Indians in the South and Trans-Mississippi West, the Indians of the North owned no slaves in the decades approaching the Civil War. Although they suffered from white racism and were even categorized in the North at times as "colored," their main concern by 1860 was maintaining their fragile existence in their homelands. Their focus was not the equality of humankind, but preserving their landbase, the source of their spiritual, medicinal, and traditional economic strength. No clearer example of this can be found than in Michigan.

Company K of the First Michigan Sharpshooters was the most famous Indian unit in the Union army fighting Confederate forces east of the Mississippi. Nearly all of the one hundred fifty men who served in the company between 1863 and 1865 were Indians from Michigan. Despite the presence of Delaware, Huron, Oneida, and Potawatomi Indians in Company K, the vast majority were Ottawa [Odawa], with a significant number of Ojibwa [Chippewa] and Ottawa-Ojibwa Indians from the Lower Peninsula of the state.[1] The unit was led by Garrett A. Gravaraet, a Franco-Ottawa Indian. Gravaraet, a second lieutenant, was personally responsible for the recruitment of one-third of the original members of the company. Until his death on June 30, 1864, Gravaraet was to serve with distinction in the Army of the Potomac in some of the heaviest fighting of the Civil War.[2]

Civil War sharpshooters were elite units conceived of by Colonel Hiram Berdan who organized the United States Sharpshooters, in two separate regiments, in the late summer of 1861. Although the First Michigan Sharpshooters was a state unit and set apart from Berdan's federal troops, both Union forces had substantially more training than regular infantrymen. Besides competitive daily rifle shooting, the sharpshooters honed their marksmanship skills by hitting a target—two figures painted on a canvas—placed at a distance of six hundred yards, a most difficult feat even with today's up-to-date target rifles. Equally important, their drill instructors cultivated a feeling of invincibility, that the sharpshooters could not be beaten down and that, when compelled to give ground, a new position was to be gained from which the action would be renewed. They were taught that Confederate infantry would advance at seventy to one hundred nine yards per minute, and that the enemy could be picked off by trained marksmen in concealed positions since they were often burdened by heavy packs and had to reload while charging. Indeed, the sharpshooters were the "first elements to encounter the enemy in movement or in stationary defensive positions." Depending on the terrain, sharpshooters "would be placed up to five hundred yards in front of the main body of infantry, their primary purpose to suppress enemy fire as much as possible." They then would "harass the enemy with carefully aimed and selected fire of their own." By 1863, employing their new Sharps NM 1859 breechloaders, these soldiers could lie low, reload, and fire ten shots a minute without changing positions, a decisive advantage during periods of heavy fighting.[3]

At the time the Civil War began in April 1861, Garrett Gravaraet was teaching school at the Ottawa community at Little Traverse Bay, Michigan. These L'Arbre Croche [Crooked Tree] Ottawa (the name designated by the French and British to the Anisnabek Indians) lived in villages along the entire coastline between Mackinac and the southern shore of Little Traverse Bay. By 1861, the widely scattered world of Michigan Indians totaled 7,755 people in seventy-two separate bands. Nearly half of them, Ottawa and Ottawa-Ojibwa, were mostly in Oceana and Mason counties and Grand and Little Traverse bays along Lake Michigan; one-quarter, mostly Ojibwa, were in the Saginaw Valley in the Lower Peninsula; and the remaining one-quarter were scattered over a wide area in the Upper Michigan Peninsula.[4]

Garrett A. Gravaraet was the son of Bear River band chief Mankewenan, Henry G. Gravaraet, a Franco-Ottawa merchant-trader at Mackinac Island, and Sophie Bailey, an Indian from Little Traverse, described in the records as "Chippewayan." Garrett was born around 1840, four years after his parents' marriage in a Roman Catholic church ceremony. His Civil War pension records reveal that Garrett's parents were living apart by the Civil War, perhaps as a result of Henry's drinking problem. Whatever his parents' marital problems, Garrett excelled in his studies. By the time of his enlistment in 1863, he had been recognized as an accomplished musician and a painter of portraiture and landscapes, as well as a skilled linguist who spoke at least four languages fluently—English, French, Ottawa, and Ojibwa. He had also completed three years of teaching at the Indian school at Little Traverse.[5]

Mackinac Island (Michikachinakong in the Ottawa language), where Garrett was born, raised, and buried, is central to both Ottawa and Ojibwa existence. The adventurous Nanabojo, the trickster-hero of Ottawa-Ojibwa culture, is given credit for creating all plants and animals as well as the geography of our modern landscape, including Mackinac Island. In both the Ottawa and Ojibwa creation beliefs, Nanabojo opened a muskrat's paws and found several grains of soil. He dried these grains in the sun and threw them into the water, resulting in the formation of a beautiful island—Mackinac. Nanabojo added soil and the island grew into the earth. Thus, the world of the Indians or Anishnabek was formed. Significantly, in Ottawa-Ojibwa beliefs, Mackinac Island was the birthplace and abode of Michobou [Michapoux], the Great Hare, who taught the people to fish.[6]

Mackinac Island was geopolitically significant even before the coming of the Europeans. Whoever controlled the island controlled the straits between Lake Huron and Lake Michigan and, with it, the major east-west trade route of the Great Lakes. Later, in the seventeenth century, the Ottawa, rivals of the Iroquois, served as valued middlemen to the French in trade between the Hurons and other Indians of the Great Lakes since by that time their four principal villages were atop the access point to the passage between two Great Lakes.[7] After 1675, according to anthropologist Charles E. Cleland, "the Ottawa were soon doing a thriving business, not only in collecting and transporting fur but in supplying the growing French community and traders with canoes, fish, game, and particularly corn."[8]

Mackinac was known by Euroamericans as "Michilimackinac" until well into the nineteenth century. To the Indians, this term referred only to the island; however, Euroamericans applied it more liberally. Soon, it was used to describe the area around St. Ignace on the Upper Peninsula north of the straits. In the late seventeenth century, Father Marquette founded a mission and the French established a trading post on that site. This post became the commercial hub of the fur trade and the most important of all the advance posts of New France until the French defeat in the Seven Years War. By the eighteenth century, the name was used by the French to designate the tip of Michigan's Lower Peninsula south of the straits. During the late eighteenth century, the term was used primarily to refer to the fort the British constructed on Mackinac Island during the American Revolution.[9]

In the early nineteenth century, Mackinac Island, still a frontier outpost, had become a cosmopolitan center with visitors, values, and styles from far beyond Michigan or Lower Canada. It reflected a somewhat different world than found in the Lower Peninsula. At the time of Garrett Gravaraet's birth, this multiethnic settlement, the regional trading center at the foot of Fort Mackinac's white stone bastions, had a three-tiered social system. According to historian James McClurken, the community's "elite was composed of fur-trade entrepreneurs, wealthy and influential French Canadians and British men, aided by a leavening of skilled and semiskilled Métis craftsmen, clerks, and laborers." McClurken added that on "the edges of this settlement were the Ottawas and Chippewa. Many of the elite had married daughters and granddaughters of important Ottawa leaders."[10]

It was from this second group—the skilled and semiskilled Métis—that Garrett A. Gravaraet sprang. He identified with his native roots. Gravaraet was no stranger to the world of the Anishnabek in the Lower Peninsula; his mother's community was there and he spent three years as a teacher at Little Traverse. Until his deathbed conversion in June 1864, he rejected Christianity.[11] Because of his Indian, French, and English language skills, he was the perfect candidate, the cultural mediator, to serve the white man in recruiting other

Indians for service. As a Franco-Indian with one foot in each world, he understood both the indigenous peoples of Michigan and the non-Indians who were rapidly transforming the landscape and permanently affecting the native cultures of the state.[12]

The ten companies of the First Michigan Sharpshooters were raised in the summer of 1863. Company K comprised twenty-four Indians who listed their birthplace as Pentwater; twenty-three from Isabella; nine from Little Traverse; seven from Saginaw; and six were from New York or Ontario reserves such as Walpole Island. The rest, fewer in number, listed their birthplaces as Bay City, Grand Traverse, Grand Rapids, Kalamazoo, LaCroix, or Northport. The average age of the company was 25.7 years. Of the one hundred fourteen soldiers who listed their occupations, seventy-five were farmers; twenty-three were laborers; eleven were hunters/trappers; three were in the maritime trades—two as sailors and one as a fisherman; one was a merchant; and one, Garrett A. Gravaraet, a musician. Captain E. V. Andress, a white man, was the major figure in raising the regiment; however, Andress was apparently dependent on the recruiting activities of Gravaraet. Of the original one hundred nine soldiers raised, Gravaraet was responsible for the recruitment of thirty, including his father, Henry G. Gravaraet, who served the company as a second sergeant.[13] It is clear that Garrett Gravaraet's leadership skills, his Indian ancestry, his father's presence in the company, and his family's reputation combined to convince many Ottawa as well as other Indians to enlist.

The younger Gravaraet's efforts should not be minimized. He successfully convinced Indians of Michigan to enlist less than one year after federal efforts crushed the Santee Sioux of nearby Minnesota. At a time when the fury of the Civil War was leading to massive casualties at Gettysburg, and the federal government was visibly hostile to neighboring tribes, Ottawa, Ojibwa, and Franco-Indians were enlisting in droves in Michigan. Moreover, Gravaraet was able to counter the strong efforts of Midwestern Copperheads and/or Peace Democrats who tried to convince Michigan's Indians to stay out of the war.

Why did so many Indians elist? Gravaraet on his deathbed affirmed that "fighten [sic] for my Country is all right."[14] Throughout the war, Michigan Indian Agent D. C. Leach frequently cited the patriotism and loyalty of the Indians to the Union cause. He often contrasted it favorably with those of disloyal white Copperheads, and those of the allegedly "wicked" Santee Sioux.[15] Undoubtedly, military bounties were inducements to poor Indians, the majority of Michigan's native population in 1861; however, few—less than 10 percent of Company K—were induced to become paid substitutes for Northerners who attempted to avoid military service, a surefire way to secure greater financial rewards. Of course, Michigan's Indians, like many other recruits, were attracted to military service by personal ambition as well as by a sense of adventure; however, after the horrors of Antietam, Fredericksburg, and Shiloh in 1862 and Chancellorsville in 1863, these reasons do not satisfactorily explain why they enlisted in such great numbers. Some may have desired to follow their ancestors' footsteps into battle, as an honorable end in and of itself. But many of those Ottawa ancestors went into battle against "Chemokmon," the Big Knives or Americans, during Pontiac's [Bewon-diac's] War of 1763, the American Revolution, and the War of 1812. The Trout, the noted Ottawa prophet, who had advocated rejecting Christianity, Euroamerican appurtenances, and land loss, had inspired the anti-American movement led by Shawnees Tecumseh and Tenskwatawa and the Ottawa Assiginac in the years before the War of 1812. Why then should the Ottawa now so faithfully serve the Americans during the Civil War?[16]

Like the Indians in the Northeast generally, the Ottawa were desperate. From 1815 onward, there had been major efforts, often nefarious, to remove all Ottawa from the Midwest to lands west of the Mississippi. As early as 1819, the Ottawa were forced to cede some of their lands at the eastern reaches of the Grand River in Michigan. In 1821, all Ottawa lands south of the Grand River in Michigan were "ceded" in the Treaty of Chicago. Between 1831 and 1833, Ottawa bands along the Maumee River in Ohio were removed to a reservation in Franklin County, Kansas. In 1833, some Ottawa, who were united with

Chippewa and Potawatomi as a community known as the Three Fires on lands south and west of Lake Michigan, were removed to Iowa.[17]

By the mid 1830s, Michigan was the fastest growing area of the United States, putting increased pressures on the Ottawa and other Indians of the state. Pushed by land speculators and traders hoping to satisfy Indian indebtedness by acquiring their lands, the United States negotiated a treaty with the Ottawa in March 1836. The Michigan Ottawa, attempting to avoid removal at all costs, were aware that the United States was waging two bloody wars of removal at that precise time—against Seminole in Florida and Creek in Alabama. They were also aware that the Cherokee Nation had undertaken a losing legal effort to withstand removal from the Southeast. In the Age of Jackson, both military and legal challenges to removal were futile.[18]

Instead of getting what they desired, namely title to fourteen reservations totaling 141,000 acres, the Ottawa received few guarantees in the Treaty of 1836, later known as the Treaty of Washington. They were forced to cede all of their remaining lands in the Lower Peninsula, covering half the State of Michigan. They retained title to these lands for a five-year period and the right of occupancy until these lands were "required" for white settlement. The United States agreed to finance an exploring expedition southwest of the Missouri River and to create an Ottawa Reservation there "as soon as the Indians desire it." The Ottawa retained the right to hunt on their former lands; they were to receive $30,000 annually for twenty years, as well as a $5,000 annuity for education for twenty years, $3,000 for missions, $10,000 for agricultural equipment, $2,000 for medicine and health care, $2,000 for tobacco, and $150,000 in provisions. Special sizable financial payments were also included to pay off traders' debts to Franco-Indians and their children in lieu of providing them with land, and to the chiefs and headmen of the Ottawa themselves, a move that was undoubtedly intended to "buy cooperation."[19] Ironically, the annuity money provided in the Treaty of Washington allowed some Ottawa to purchase a small portion of their lands back.[20]

The Treaty of Washington was followed by repeated attempts to coerce the Ottawa to remove west, a movement led by Henry

Schoolcraft, head agent of the Michigan Indian Superintendency. In response, some Ottawa petitioned Washington to become United States citizens rather than face removal. Their precarious existence was also shaped by major economic and environmental changes. In the northwest portion of the Lower Peninsula, white intruders began squatting on Indian lands and cutting Indian maple groves.[21] By the 1850s, most of the Indian fishing grounds were depleted, leading a sizable number of Ottawa men to abandon their traditional life as fishermen and hunters and become farmers, a fact confirmed in the occupational columns of muster rolls of Civil War recruits.[22]

In the spring of 1855, the Ottawa signed the Treaty of Detroit with the United States government. This allotment agreement "allowed" Indian heads of families to select fee simple lands of eighty acres— forty acres for single adults over twenty-one years of age—from townships. The treaty, a harbinger of the Dawes General Allotment of 1887, provided that, after these selections were concluded, the remaining Ottawa lands would be put up for sale to the general public.[23] Under the treaty the Ottawa had to select and register their allotments with the federal Indian agent by 1861. Thus, the lands of the L'Arbre Croche Ottawa were incorporated into Michigan as Emmett County. The Ottawa community at Harbor Springs became an incorporated town much like other communities in the state, although Indians held the major offices until after 1870.

While the Civil War was being waged in 1861 and 1862, American settlers were moving in on some of the best Indian lands, especially those held by the Ottawa in Oceana and Mason counties. These were prime farmland and pine forest. The Ottawa as well as their Ojibwa neighbors quickly saw that it would be necessary to readjust their treaties in order to guarantee them and their progeny a larger and more permanent landbase. Thus Ottawa and Ojibwa enlisted in the Civil War in part in hopes of gaining the trust and leverage for a new treaty arrangement.[24]

The recruitment of the Ottawa in the summer of 1863 is recorded in a county history of Oceana County. During a July Fourth celebration at the Indian community at Pentwater, Captain Andress addressed the Ottawa audience, aided by Chief Pay-baw-me as well as an Indian interpreter, encouraging community members to enlist. Louis Genereau, Jr., the son of the interpreter, and twenty-four others stepped forward and were soon sworn into service. Several days later, they departed by steamer from the harbor under the watchful eyes of nearly all the Indians of the reservation. The scene was later described as follows: "Many of the squaws had come to see them off, and there could be seen the old grey-headed squaw taking leave of her son. A mother with a papoose on her back bidding her husband goodbye after the Indian manner. In another quarter a younger squaw casting shy glances at her departing brave." The ship left the dock as the onlookers gave "three heavy cheers" to their men going off to war.[25] Among those departing that day was Antoine Scott, later cited by the Adjutant General's Office for valor at the Battle of the Crater: "Before Petersburg, July 30, 1864, instead of screening himself behind the captured works, this soldier stood boldly up and deliberately fired his piece until the enemy was close upon him, when, instead of surrendering, he ran the gauntlet of shot and shell and escaped."[26] Scott's actions, a diversionary tactic, helped save some of his trapped Indian comrades.

Even before its ranks were filled, the First Michigan Sharpshooters were called into action. Under the leadership of Colonel Charles V. De Land, some of these Indian troops were sent off to Indiana and Ohio to combat Confederate marauders led by General John Hunt Morgan who had made incursions into the North in July, 1863. After their mission was accomplished, the Indian troops returned to Dearborn where they were joined by new recruits and subsequently trained as sharpshooters. By mid-August, instead of serving as sharpshooters, the regiment was ordered to Chicago where it guarded rebel prisoners incarcerated at Camp Douglas.[27]

The Indians hardly made an impression on their fellow Union soldiers in their first six months of Civil War service. Indeed, one Union soldier at Camp Douglas even wrote disparagingly in his diary on September 27: These "Chipawa [sic]" Indians "who are formed to gather as Guards, calling themselves the 'Michigan Sharpshooters,' . . . are a desperate set of men, but as we all know, they only fight from behind trees and bushes."[28] Nor was this the only misreading of the regiment's future contribution to the Union war effort. On February 14, 1864, the First Michigan Sharpshooters were assigned to the Second Brigade, Third Division (Wilcox's), Ninth Army Corps and sent to Annapolis, Maryland. Their tenure at Annapolis was unfavorably noted by another Union soldier of the Thirteenth Massachusetts. Writing to his aunt, Jeremiah Stuart observed that the "Reg't of Sharpshooters" has a "Company of Indians" whom the Union soldier deemed "a drunken lot."[29] Several weeks later, with De Land in command, the Indian sharpshooters joined the Army of the Potomac, almost precisely when General Ulysses S. Grant assumed supreme command.

The Indian sharpshooters were eventually attached to Burnside's Corps. During the spring and summer of 1864, their presence was frequently noted in combat as well as in the daily events of camp life. Besides their distinctive physical appearance, the Indians in this unit were set apart from other soldiers in the Army of the Potomac by their "battle flag." One startled soldier of the Twentieth New York, writing to his sister back home in the Hudson Valley, observed that the Indians' unusual standard was a "large live Eagle" which was perched "on a pole some six feet long on a little platform."[30]

On May 4 and 5, the First Michigan Sharpshooters crossed the Rapidan River, a seemingly innocuous move but one that turned out to be their boat to Hades. From that time through July 30, 1864, the regiment found itself involved in the most intensive fighting of the Civil War. From Spotsylvania to the Crater, the Indian sharpshooters were used, sometimes against their training and better judgment, in dreaded human wave frontal assaults. Although they were cited for heroism, the Indians took heavy casualties in nearly every engagement in Grant's meat-grinder efforts to draw Lee's army out of its trenches by flanking the Confederate army from the right.

On May 5, Lee's advance units surprised Grant's massive army near the Wilderness Tavern in a forest between the Orange Turnpike and Orange Plank Road, at almost exactly the same spot where the

Battle of Chancellorsville had been fought a year earlier. The Union army immediately struck back. This Battle of the Wilderness was played out in woods so thick that soldiers seldom had a clear shot at their enemies. Entire brigades became lost in the forest and the organizational structure of both armies disintegrated. Muzzle flashes from thousands of rounds of rifles set the underbrush on fire, and many of the wounded who were unable to flee were burned to death. In two days of fighting, the Union suffered nearly eighteen thousand casualties and the Confederates nearly eleven thousand, about seventeen percent of each army![31]

Despite Lee's apparent "victory" over superior numbers, Grant's army did not retreat. His next objective was the crossroads at Spotsylvania Courthouse, a few miles south. He hoped to [which he believed would] force Lee to fight in open territory with his army in safety poised between Lee and Richmond. Lee foiled Grant's chess move by swiftly dispatching General Richard Anderson and his forces to reach Spotsylvania first. Grant's forces were delayed when rebel cavalry attacks blocked the road. By May 8, Anderson's men hastily improvised breastworks and a five-mile line of trenches in what appeared to observers as the shape of an inverted **U**. Grant's exhausted troops had lost the race. The Union general, in response, tried to outflank Lee on the west end of the Confederate line, but Lee shifted troops to meet every challenge.

On the afternoon of May 10, Grant, mistakenly believing that Lee's center was weakened by Union flanking movements, ordered two frontal assaults. The first failed; however, the second, under the heroic efforts of Colonel Emory Upton, achieved a temporary breakthrough. The failure of a supporting division to take advantage of the opening allowed the Confederates to counterattack, forced Upton's men back, and inflicted heavy casualties on Union troops. Yet Grant was not defeated.

In the rain and fog on May 12, at 4:35 A.M., Union General Winfield Scott Hancock's Federal Second Corps initiated a third assault on the Confederate lines with twenty thousand federal troops. This large-scale assault was directed at the tip of the so-called "mule shoe" salient, considered the weakest point of Lee's fortifications because its convexity caused the fire of defenders to converge. Within fifteen minutes, Union troops poured through gaps they had made in the line. After forty-five minutes, Union troops had reached the Confederates' second line of entrenchments and had captured between two thousand and four thousand prisoners, including General Anderson. They seized twenty artillery pieces, and cut off the famous Stonewall Brigade. After Confederate General John Brown Gordon's counterattack, Hancock was driven back to the first line of the southern entrenchments which he and his troops managed to hold.

While this was occurring, the Union's Sixth Corps assaulted the Confederate trenches a few hundred yards down the west side of the salient, at the so-called "Bloody Angle." In some of the most intense fighting of the war, the two armies slugged it out in the rain. Surrounding trees were splintered and shattered by musket balls and trenches were filled with mud and blood. Men on both sides became killing machines and troops could not be brought up fast enough to fill in for those who had been shot. In twenty hours of fighting, each side suffered seven thousand casualties. Eventually, after midnight, Lee's forces abandoned their mule-shoe entrenchments; however, Lee avoided defeat by shifting troops to reinforce his interior lines.[32]

The First Michigan Sharpshooters at the Battle of the Wilderness succeeded in withstanding a charge by double their number; however, they took heavy casualties when a line officer gave an order to retreat without any authority to do so. According to the War Department's *Official Record*, at Spotsylvania, the company was exposed all day on May 11 to "a raking fire from the enemy's skirmishes, and from which the regiment suffered severely" until De Land was able to strengthen his skirmish line and drive the Confederates back out of range. After reinforcing his lines further that night, De Land led his regiment in a charge against the enemy in the early evening hours of May 12. They "advanced rapidly about 500 yards under a heavy and destructive fire of musketry, grape, and canister from the enemy." Reaching within fifty yards of the enemy's lines, De Land's men were finally halted. He then "ordered the men forward to the

first line of the enemy's works, which was carried, and jointly occupied by the Sharpshooters and the Twenty-seventh Michigan Infantry." However, after a few minutes, the Indians and their comrades-in-arms "became exposed to a murderous cross-fire of shell,
grape, and canister. To advance was impossible; to retreat difficult."
With their command breaking down because of casualties and running out of ammunition, De Land "decided to hold the ground until
the last possible moment in hopes the line would be organized or
some support sent to our aid." For one hour, the Union forces accomplished this feat. The Confederates charged the Union ranks
twice, but De Land's men, fighting "with a determination and gallantry unsurpassed," drove them back with their bayonets. Indeed,
his Michigan men, who were finally ordered to retreat, "were the last
to contest the field."[33]

The Indian sharpshooters had borne a heavy toll in the week's
fighting at the Battles of the Wilderness and Spotsylvania. Of the
thirty-four men of the First Michigan Sharpshooters killed in action,
at least thirteen were Indians from Company K. Included in these
ranks was Sergeant Henry G. Gravaraet, who was killed instantly at
the Battle of Spotsylvania when a Minie bullet from a muzzle-load-
ing rifle struck him in the head.[34] Later, Colonel De Land cited
Henry's son Garrett, along with twenty other officers, for their "con-
spicuous coolness, courage and gallantry" in the campaign.[35] A subsequent article reported a "company of civilized Indians" at Spotsylvania "in command of the gallant and lamented young Gravaraet, an
educated half-breed—as brave a band of warriors as ever struck a
war-path." According to this news story, this Indian company "suffered dreadfully, but never faltered nor moved, sounding the war-
whoop with every volley, and their unerring aim quickly taught the
rebels they were standing on dangerous ground. . . ."[36]

The Battles of the Wilderness and Spotsylvania were only the horrid beginnings of these Indians' misfortunes. After crossing the Pamunkey River on May 28, Grant was to meet Lee's forces again, this
time entrenched behind Totopotony Creek, within ten miles of

Richmond. Philip Sheridan's cavalry seized a crossroads near Cold Harbor, soon being reinforced by Union foot soldiers on June 1. Grant had to delay his attack on the following morning because one of his corps had become lost and his men, forced-marched for days, were too weary to fight. In the meantime, the Confederates built a six-mile line with flanks protected by the Chickahominy River and Totopotony Creek. Foolishly, Grant attacked on June 3 with fifty thousand men against by then thirty thousand well-entrenched Confederates. Lee won the day at Cold Harbor, inflicting seven thousand casualties on the Union troops.[37]

Luckily for the Indian sharpshooters, they were not directly involved in Grant's suicidal assault at Cold Harbor. Perhaps because of the regiment's heavy losses at Spotsylvania, the Indian sharpshooters were employed on the periphery, in the supporting lines from May 28 to June 4; however, their role was to change when they reached the outskirts of the Confederate citadel of Petersburg by mid-June. In Grant's thinking, if Petersburg fell to Union forces, the Confederates would have to evacuate Richmond, Lee's Army of Northern Virginia would be cut off, and the war would end.

Outnumbering Lee's forces five to one, federal troops attacked Confederate fortifications on the evening of June 14 in an action that was to continue intermittently through June 18. On the morning of the 17th, General Gouverneur Warren, the hero at Gettysburg, deployed his 5th Corps on the federal left, while General Robert Brown Potter's Second Division, Ninth Corps initiated a surprise attack which caught the Confederate defenders on the exterior defenses of the Petersburg fortifications asleep on their arms. Potter's forces, which included the Indian sharpshooters, captured six hundred Confederate troops at Shand House, just east of the city; nevertheless, the Ninth Corps was unable to penetrate the main Confederate lines one mile from the city.

The Union troops took heavy casualties in their assault and induced a substantial Confederate response. At dusk on June 17, Confederate forces under General Archibald Gracie, who had been sent from Richmond, launched a counterattack that recaptured some of the positions taken by the Ninth Corps during the day.[38]

During the engagement the First Michigan Sharpshooters were on the extreme left. Because of the Union failure to connect the line after the capture of the rebel works at Shand House, the rebels were able to pour in their troops. The First Michigan Sharpshooters, faced with severe fighting, repulsed the enemy in two successive and vigorous charges, taking two officers and eighty-six men prisoner, capturing colors of the Thirty-fifth North Carolina Volunteer Infantry, and exhibiting "distinguished gallantry on the occasion."[39]

Disaster soon struck when the left of the regiment became surrounded by rebel forces. When the regiment's troops attempted to force their way out of the encirclement, most sharpshooters succeeded in getting through the rebel lines but many were taken prisoner and thirty-two were killed in the day's fighting. Twelve Indian sharpshooters were captured by Confederate forces on June 17; seven of these men subsequently died as prisoners of war at Andersonville. One other was listed as missing in action.[40] Two Indian sharpshooters were killed in the heavy fighting, including Second Lieutenant Garrett A. Gravaraet, who died of wounds less than two weeks later at the federal Armory Hospital in Washington, D.C.[41]

At the battle Gravaraet had been shot in his left arm, fracturing his humerus near his shoulder.[42] According to one source, he was wounded in the "disastrous charge" before Petersburg. Though he was ill at the time, Gravaraet had "placed himself at the head of his men, waved his sword above his head, and called them to follow."[43] At one of the field hospitals of the Army of the Potomac, military surgeons amputated the arm, a most common and often quite barbaric procedure at Civil War medical facilities since surgeons knew of few other ways to stop blood poisoning, bone infection, or gangrene.

Although Washington's hospitals rated far better than most Union medical facilities, by the time Gravaraet reached the city, it was already too late. It is important to remember that a Civil War soldier was eight times more likely to die of a wound and ten times more likely to die of disease than an American soldier in World War I, when antibiotics were still unknown. The medical advances of Pasteur and Lister and the modern science of bacteriology were yet to come; moreover, Civil War rifles, with their low muzzle velocity and large calibers, caused grotesque wounds. During the conflict, regimental surgeons desperately tried to use porous bags filled with earth as an absorbent for closing wounds.[44] The horror of these field facilities was vividly described by Dr. William Keen, later President Grover Cleveland's physician and a leading surgeon, who wrote in 1918 of his experience in a field hospital during the Civil War:

> We operated in old blood-stained and often pus-stained coats, the veterans of a hundred fights. . . . We used undisinfected instruments from undisinfected plush-lined cases, and still worse, used marine sponges which had been used in prior pus cases and had been only washed in tap water. If a sponge or an instrument fell on the floor it was washed and squeezed in a basin of tap water and used as if it were clean. Our silk to tie blood vessels was undisinfected. . . . The silk with which we sewed up all wounds was undisinfected. If there was any difficulty in threading the needle we moistened it with . . . bacteria-laden saliva, and rolled it between bacteria-infected fingers. We dressed the wounds with clean but undisinfected sheets, shirts, tablecloths, or other old soft linen rescued from the family ragbag. We had no sterilized gauze dressing, no gauze sponges. . . . We knew nothing about antiseptics and therefore used none.[45]

While on his deathbed at the Washington Armory Hospital, Gravaraet penned a most revealing letter to his mother and sister describing what had happened to him as well as to his deceased father. He apparently had a deathbed conversion to Christianity. Clearly expressing a fervent loyalty to the cause of the North, the dying Indian officer wrote:

> On Friday last during the first charge on the enemy's outworks near Petersburg, I was wounded in the left arm with a minnie ball and the arm had to be amputated too, below the shoulder, which was done that evening. I think I shall be discharged before long and come home if my

arm does well. The Dr. thinks it will do well. I've had no opportunity to write about father's death. Don't be discouraged about me.

Mother's kind teachings and progress is all that has kept me up. I have thought of them a great deal. I feel determined to become a Christian if possible. This fighten for my Country is all right. It has brought me to my senses. I expressed from Washington Junction early in May. Four Hundred Dollars to Hon. D. C. Leach [Indian agent] to be given by him to mother—That is I enclosed that amount in a letter to Mr. Leach and gave them the letter into the hands of our paymaster who promised to have it expressed from Washington. Now I want to know if you have received it. . . .[46]

Although it appears from Gravaraet's letter that his patriotism was to the Union, one may interpret his statement "fighten for my Country" in an entirely different way. Although Gravaraet was a product of two worlds, he, as well as the numerous Ottawa and Ojibwa Indians in his company, saw *their* country as the Indian world of the Great Lakes. To prevent further loss of this universe, they were willing to fight and even die for another country, the United States.

After Gravaraet's body and personal belongings—$130—were sent back to Michigan, the "Assistant Ward Master" of the hospital wrote his mother that, after suffering "a great deal," the Indian's death was caused by complications from his amputation when "mortification set in and struck to his heart." Assuring his mother, a Catholic, that the priest as well as the local Michigan congressman visited him several times, the administrator maintained that Gravaraet had been "a good soldier and was liked by all."[47] The day before, in a letter which crossed in the mail, Richard Cooper, writing for the twice-bereaved Sophie Gravaraet, expressed his anguish over her losses in the war. Cooper insisted that the death of Mrs. Gravaraet's son "will be the means of killing Mrs. Graverate. It is only a few days ago, she got word about her husband Sergeant Graverate . . . been killed, and now her only son Garret. . . ."[48]

Gravaraet was buried on Mackinac Island. At age twenty-four, he had returned to the land of the Great Hare. Perhaps he was more fortunate than his fellow comrades-in-arms who continued to suffer the fate of trench warfare and combat at Petersburg. By this time, the Indians had won the respect of their comrades. One Union soldier wrote admiringly of their courage and sacrifice. On July 24, 1864, he described how these Indians had been "all through the present campaign" including the "awful fights of the Wilderness" and that there were "only some 20 of them left out of over 100 that commenced the campaign."[49]

The Indian Sharpshooters' last major military engagement was at the Battle of the Crater on July 30, 1864, a Union fiasco which is fully described for different reasons in the following chapter. Being fired on from all sides, the Indians of the First Michigan Sharpshooters found themselves surrounded and with little ammunition.[50] In one of the more remarkable accounts of the battle, Lieutenant Freeman S. Bowley of the Thirtieth United States Colored Troops described their actions. A few of these Indians, he noted, "did splendid work. Some of them were mortally wounded, and drawing their blouses over their faces, they chanted a death song and died—four of them in a group."[51]

The First Michigan Sharpshooters served through the nine-and-a-half month ordeal at Petersburg and through the Appomattox campaign. The company's survivors—less than two-thirds of the original enlistees—were mustered out of service at the end of the war.[52] D. C. Leach, the Indian agent of the Michigan Indian Agency, later summarized the unit's remarkable war record at the same time he argued for tolerance and respect for Michigan's Indians. Leach insisted that from "the first outbreak they manifested a lively interest in all matters pertaining to the war, and an earnest desire that the government should in the end triumph over its enemies and restore its authority throughout the land." The Indian agent added: "Very much to their credit and praise it is to be mentioned, that when offered an opportunity of engaging in the military service of the country, they promptly and cheerfully came forward and assumed all the duties and responsibilities of the soldier."[53]

What Leach failed to note was that the Michigan Indians had little choice about serving. Their need to gain assurances that Washington would allow them to remain in the state motivated their entry into war. Rather than be accused of "Copperheadism" or be grouped with so-called "hostile Indians" in nearby Minnesota, they chose the Union, a warpath which tragically led many of them to perish on Virginia's bloody battlefields.

8

Among the United States
Colored Troops

The Pequot

IN THE TRENCHES BEFORE PETERSBURG WERE OTHER INDIANS SERVING in important but less documented capacities than the First Michigan Sharpshooters. One of them was Private Austin George, a Mashantucket Pequot Indian from southeastern Connecticut, who was a member of the Thirty-first United States Colored Infantry of the Army of the Potomac. George was one of at least three Indians from the Ledyard–North Stonington area who served in the Union army.[1] Some historians have incorrectly assumed that the troops of the United States Colored Infantry, as it was officially called, were entirely African Americans. Not so. For whites, "colored" meant Indian as well as black, even well into twentieth century. Because these soldiers have been labeled African American, black, or Negro, many Native Americans, especially in southern New England, have been written out of Civil War history.[2] Returning them to its pages offers a fascinating look into the gap between racist categories and individual actions.

George was a Mashantucket Pequot who also had Mohegan ancestry. He appears on the Pequot Overseer's Reports from 1860 through 1873, but does not appear on Mohegan documents in the same period.[3] In his Civil War military records, his Indian heritage is described in three distinct ways. Upon his enlistment, the recruiting officer recorded the word "Indian" on his descriptive muster-in roll.[4] In his pension record, an examining surgeon in 1889 stated: "This man belonged to [the] Mohegan Tribe of Indians."[5] Two years later, another examining surgeon maintained unequivocably: "Is a full blood Indian 'Pequot.' No African blood. Lives alone on reservation. Bones Large."[6]

George was born in New London County, Connecticut around 1828. Although no photograph of the man has survived, George's military records provide [clues to some basis of ascertaining] his physical appearance: He had black hair and black eyes, was classified as [being] dark or "colored" in complexion, and was between 130 and 175 pounds in weight and approximately five feet seven inches in height, about the average size for Civil War recruits. These records also indicate that he lived at Ledyard and had some schooling, although of a limited nature. Tribal records reveal that he married Sabrina Nedson, another Pequot, in Ledyard in 1851. In one genealogy of southeastern Connecticut, George, in 1859, is listed as the father of a son borne by another woman. No further information about his marriage or his son has been found, and from 1864 to 1895 his military/pension records list George as "single." These same records refer to his occupation as "whaleman," although his recruiting officer simply categorized him as a "sailor."[7]

We know little of George's early life; however, central to the upbringing of Pequots then and now are family stories about the horrors that befell these southeastern Connecticut Indians in the seventeenth century. George, like other Pequot tribesmen, was dramatically affected by events that had transpired well over two hundred years earlier. The War of 1637, the so-called Pequot War, was the first serious one between colonizers and the indigenous populations in New England, and it remained an important part of the Indians' psyche. The war and the colonial policies that followed nearly exterminated the Pequot, then the most powerful Indian group in southern New England; it opened southeastern Connecticut to English colonization and established English hegemony over the Indians of southern New England;

and it allowed for future Puritan missionary endeavors in the region.[8]

Just before dawn on May 26, 1637, an army of English soldiers led by Captains John Mason and John Underhill, Mohegan-Pequot under Uncas, and a contingent of Narragansett and Eastern Niantic assaulted the Pequot's eastern fort on the Mystic River. This attack occurred while most of the Pequot men were away and resulted in the deaths of between three hundred and seven hundred noncombatants, women, children, and old men. Many of the Indians were killed when Mason ordered the wigwams burned. The English and their allied Indians surrounded the village and cut down those trying to flee. The massacre lasted less than an hour and all but seven Pequot perished. Two English men were killed and twenty wounded, while twenty Indian allies were also wounded. The leaders of the expedition defended their actions as "God's will."[9] Even before the formal cessation of hostilities, Massachusetts Bay celebrated an official day of thanksgiving on June 15, 1637, "in all the churches for the victory [of May 26, 1637] obtained against the Pequods, and for other mercies."[10]

In addition to the sacking of Mystic fort, this largely one-sided war, which spread into the swamps of southeastern Connecticut, had other dire consequences for the Pequot. Perhaps as many as 1,500 Pequot, 40 to 50 percent of their prewar population, were killed.[11] Many of the Pequot not in the fort during the conflagration were captured, killed in skirmishes, or executed in the months that followed either by the English or by their Indian allies, including the Mohawk. Some Pequot prisoners of war were loaded on board the ship of Captain John Gallup, who subsequently threw them overboard to drown them. Others were enslaved, assigned to the "protection" of colonists or to Indian leaders—Uncas the Mohegan, Miantonomo the Narragansett, or Ninigret the Eastern Niantic—or sold into slavery and sent to Bermuda, the Bahamas, and the West Indies. The war formally ended in September 1638, when sachems for the remaining Pequot were forced to sign the Treaty of Hartford, also called the Tripartite Treaty. By the humiliating provisions of that accord, the Pequot nation was officially declared to be dissolved. Even the use of the designation "Pequot" was soon outlawed by colonial authorities. Until the 1650s, the Colony of Connecticut did not allow the Pequots to resettle in their homeland.[12] Two generations later, Cotton Mather, the venerable New England cleric, continued to rationalize his ancestors' actions against the Indians: ". . . in a little more than one hour, five or six hundred of these barbarians were dismissed from a world that was burdened with them."[13]

Although the Pequot attempted to rebuild their community, the legacy of the War of 1637 remained. As "dependent peoples," their lives were circumscribed economically and politically over the next two hundred years by colonial and state legislation. The State of Connecticut appointed overseers to manage their small landbase and tribal funds as well as lead these unfortunate people to "civilization."[14]

With this indelible memory still alive two centuries later, the Pequots of the Civil War era remained extremely wary and, at times, resentful of their white neighbors. No doubt for them the Civil War was far less appealing than it was for some others. Nonetheless, albeit in the late winter of 1864, Austin George enlisted. He volunteered for service in nearby Norwich, Connecticut on March 16, and was assigned to the Thirtieth Connecticut Colored Infantry. Governor William Buckingham had authorized the recruitment of the Thirtieth Infantry on January 12, 1864; however, only four companies were organized. These companies were later consolidated with other units organized at Hart's Island, New York, forming the Thirty-first United States Colored Infantry. This regiment, as well as other "colored" units, was largely the result of the long and extensive lobbying effort by the Association for Promoting Colored Volunteers, the Union League Club, and powerful New Yorkers such as William Cullen Bryant, Peter Cooper, Horace Greeley, Alexander Van Rensselaer, and James Roosevelt. After its establishment and consolidation, the regiment was assigned to the Third Brigade, Fourth Division, Ninth Army Corps.[15]

George was a member of F Company, which included at least one other Indian. Of the 131 soldiers in the company, forty of the recruits had been enlisted in the Thirtieth Connecticut Colored. Thirty-three men in the company were listed as substitutes, at least 27 of whom were African American freedmen from Virginia. Of the 98 nonsubstitutes, 24 were native New Yorkers, 17 were from Virginia, 12 from Kentucky, and 11 from Maryland. George was one of only two who claimed Connecticut birth. He was thirty-six years old, ten years older than the average age for nonsubstitutes; only twelve soldiers were thirty-six years old or older. Of the 98 nonsubstitutes, nearly half listed their occupation as laborer (30) or farmer (17). Eight listed their occupation as "sailor."[16]

George's enlistment was largely, but not entirely, prompted by economic factors. The New London whaling industry, already in decline since 1849, suffered considerably in the Civil War and went out of existence soon after. As part of the North Atlantic blockading squadron, the Union navy purchased much of New London's great whaling fleet, mostly from the Haven (later Williams and Haven) shipyards, filled them with stone, and sank the vessels in the channels of major southern ports in order to strangle the Confederate naval machine and starve the South into submission. Other New London whaling ships were leased to the federal government as troop transports and supply vessels.[17] Instead of building more whaling ships, southeastern Connecticut turned to the war effort. The famous Mallory yards of Mystic sold off its entire whaling fleet of thirteen sloops and schooners. In its place, the Mallorys and others built fifty-six steamships, or sold ships to private parties who refitted these vessels with thirty-pound Parrott guns for the Union navy. Only Boston, a port nearly twenty times larger than Mystic, had greater productivity in New England during the Civil War.[18]

A whaleman with wanderlust, to be sure, had no temperament for shipbuilding. Factory work, which boomed in southeastern Connecticut during the Civil War—especially at the Attawaugan Textile Company in Norwich, the Norwich Arms Company, and the Joslyn Arms Company of Stonington—was equally unappealing.[19] Nonetheless, George and other Indians in the region had to find some way to sustain them after the sharp decline of whaling. The minuscule Pequot landbase had been reduced considerably in the mid-

1850s and could not provide enough sustenance. Despite tribal protests, a Connecticut law had been passed allowing the auctioning off of six hundred acres of Mashantucket Pequot lands on January 1, 1856. As a result of the authoritarian and corrupt Connecticut overseer system, Pequots were denied their benefits and the monies due them. Thus, by 1864, members of the George family were described in the Stonington town accounts as being "on expense," namely as receiving public assistance.[20]

As was true of many Union soldiers by 1864, Austin George was entitled to a hefty bounty for volunteering. For example, by 1864, the Town of Ledyard was paying out bounties of $150 and the State of Connecticut $600 to any recruit who signed up.[21]

George served in a segregated unit and almost all of his comrades-in-arms were African Americans. Although it was common practice in southern New England to group Native Americans and African Americans together as free persons of color, we do not know if George intentionally sought service in the Thirtieth Connecticut Colored Infantry Regiment or if he was placed there. He may have requested it, because of his familiarity with blacks and his Pequot people's memories of past white treachery. Blacks and Indians had participated in the whaling industry in southeastern Connecticut. Moreover, one of the main slave escape routes in New England on the underground railroad, the New London–Norwich corridor, passed right through North Stonington, which also had a major anti-slavery society. The town was the home of the shoemaker James Lindsey Smith, ex-slave and abolitionist lecturer. Although we do not know George's views about slavery, he had to be aware of these well-documented abolitionist activities.[22]

The Indians of southeastern Connecticut in general did not beat down the doors to join the war effort. After the bloodletting at Antietam and Shiloh in 1862, few individuals, let alone the resentful Pequot Indians, saw the conflict in romantic or patriotic terms. Nonetheless, the vast Union war machine needed bodies and recruiters began beating the bushes to get soldiers. By 1863, the United States had instituted the first draft in American history.

In that year, there were attempts to conscript Indians in the Norwich area to fill district quotas. In reaction, the Mohegan, separate but culturally related to the Pequot, sent an official protest to the War Department, asserting that their tribesmen could not be legally drafted. They insisted that all-too-eager Norwich and Montville recruiters had "taken the liberty to enroll some of the said Mohegan tribe for the present draft and without our consent." The protest insisted that Article I of the Constitution of the United States legally exempted the Mohegan, a small community "already reduced by war and other pestilence," from the draft.[23] There is no record of whether this protest had any effect.

Even while joining the North's avowed thrust against the South's peculiar institution, the Thirty-first United States Colored Infantry, as well as other "colored" regiments, were seriously affected by white racism. The 180,000 "colored" troops were paid less than their white counterparts throughout much of the war. Even as late as August 1864, George was being paid $7 per month, far less than the $13 per month that white privates received in the Union army. The "colored" regiments received poorer medical care, having twice the death rate from disease as white troops. Not surprisingly, all commanding officers of these "colored" units were white, and many of them had blatantly racist attitudes about their companies. The War Department originally planned to use the "colored" regiments to guard supply dumps and wagon trains, garrison forts, and to perform rear-area duties, thereby releasing white regiments believed to be more "capable," for combat. Thus, when the Thirty-first United States Colored Troops were sent to Virginia in May 1864, they were assigned to guard Union railway facilities. White troops meanwhile were released to fight the bloody Battles of the Wilderness and Cold Harbor.[24]

By mid-June, George and his comrades were digging trenches at Petersburg, Virginia. These trenches were a complex undertaking with abatis (felled trees), cheveau-de-frise (sharpened stakes), and protected ditches. The trench warfare at Petersburg paralleled the later World War I experience. The thirty-five-mile Confederate defense line, which began west of Petersburg, protected the Bermuda Hundred peninsula, then crossed the James River to northeast of Richmond. Indeed, the area was the gateway to the Confederate capital. Petersburg also served the Confederacy because of its rail link to the maritime South Atlantic supply line at Wilmington, North Carolina. The siege at Petersburg, in all, involved six major battles, eleven engagements, forty-four skirmishes, six assaults, nine actions, and three expeditions. Despite Grant's overwhelming numerical advantage—Union forces averaged 109,000 men while Lee's Confederate troops averaged 59,000 men—the campaign lasted nine and a half months.[25] In time, as manpower disappeared into this killing machine, the colored troops were then thrust right into the heart of the action.

The siege began in the hot, sultry months of 1864. The development of bigger and more powerful mortars and more accurate and deadly rifles meant that Union troops were unable to go out, get up, stretch, or even stand for fear they would be picked off by the Confederate lines less than two football fields away. Federal orders "instructed soldiers to duck when they saw the distant puff of smoke from a sharpshooter's rifle."[26] In this mole-like existence, sleep was intermittent at best. Vermin, filth, disgusting odors, and lack of privacy tested the troops further. After six weeks of dry weather, heavy rains began in July, filling the trenches with mud and adding to the misery. Whatever romanticism or sense of adventure they had upon enlistment, the Union troops quickly learned the grim reality of the death struggle outside the besieged Petersburg citadel.[27]

As the opposing armies faced off before Petersburg, Colonel Henry Pleasants of the Forty-eighth Pennsylvania Infantry Regiment, which included many coal miners, proposed building a ventilated tunnel more than five hundred feet long—unheard of in any previous military operation—that would breach the Confederate fortifications since General Ambrose Burnside's Ninth Corps lay within 150 yards of the Confederate Elliott's Salient. Ironically, behind the southern lines at this point were Catawba Indian soldiers of the Seventeenth South Carolina. Pleasants's brilliantly conceived plan was to place four tons of gunpowder in lateral galleries at the end of the tunnel which would be triggered at a set time. After the explosion, Union forces would fan out around both sides of the newly formed crater and then would press through the gap in the Confederate fortifications and seize Petersburg. Though the plan was dismissed as unfeasible by army engineers and stonewalled by the Union brass, the troops of the 48th Pennsylvania improvised, making their own tools, securing their own lumber to timber the shaft, and borrowing a theodolite from a civilian to triangulate for distance and direction. From June 25, 1864 onward, the mine construction project continued until its completion in late July.[28]

Since the Army of the Potomac had been worn down by intense combat, with heavy casualties in May and June, 1864, General Burnside recommended to Grant and Meade that fresh soldiers, the United States Colored Troops, General Edward Ferrero's Fourth Division Infantry, lead the assault after the explosion of the mine. Ferrero and his troops were to rush through the breach in the Confederate lines and open the way for the Union army to take Petersburg along the Jerusalem Plank Road and Cemetery Ridge. While the mine was being dug, the "colored" troops, including the Thirty-first United States Colored Troops, were specifically trained for this delicate mission.

A half a day before the gunpowder was set to be detonated, Meade, with Grant's approval, changed the plan, ordering Burnside to send in his "white" divisions first. Apparently, Meade did not have confidence in the untested United States Colored Troops, while Grant feared that he would be criticized by abolitionists and radical Republicans if these raw recruits took heavy casualties and served as cannon fodder for Confederate batteries. The Battle of the Crater, also called the Battle of the Petersburg Mine, which soon followed was the Civil War's version of the folly known as the Charge of the Light Brigade. Indeed, the Crimean War's Battle of Balaklava was in some ways mild compared with the terrible events that transpired on July 30, 1864, before Petersburg, Virginia.[29]

General James H. Ledlie was chosen by drawing straws, not because of overall ability, to lead the "white" troops' assault. Five months later, Grant would label Ledlie the worst division commander in the Ninth Corps; however, the supreme commander had never objected to Ledlie's leadership before the assault. Grant was also well aware that officers in Ledlie's command had blamed him for incompetence, cowardice, or drunkenness in a botched attack on the Confederate lines on June 17. When he was accused of being drunk at the Battle of the Crater, Ledlie claimed he had been administered rum by an army surgeon after being wounded by a spent ball.[30]

Although Meade deserves plenty of censure, the primary blame for the disaster at Petersburg rests with Grant. In addition to the use of war-weary troops, Grant's authorization of a change of plans only fifteen or sixteen hours before the mine was sprung did not allow the troops time to rehearse their roles. It is little wonder that Grant took overall responsibility for the fiasco, later writing: "It was the saddest affair I have witnessed in the war."[31]

When the explosives failed to detonate at their designated time, 3:30 A.M., because the army brass had denied the miners a suitable fuse line, Pleasants and two assistants re-lit the line and raced back to the mine's entrance as the flame traveled to the black powder. The explosion, which finally occurred at 4:44 A.M., blew a hole 170 feet long, 60 feet wide, and 30 feet deep, burying numerous rebels and scattering and destroying two guns of an artillery battery in the flying debris. Two hundred seventy-eight Virginians and South Carolinians, including members of the Seventeenth South Carolina, were killed in the explosion. Immediately after, one hundred ten Union guns and fifty-four mortars began opening up on the Confederate lines.[32]

Instead of charging right away, Ledlie's men, deafened by hearing the terrific explosion and witnessing the immense red flames, lightning flashes, and billowing smoke, recoiled from the horrible scene. Ten minutes were lost regrouping Union forces. Meanwhile, no one in the Union command had bothered to order the removal of the abatis before their lines which had prevented Confederate assaults on the North's positions. Now the same abatis had to be removed before a Union charge could be made.

The unprepared and battle-fatigued white soldiers went forward but stopped to gawk at the awesome sight of the crater. In the smoke and confusion, Union forces went into the crater instead of fanning out right and left as the Union plan had intended. The other "white" divisions, which included Michigan's Indian sharpshooters, Seneca Indians of the Fourteenth Heavy Artillery, and Indians from Wisconsin in the Thirty-seventh Wisconsin Volunteer Infantry, followed. They soon became sitting ducks for regrouped Confederate artillery and mortars. The heat of that early mid-July morn only added to the oppressive conditions. Eventually no "air was stirring within the crater." According to one officer of the Fourteenth New York Artillery: "It was a sickening sight: men were dead and dying all around us; blood was streaming down the sides of the crater to the bottom, where it gathered in pools for a time before being absorbed by the hard red clay."[33]

The Union command held back the United States Colored Troops for two hours after the mine was "sprung." Finally, while General Ferrero squirreled himself away in a bunker far from the fighting, his "colored" troops began their charge. At 7:30 A.M., Confederate General William Mahone initiated his counterattack, approximately the time the Union's "colored" troops had pushed past many of the frantically retreating white troops. George and his comrades-in-arms in the Thirty-first United States Colored Infantry were among the first units hit by Mahone's counterattack. The regiment's colonel, W. E. Ross, as well as his next officers in rank, were shot during the foray. The Thirty-first was leaderless at the crucial time of the battle, and its organization collapsed.[34]

Colonel, later General, Henry G. Thomas, who headed the Second Brigade of General Ferrero's Fourth Division at the battle, described the confusion: "The instant I reached the First Brigade I attempted to charge, but the Thirty-first was disheartened at its loss of officers and could not be gotten out promptly."[35] In another account, Thomas stated: "The men of the 31st making the charge were being mowed down like grass, with no hope of any one reaching the crest, so I ordered them to scatter and run back."[36]

Encountering Mahone's counterattack, the Thirty-first and other "colored" regiments had nowhere to take cover. Their forward

progress was halted by bodies strewn in the crater and over the battlefield. They could not "make a decent charge" since "the pits into
which we were sent were entirely occupied by dead and dying rebel
troops and our own, from the First Division of our corps—General
Ledlie."[37]

After the war Thomas had the highest praise for the "colored"
troops. He described how one group of soldiers "defended the in-
trenchments we had won from the enemy, exhibiting fighting qualities that I never saw surpassed in the war." A handful of these troops
"stood there without the slightest organization," each man for himself "until the enemy's banners waved in their very faces. Then they
made a dash for our own lines, and that at my order."[38] It should be
noted that Confederate forces exacted retribution on these "colored"
troops, many of whom were ex-slaves. They bayoneted, shot, and executed prisoners and left wounded Union "colored" troops to rot behind their lines.[39] On the day after the battle, General Gouverneur K.
Warren, a hero of the Battle of Gettysburg, reported that the Union's
"helpless wounded are still lying close to the enemy's line and they
give no help." The shocked Warren added: "The wounded seem to
be mostly colored men that are writhing with their wounds in this
insufferable scene and I think the neglect of them must be intention-
al. I think we should offer to fire upon the enemy if he refuses to go
and take care of these men."[40] Finally, two days after the mine was
triggered, a truce was declared so that both sides could gather their
wounded and bury their dead.[41]

In all, the Union took nearly 3,800 casualties while the Confederate total was less than 1,500. The Thirty-first United States Colored
Infantry lost 136 men in this fiasco. Seven soldiers in George's Company F alone were killed in the battle, including private Clinton
Mountpleasant, a Tuscarora Indian from western New York. In total
at the Crater, the "colored" troops suffered more than 40 percent of
the casualties, despite the overwhelming number of white soldiers in
the battle.[42]

Austin George was one of the casualties of the battle and the
events of July 30 changed his life forever. He was shot in the left

shoulder, an injury described in his medical file as a "flesh wound near scapula."[43] Despite this reference, his medical and pension records indicate that the wound was hardly superficial. In an affidavit dated August 14, 1866, Second Lieutenant W. C. Williams of the Thirty-first indicated that George was "wounded in the line of duty to wit on the 30th day of July 1864, while charging on the enemy's works in front of Petersburgh Va. received a gun shot wound in his shoulder from the performance of military duty and was sent to the hospital."[44] The examining surgeon's report on the same day shows that George was inches away from a very different medical file description: "The ball struck near the top of the left shoulder-blade, about three inches from the spine, pinned under shoulder blade and came out [after surgery] near armpit." The doctor continued: "The injury has impaired the motion of the shoulder joint, unfitting him for full manual labor."[45] In a later affidavit to secure an increase in George's pension, Gilbert Billings, a neighbor who had known George nearly all his life, indicated that he saw the Mashantucket Pequot while the Indian was home on furlough in October 1864. Billings insisted that he had seen "his wound there . . . and it was very bad indeed."[46]

The more seriously wounded were evacuated by the Union army from Petersburg on flatcars "piled like logs . . . with here and there a half-severed limb dangling from a mutilated body."[47] Those who were ambulatory, such as George, had to make their own way for help since assisting such companions could be "construed as a cowardly attempt to escape combat."[48] George and the other ambulatory wounded waited for days for medical attention.

Four days after the battle, George was admitted to the Union hospital at City Point, considered to be the outstanding field hospital of the war. The huge facility of six thousand iron beds contained ninety pavilions and 324 tents. Despite its acclaim, the hospital had less desirable features such as open ditches serving as latrines that were situated too close to the medical tents. The latrines were covered with mosquito nets and treated with sulfite of iron to reduce the likelihood of typhoid fever.[49]

George was evacuated from City Point, first to the floating hospital on board the transport, the U.S. *Baltic*, and later to Summit House, a major Union hospital in Philadelphia. On board the *Baltic*, military surgeons performed surgery on him on August 17, extracting a "ball from wound of entrance." For the "luckier" wounded such as George, who made it to surgery rather than amputation, chloroform and ether were used as anesthetics. Yet for eighteen days he had borne the pain of a Confederate bullet lodged in his body as a memento of the tragedy at the Crater. George's wound, which resulted in a permanent disability, was then treated in Philadelphia, much to his fortune, because of the quality of the care provided in a city known for its medical facilities. George was a patient in Philadelphia from August through December 1864, except for a two-week furlough to visit his Connecticut home in October.[50]

Although being shot was by far the worst experience that he faced in the war, it is clear that the private suffered one hardship after another in military service. George injured himself falling off a horse, hurting his right shoulder. This same shoulder was also injured when timber fell on him while dissembling winter quarters and was reinjured during the digging of breastworks at the Petersburg siege. He later insisted that he developed a permanent condition of rheumatism in his shoulders as a result of lying on the ground in front of Petersburg. On one occasion, he was admitted to the field hospital at Fort Monroe, Virginia with diarrhea/dysentery. As was true of a substantial number of Union soldiers, George was also treated for syphilis.[51] Venereal diseases were among the leading illnesses contracted, only behind dysentery, typhoid, pneumonia, and malaria in their frequency. Syphilis totaled nearly eighty thousand cases alone.[52] By the 1890s, an examining surgeon noted that George exhibited signs of senility, indicating, perhaps, that this illness continued to riddle his body long after the war.[53]

On January 17, 1865, after five months of recuperation at Summit House Hospital in Philadelphia, Austin George "went over the wall." This action—there were 278,044 desertions in the Union army— was common at military hospitals during the war. More than 33,430 soldiers and sailors deserted at United States general hospitals. George was apprehended six weeks later by one Captain William Holden who was paid $30 plus expenses for his efforts. He was immediately returned to his regiment, which in March 1865 was tightening the noose on Lee's Army of Northern Virginia.[54]

Perhaps "going over the wall" was an apt end for a Pequot in service in a white man's war, a Pequot identified and stigmatized as colored, a Pequot put through the shame of underpaid ditch digging and the hell of the fight in the crater. Though a substantial number of Civil War veterans, like their modern counterparts, suffered from stress disorders, George had more cause to go over the wall than most. George's resentment of Northern whites could not have lessened at all with army life. His leaders had sent him on a suicidal mission. Instead of being punished for cowardice and/or incompetence at the Battle of the Crater, General Ferrero retained his command and was promoted to brevet major general for meritorious service, while George was being given the pittance of $7 per month, lying wounded in a Philadelphia hospital that hadn't even admitted him for some days. It should be pointed out that George was never officially prosecuted nor did he receive a dishonorable discharge. Almost immediately after his discharge, he was in fact awarded a Civil War pension, recommended to the Bureau of Pensions by Second Lieutenant W. C. Williams, his company's commanding officer.[55]

When George returned in March 1865, the Thirty-first was about to cross the James River and take its position on the left of the Army of the Potomac at Hatcher's Run. Subsequently, the regiment was under constant siege, but helped pierce the rebel lines on April 1 and 2, resulting in the Confederate abandonment of Petersburg and Richmond. For the next six days, the regiment participated in the operations which led to Lee's surrender at Appomattox. In thirty hours on April 7 and 8, it covered an unbelievable distance of sixty miles in Grant's relentless pursuit of victory.[56]

On June 8, 1865, Austin George was mustered out of the Thirty-first United States Colored Infantry at Fort Monroe, Virginia. Unable to do heavy shipboard work in the new seal-hunting industry which arose after 1867, he returned to Ledyard where he worked as a subsistence farmer and/or farm laborer. Two weeks after his discharge, he filed for his invalid military pension under a congressional act of July 14, 1862. On December 18, 1866, he was awarded a half pension of $4 per month as a result of his disability in his left shoulder. Although this award was reduced to $2 per month in September 1871, it was again increased to $4 per month in June 1878, since he experienced numbness in his highly scarred left shoulder. From this time until his death on November 11, 1895, George was unable to secure an increase in his pension, despite his frequent appeals and the continuing deterioration of his physical condition.[57]

Austin George's Civil War service was fifteen months of hell followed by thirty years of misery. His Indian nation's history, at least since 1637, had been a similar short hell and long misery. On March 1, 1888, he stated in an affidavit that he did not know the present addresses of any of his comrades in his regiment.[58] At a time when the Grand Army of the Republic played a significant social and political function, frequently uniting Union veterans in pageants, picnics, and reunions, one Pequot had had enough, isolating himself from more mental anguish about the nightmare, that horrible pit, the Petersburg Crater.

9

Union Officers

Two Seneca Brothers from New Bern to Appomattox

As in the sad case of Austin George, American Indians in the North put themselves in harm's way in a Union war effort that often was unappreciative of their sacrifice. Although white prejudice toward their service varied from one area to another in the North, American Indians had to overcome racist restrictions in recruitment and long delays in securing commissions. Despite these barriers, some Indians were able to persevere and rise in the ranks of the Union officer corps, playing remarkable roles even in the outcome of the war itself. No better examples of success in the face of most difficult circumstances are there than the outstanding military careers of two Tonawanda Seneca officers from western New York, Isaac Newton Parker and Ely Samuel Parker.

At military headquarters at City Point during the never-ending Petersburg campaign, Ely Samuel Parker, a Seneca Indian sachem, was serving on Grant's staff. Both Ely Samuel and his brother Isaac Newton were officers in the Union army. The extensive correspondence of these two exceptional brothers provides an unmatched firsthand portrait of American Indian involvement in the Civil War. Both men were thoroughly at home in both the Indian and non-Indian worlds.

Their remarkable wartime letters reveal every aspect of an Indian officer's involvement in the Union army: recruitment, training, company life, and combat. Besides their views of the South and southerners, white, black, and Indian, their correspondence describes the harsh realities, racial prejudices, as well as the deaths of trusted Indian and non-Indian comrades-in-arms.

Isaac Newton Parker, who preferred to call himself "Newt," was a noncommissioned officer, eventually the Third Sergeant and Color Bearer of D Company of the 132nd New York State Volunteer Infantry. He was stationed in the vicinity of New Bern, North Carolina from 1863 to 1865, guarding the rails at this major transportation nexus. Unlike his brother who served as the sole Indian at the power center of the Union high command in 1864 and 1865, Newt served with twenty-four other Iroquois in an integrated unit which was popularly called "the Tuscarora Company."[1] Ely Samuel Parker, the first Native American to serve as commissioner of Indian Affairs, received a commission in the Union army in May 1863. Parker served as assistant adjutant general, division engineer, and, most importantly, as General Grant's military secretary. By the end of the war, he had been promoted to brigadier general and served as Grant's scribe drawing up the articles of surrender which General Robert E. Lee signed on April 9, 1865 at Appomattox Court House.[2]

The two brothers came from an extraordinary Seneca family. They were the sons of Chief William Parker, Jo-no-es-sto-wa, a Seneca who had been wounded serving the Americans during the War of 1812. Their mother, Elizabeth Johnson, Ga-out-gwat-twus, was the daughter of Jimmy Johnson, a nephew of the Seneca orator Red Jacket and the leading disciple of the Seneca prophet Handsome Lake, who was also in Parker's lineage. Thus, it was no coincidence that the Parkers had leadership skills. It is also not surprising that the Parkers' two-story log homestead on the Tonawanda Reservation became the center of political activity attempting to overturn fraudulent treaties and that both brothers devoted more than a decade of their lives to that effort.[3]

During the Parkers' formative years, the Seneca Indians, the "Western Door" of the famous Iroquois Confederacy, faced one of the worst crises in their history, affecting their lands and tribal existence. In 1826, 75 percent of the Tonawanda Reservation, which had been established in 1797 by the Treaty of Big Tree, was sold off by the Seneca. In January 1838, at the blatantly corrupt Treaty of Buffalo Creek, initiated by the Ogden Land Company and its supporters, and consummated through alcohol, bribery, forgery, and intimidation, the Tonawanda Seneca were defrauded of their remaining lands. Despite appeals to overturn the 1838 treaty, a second treaty in 1842, the so-called "Compromise Treaty," formally recognized the legality of the sale of the Tonawanda as well as the Buffalo Creek reservations. For the next decade and a half, the Tonawanda Seneca attempted through legal action to overturn the Treaty of 1842. Through the efforts of their attorney John Martindale, a white man who later served as the commanding general of the military district of Washington, D.C. during the Civil War, the Tonawanda Seneca's case reached the United States Supreme Court. Before its adjudication, the United States Senate had worked out a resolution of the continuing controversy by allowing the Tonawanda Seneca to use money set aside for the Indians' removal to Kansas. With this money, the Indians purchased back 7,500 acres of tribal lands from the Ogden Land Company. This "settlement" was confirmed in a new federal treaty with the Tonawanda Seneca in 1857.[4]

The Parker family witnessed these events and lobbied to regain tribal lands. During this time, many prominent people of the day visited the family's homestead. One frequent guest was Lewis Henry Morgan, the "father of American anthropology," who was aided by the Parkers, both Newt and Ely, in producing his ground-breaking ethnography, *The League of the Ho-de-no-sau-nee, or Iroquois*, in 1851. Morgan's continuing interest in the Parker family and their welfare continued through the Civil War.[5]

Born in 1833, Isaac Newton Parker was the second youngest child of six brothers and a sister. He was a product of the Seneca world of Tonawanda, the Baptist mission school there, and the New York

State Normal School at Albany. According to his grandnephew Arthur C. Parker, Newt Parker received a "polished education" and was a "keen student of fine literature." Nevertheless, his drinking problem "brought with it unreliability" and hindered his success in life. In the 1850s, his amorous escapades and his wanderlust proved embarrassing to his family.[6] Previous to his enlistment in the war effort, he had been a farmer and a teacher, and had traveled extensively throughout the eastern half of the United States as an entertainer in a troupe with his brother Nicholson.[7] Although there are no extant photographs of Parker during the Civil War, Union army records indicate that Isaac Newton Parker was five feet, eight and a quarter inches tall, an average height for that time, and that he had black hair, dark eyes, and a dark complexion.[8]

The recipient of most of Parker's correspondence was his wife, Sara Adelaide Jemison, a teacher at the Cattaraugus Indian Reservation. We know too little about Sara, her marriage to Parker, their child Trent, and her death. We do know that they had known each other since the mid-1850s. Sara was related to Chauncey C. Jemison, a Seneca farmer and teacher as well as a Parker family friend. She was apparently more of a practicing Christian, in contrast to her less-than-observant husband. Sara was also a friend of Newt's sister Caroline while Newt was a friend of Sara's brother Tommie. Indeed, Newt's and Tommie's escapades and heavy drinking often got them into difficulty with conservative reservation residents. Tommie's "battle with the bottle" eventually led Newt to distance himself from him because Parker's family, friends, reservation folk, and missionaries were beginning to speak badly about him. Tommie's alcoholism became worse and continued to be a subject of Sara's and Newt's correspondence.[9]

In 1859, Sara and Newt started corresponding on a wide variety of subjects. In November of that year, he addressed his letter to her, "*Dear Friend Sarah.*" By January 3, 1861, his letters began "My Dear and Loving Sara." After being encouraged by Martha Hoyt Parker, Newt's sister-in-law, the two planned to marry.[10] Because of their long-distance courtship—Cattaraugus and Tonawanda Indian reservations are separated by approximately seventy-five miles—he had much catching up to do regarding her medical condition, reservation occurrences, gossip about family and friends, personal medical concerns, and his travels as an Indian entertainer. He was especially annoyed by the gossip of reservation residents who spread rumors of his alleged amorous affairs, including one with a Penobscot woman named Elizabeth, which he had to spend time countering and explaining to his soon-to-be wife.[11]

Despite this rumor, Sara and Isaac Newton were married in the last week of February 1861, and Newt's letters reveal a deep affection for his wife. In December of that year, their son Trent was born. After this date, we learn little about Sara from Newt's letters. We do know that she lived for a time in Buffalo and suffered from deteriorating health, including eye problems, throughout the Civil War period. In the spring of 1864, her correspondence with her husband abruptly ends. Despite the author's careful checking of church and cemetery records in and around the Cattaraugus Indian Reservation, tribal and museum records, and discussions with Nicholson Parker's great granddaughter, the fate of Sara Adelaide Jemison Parker remains a mystery.[12]

Newt Parker's military service began in the late spring of 1862, after several aborted attempts to volunteer for service. The twenty-five Indians, Onondaga, Seneca, and Tuscarora, of the Tuscarora Company were mostly farmers recruited from May 12 to August 26, 1862. Newt Parker and two other Senecas—Benjamin Jonas of Cattaraugus and Henry Sundown of Tonawanda—volunteered on June 18, 1862 at Buffalo.[13] Their enlistment was possible only after they first fought a battle against prejudice in order to be allowed to enter military service.

Until 1862, many Iroquois, including Seneca, had been repeatedly rejected for service by New York recruiters because of overt racism and because there the legality of Indian service was in question since almost no Indians at that time were United States citizens. As earlier chapters make clear, admitting Indians into Union service varied from locale to locale. Unlike the Delaware Indians in Kansas, an underpopulated and besieged frontier state adjacent to Confederate territory, the Indians of New York lived in a populous state far from Dixie.

Although Seneca Indians were allowed immediate entry into the military in other areas of the North such as Pennsylvania, time and time again they were rejected in western New York State. Sarcastically writing about his rejection, Newt Parker commented to his wife Sara: "Glory to God!!! I.N. Parker is not accepted in the volunteers service for the 'U.S. Army.' The officer of the 'Mustering Office of the U.S. Office' could not accept *me* because there is no regulation, that is no law for accepting the 'red man' in 'U.S.' law on the subject." Later, Parker and other Tonawanda Seneca went to Geneseo to join General Samuel W. Wadsworth's "Wadsworth Guards" but they were discharged again because they were Indians.[14] Before Parker's enlistment was rejected and he was dismissed from service for this second time, he returned to his home at Tonawanda, proudly dressed in his military uniform. Finally, heavy Union battlefield losses at First Manassas and Shiloh and the persistent lobbying by Iroquois Indians and their non-Indian allies forced local New York recruiting officers to accept the enlistment of Iroquois Indians in the spring of 1862.

The 132nd New York State Volunteer Infantry was known as the second regiment of the Empire or Spinola's Brigade and Hillhouse Light Infantry. It was formed in July 1862 out of several earlier incomplete units, including the Fifty-third New York State Volunteer Infantry, known as the Vosburg Chasseurs and recruited by Colonel George A. Buckingham, which included these same twenty-five Iroquois Indians who were from the Allegany, Cattaraugus, Onondaga, Tonawanda, and Tuscarora reservations; most of Company D included native-born Americans and naturalized citizens of German birth recruited at Buffalo, Brooklyn, Lewiston, Manhattan, and Syracuse.[15]

With the exception of Clinton Mountpleasant and a handful of other Iroquois, almost all Iroquois soldiers served in integrated units as officers and ordinary volunteers in the Union army and navy and received the same pay as their white counterparts. Of the twenty-five Iroquois in the Tuscarora Company, one served as corporal, two as sergeant, and one as lieutenant. Parker's writings and the letters of his white comrades in the 132nd New York State Volunteer Infantry also reveal mutual admiration and bonding between Indian and non-Indian soldiers. The Iroquois soldiers were cited for meritorious service twice in the official war department records of the Civil War. There was little, if any, evidence of racial prejudice in the company as reflected in Parker's letters after his enlistment in June, 1862.[16]

Much of the recruitment of the Indians was done by Cornelius C. Cusick, a Tuscarora sachem who had lobbied hard to overcome enlistment barriers. Cusick was born on the Tuscarora Indian Reservation in western New York on August 2, 1835. His family was among the most prominent ones in Tuscarora history. Cusick's grandfather was Nicholas Kaghnatsho [Cusick], the bodyguard and interpreter for General Marquis de Lafayette during the American Revolution. Because of Cusick's recruiting activities and his remarkable leadership of both the Indian and non-Indian troops in the unit, Company D was soon being referred to as the Tuscarora Company.[17] Although there were accusations that Cusick as well as Parker had profited from recruiting Iroquois soldiers for military service, no evidence of these charges has been substantiated. Later, after the Civil War, Cusick served with distinction as a captain in the regular army on the Trans-Mississippi frontier until his retirement in 1891. Subsequently, he was appointed honorary and special assistant in the Department of American Archaeology and Ethnology at the Columbian Exposition in Chicago.[18]

Parker had several reasons to enlist in the Union army. Growing up in the era of significant Seneca land loss, patriotism to the United States was not one of them.[19] From childhood, he and his brothers had been inculcated with a sense of *noblesse oblige*. As an educated person, Parker had an obligation to serve his community with the skills he had acquired in the white man's world. Going off to war also satisfied his lifelong wanderlust. As a man frequently faced with debt, Civil War military service allowed him to make a steady but small income. Perhaps most important, the war also offered him a way to follow in his father's footsteps, as a warrior in mortal combat, a time-honored route to influence and status among his Seneca people.

Moreover, the Tonawanda Seneca's well-respected white attorney, John Martindale, played a major role in the Union war effort, a fact not lost on Parker or the other Indians of Company D.

The Iroquois troops were transferred into the 132nd New York State Volunteer Infantry when the Fifty-third New York State Volunteer Infantry, a fancy-dressed Zouave regiment, was disbanded in the summer of 1862. After receiving assurances of getting a $25 bounty, a $2 premium, and a month's pay of $13 for enlisting, the twenty-five Indians were sent to Camp Scrogg in New York City. There they trained on the parade grounds and received regimental inspection. On September 28, 1862, the regiment was sent to Washington, D.C., and temporarily encamped adjacent to the Capitol. A week later, the Indians were mustered into service for three years and sent to Suffolk, Virginia for reconnoitering, constructing works of defense, and outpost duty at Camp Hoffman at Fort Monroe under General John Peck of Syracuse, New York.[20]

On Christmas eve, 1862, the unit was transferred to New Bern, North Carolina, which had been captured by Union General Ambrose Burnside in March of that year. Ironically, the Iroquois soldiers found themselves in the precise area that the Tuscarora had been removed from one hundred and fifty years earlier. One of the towns in the environs of New Bern is even named Tuscarora. They were now assigned to guard the Union railways and prevent the Confederacy from resupplying its forces by sea. Commanded by Peter J. Claassen, a non-Indian, the regiment was associated with the Second Brigade, Fifth Division, Eighteenth Army Corps from March 1863; unattached, on outpost duty, at Batchelder's Creek near New Bern from May 1863; in Palmer's Brigade, Peck's Division, Eighteenth Army Corps, from January 1864; in the Department of Virginia and North Carolina from April 1864; in the Provisional Corps, North Carolina from March 1, 1865; in the First Brigade, Second Division, Twenty-third Army Corps from April 2, 1865; at Salisbury, North Carolina from May 1865 until it was relieved of its duties and transferred to New York City, honorably mustered out of Union military service on June 29, 1865.

From October 1862 to April 1865, the 132nd New York State Volunteer Infantry faced a variety of military actions. In the fall of 1862, it fought an engagement at Blackwater, Virginia and skirmishes at Franklin and Zuni, Virginia. In the late winter and early spring of 1863, it fought skirmishes at Pollocksville, Trenton, and Sandy Ridge, North Carolina; engaged the enemy at Blount's Creek, Blount's Mills, Blount's Ridge, New Hope Church School House, and Swift Creek, North Carolina; and defended the strategic Union facilities at New Bern, North Carolina. The following year, the unit engaged the enemy at Batchelder's Creek and at Jackson's Mills and Foster's Mills. It also saw action at Gardner's Bridge and at Butler's Bridge, North Carolina, where Sergeant Parker planted the regimental colors after an attack and capture of the Confederate's bridgehead. In the winter and early spring of 1865, the regiment participated in General William Tecumseh Sherman's Campaign of the Carolinas, supplying an escort for Sherman's supply wagon train from Goldsboro to Kinston, North Carolina. It fought in the three-day Battle of Wise's Forks and skirmished with the enemy at Snow Hill in March and joined in receiving the surrender of Joseph E. Johnston at Bennett House, Durham Station, North Carolina on April 26, 1865.[21]

In his three-year service in the regiment, Parker worked in a variety of positions. At first, he was assigned to headquarters, working as a scribe. He then was made an orderly sergeant and served in camp duty. Finally, an assignment to the signal corps as color bearer placed him in harm's way, since the Confederate forces always attempted to shoot the color bearer to prevent the Union advance. Parker survived and was cited for his role in this position in December 1864.[22]

Camp life of the 132nd in North Carolina was unenviable: parade drills, forced marches with little consequence through ankle-deep mud, and delayed wages. At times, work details relieved some of the anxiety and monotony of army life. There were also more pleasant sides. The camp had a bowling alley and theatre, and the general anxiety about the war was broken by occasional parties and entertainment. Whiskey rations, often referred to as an "army gallon," were dispensed to the troops. Parker also reported the visit of Negro singers or minstrels. On one occasion, troops came together to honor their white captain, Thomas Green, with a party and the presentation of a gold watch. The letters once again reveal that the soldiers, Indian and non-Indian, bonded with little prejudice.[23]

Parker's letter to his sister-in-law on April 1, 1864 reveals his deep feelings about his comrades-in-arms. At the Battle of Batchelder's Creek in February, 1864, Parker reflected on the gruesome death of First Lieutenant Arnold Zenette, a non-Indian and the quartermaster of the Tuscarora Company, which he described in grisly detail. Zenette was attempting to supply ammunition to men in the entrenchments. According to Parker, the quartermaster was first captured, then robbed, and finally tortured to death by Confederate soldiers.[24]

In all, the regiment lost one officer and six enlisted men in combat; seven enlisted men and one officer died of disease and other causes; and seventy-one enlisted men died as prisoners of war. At least twenty-eight men died when torpedo mines stored at Batchelder's Creek, North Carolina accidentally exploded on May 26, 1864. As for the Iroquois Indians in the regiment, one Indian, Sergeant Foster J. Hudson, a Seneca, was killed in action; another Seneca, Private William Kennedy, died as a prisoner at Andersonville. Although no Indian casualties occurred during the torpedo accident, Parker was thrown fifty feet into the air by the explosion.[25]

His letters to and from Sara reveal diverse wartime concerns. They also brought with them other concerns. Kept in the dark by military supervisors and isolated from the news on other fronts of the war, Parker told his wife on February 3, 1863, that she probably knew more about what was happening in the war than he did. When bounty agents began to conscript under-age Seneca recruits for military service and when some Iroquois recruits were not paid their promised bounties, Sara informed her husband of these doings. News from home brought other problems and weighed on Parker heavily. He was especially concerned by his parents' failing health and his inability to be granted a furlough to visit home. Only after his father died in the spring of 1863 did Parker receive a furlough which he used to attend the funeral. Equally vexing was his separation from his wife Sara. As the war continued, their relationship was increasingly strained, and Newt was frequently disturbed about her failure to write to him.[26]

By the fall of 1863, Parker's enthusiasm for military service had cooled. When his sister Caroline incorrectly informed him that an Indian named Ed Green had reenlisted for military service after being discharged because of a persistent dry cough, Parker reacted by labeling Green a "Great Fool" who had reenlisted "for money I reckon."[27] His later attempts to secure a commission as captain failed, despite a personal recommendation by Lewis Henry Morgan about Parker's character and leadership qualities, which Morgan forwarded to General Benjamin Butler.[28]

In early January 1864, General Robert E. Lee urged Jefferson Davis to sanction an attack on the Union army depot at New Bern in order to capture the large amounts of provisions stored there. Lee was also intent on recapturing the Union railroad there, which had been guarded by the Tuscarora Company and other Union forces since late in 1862; however, Lee badly underestimated his enemy's abilities and chose the wrong commander, General George E. Pickett, to lead the strike.

With thirteen thousand men and fourteen navy cutters, General Pickett moved on New Bern on January 30, 1864, dividing his troops into three columns. Confederate General Seth M. Barton and his men were to cross the Trent River near Trenton and proceed to the south side of the river to Brice's Creek below New Bern. He was to take the forts along the Neuse and Trent rivers and enter New Bern via the railroad bridge, thus preventing Union reinforcement by land or water. Colonels James Dearing and John N. Whitford and their men were to move down the Neuse River and capture Fort Anderson. Generals Robert F. Hoke and Pickett and the remainder of the expeditionary force were to "move down between the Trent and the Neuse, endeavor to surprise the troops on Batchelder's Creek, silence the guns in the star fort and batteries near the Neuse, and penetrate the town in that direction." The Confederate navy was to descend the Neuse, capture Union gunboats, and cooperate with the three Confederate columns.[29]

The Confederate operations went badly from the outset. Pickett had failed in planning beforehand, underestimating, as Lee did, the task at hand. General Hoke moved quickly to reach Batchelder's Creek before the bridge was taken out by Union forces, but the firing of pickets had warned the Union forces of the enemy's approach. The Union troops destroyed the bridge to prevent the Confederates' advance. Hoke also failed to capture the Union train and enter the city by rail. Finally, by felling some trees, two of Hoke's regiments crossed over the creek. Despite Union reinforcements, Hoke routed the blues that he met. His men then marched to within a mile of New Bern and waited to join Barton's forces.[30]

General Barton's men never reached Hoke. After passing through low swamp country with vast mud holes caused by winter showers, Barton came in view of the enemy's breastworks close to Brice's Creek at 8:00 A.M. on February 1. Instead of attacking immediately, which might have caught the Union forces by surprise, he ordered a reconnaissance while bringing up his artillery. The reconnaissance found that Union forces were more entrenched than previously thought. Barton reported to General Pickett his conclusion, that his troops were "unprepared to encounter so serious" and "insurmountable" a defense. In the meantime, Union forces were alerted and their artillery began to hit Barton's position. Pickett then ordered Barton to join the troops before New Bern for an assault on that front. To do so, Barton would have had to cross the Trent River and retrace his steps, which would have taken more than two days. When Pickett was informed that Barton and his men could not reach him until February 4, Pickett withdrew on February 3 and admitted failure. Although the Union forces suffered more than twice as many casualties—one hundred compared to the Confederate forty-five—the Confederates failed to capture the supplies they so desperately needed.[31]

Union forces in the fight included the Ninety-ninth and 132nd New York State Volunteers and Twelfth New York State Cavalry. Under Claassen's command, the Union forces in Company D held their ground until the Confederates brought up their artillery pieces. The Indians were part of the Union picket post holding access to Batchelder's Creek on the Neuse Road Bridge and at an old mill near the railroad. They did so until overcome by overwhelming Confederate numbers. Claassen, later cited the Indians of the Tuscarora Company for heroism in the official record, as did Generals Butler and Peck.[32] Captain Charles G. Smith, the General Officer of the Day (February 10, 1864) of the 132nd New York State Volunteer Infantry, commended Cusick and several other commanders at Batchelder's Creek for their "individual instances of coolness and heroism." After lauding one "Lieutenant Haring" for his bravery in defending the Neuse bridge, Smith added: "In this he [Haring] was nobly seconded by Capt. Thomas B. Green, Lieutenant Cusick, and Companies D and G, with Lieutenants Gearing & Ryan, who were both badly wounded, the respective companies losing heavily."[33] Later, Captain R. Emmett Fiske, also of the 132nd New York State Volunteer Infantry, wrote of the fight at Batchelder's Creek: "Lieutenant Cusick with some thirty of his warrior soldiers of his tribe, engaged the rebel advance in a sharp skirmish for several hours and by desperate fighting prevented the dislodgement of the picket reserves and the capture of the outpost camp."[34]

The bloody skirmish was later described by Parker in shorthand fashion. The Seneca sergeant wrote about the swampy terrain, made a map of the battlefield, and mentioned the capture of Private William Kennedy, a Seneca Indian, who was sent off to Andersonville Prison where he later died. Indeed, the regiment paid a costly price. The 132nd New York lost five men, six others were wounded, while fully eighty were captured.[35]

In June of 1864, Colonel Claassen's men were sent on a forced march—seventy-three miles in thirty-nine hours—to the vicinity of Kinston, North Carolina. While on reconnaissance at Jackson's Mills, Lieutenant Cusick, "leading his Indians in a flank movement, distinguished himself by materially assisting in the capture of the commandant of Kinston, N.C. . . . together with five of his officers and upwards of fifty of his rank & file." They also captured fifty-one noncommissioned officers and privates and inflicted thirty to forty casualties. Captain Thomas B. Green, his officers and men were cited in the official record for the success of the operation which was attributed to their "endurance and determination."[36] Claassen later wrote that at Jackson's Mills, North Carolina, Cusick and his "dusky warriors" lying in wait in a "roadside thicket, with instructions to closely guard the rear," completely trapped the rebels.[37]

After the engagement at Jackson Mills, Newt Parker's correspondence to his family ends. The Tuscarora Company's last major encounter with Confederate forces occurred on March 7–10, 1865, at Wise Forks, North Carolina. One of the casualties at the skirmish was Foster J. Hudson, Seventh Sergeant of the company and a Seneca Indian from the Cattaraugus Reservation. Once again Parker was the conveyor of the bad news to his fellow Seneca. In a letter to Asher Wright, the well-respected Presbyterian missionary to the Seneca, he graphically described Hudson's death. On March 7, 1865, his Seneca comrade had been shot in the left knee joint at Jackson's Mills, North Carolina. After he fell with his wounds, Confederate soldiers robbed him of his watch. D Company recaptured him, and he was then sent to the military hospital at New Bern, since the bullet was lodged deep in the joint. Subsequently, military surgeons amputated his leg. Although there were hopes of recovery, Hudson died on March 23 of a hemorrhage just seventeen days before the end of the war.[38]

Parker and eight other Iroquois Indians of the Tuscarora Company were mustered out of service on June 29, 1865. Benjamin Jonas and Henry Sundown, who had volunteered with Parker at Buffalo on the same day in 1862, left service with him.[39] On December 31, 1866, Lewis Henry Morgan, once again serving as Parker's patron, recommended the Seneca for a commission as a second lieutenant in the United States Army, writing to Congressman Burton C. Cook of Illinois: "In October last I wrote to Lieu. Gen. Sherman, asking him if he would take Isaac N. Parker into the Military Service, in his District, and in due time have him promoted with a commission in the regular Army if he deserved it." Morgan added: "Mr. Parker is a

Seneca Indian the youngest brother of Colonel Ely S. Parker of Genl. Grants staff, and the equal of his brother in capacity."[40] Two months earlier, Morgan had sent a similar recommendation to Secretary of War Edwin M. Stanton. On September 18, 1867, Stanton granted the request for a commission and Parker was appointed a second lieutenant in the Thirty-sixth United States Infantry. Unfortunately, Parker's military career ended soon after when he failed to pass the army's physical examination because of his poor eyesight.[41]

Parker's later life is impossible to reconstruct. The few surviving records indicate that he frequently sought his brother Ely's help for employment or a special favor. Moreover, he challenged the power of the Tonawanda Council of Chiefs for some unknown reason and soon found himself out of favor on the reservation. Parker went west as a teacher. During Reconstruction, he married a Cherokee woman in Indian Territory.[42] According to his relative, the noted anthropologist Arthur C. Parker, Newt in his last years worked in Montana "where he contracted a fatal malady. He fell dead from his horse as he journeyed over the prairie and was buried on the plains near the spot where he died."[43]

Ely Samuel Parker, Isaac's second oldest brother, offers even more of a wartime success story. He was born in 1828. Although his first name was given to him in honor of the respected local Baptist minister on the Tonawanda Reservation, Ely was also bestowed with a Seneca name at birth: "Ha-sa-no-an-da," meaning "Leading Name." Much like his naming, his entire life—upbringing, education, and work experiences—was in two worlds. While acquiring a great knowledge of the Gaiiwio or Old Way of Handsome Lake, the Iroquoian religion, from his grandfather, he was also educated in the new ways of his white teachers at the local Baptist school and Cayuga Academy in Aurora, New York. In 1844, Parker met Lewis Henry Morgan at a bookstore in Albany; the chance meeting changed both men's career directions, led to Morgan's visits to the Tonawanda Reservation, and dramatically influenced the development of American anthropology. By the late 1840s, he was reading law at Ellicottville, near the Allegany Indian Reservation, and receiving on-the-job engineering experience on the Genesee Valley Canal. As early as 1853, he was adding to his growing resumé by serving in the New York State Militia as a captain of engineers with the Rochester regiment. In the same period, Parker was selected as a sachem, one of the honored leaders of his people, and bestowed with the name "De-ne-ho-ga-wa," the "Open Door."[44]

Parker was a physically imposing figure. Although he was slightly above average height at five feet eight inches, he carried two hundred to two hundred thirty pounds on a wide muscular frame. During the war, he was frequently referred to in camp by officers and enlisted men as "the Indian" or "Grant's Indian," as well as "Big Indian" and "Falstaff." His work duties were such that he basically was a lone Indian in a white world, a world that just happened to be at the innermost power center of the Union military command. Although he was highly educated and had a perfect command of English, his physical appearance separated him from Grant's staff and his troops.[45]

Despite his past military experience, his extraordinary intelligence and his friendship with Grant since 1860, Parker sat out the first half of the war waiting for a commission to make use of his diverse talents. He was active in Tonawanda tribal affairs and watched over his family's homestead as well as his aged parents. Finally, in June 1863, after receiving a commission as a captain in the Union army, Parker left the Tonawanda Reservation to join General John E. Smith's command as division engineer of the Seventh Division, Seventeenth Army Corps. By the time he arrived at Smith's headquarters at Vicksburg on July 7, the great battle for this strategic city was over and the Union forces under General Grant had control of the Mississippi River. On September 18, Parker was assigned as assistant adjutant general on Grant's personal military staff. For the next two months, Parker's combat experience was limited.[46] All this was to change in November 1863, at Chattanooga, Tennessee.

The City of Chattanooga had considerable strategic value, guarding a gap in the Cumberland Mountains and dominating the Tennessee River. It was also a major railroad terminus connecting two major east-west railroads, thereby serving as a gateway to the rich farmlands of the South and the industry of Atlanta. The Confederates held a seemingly impregnable position along Missionary Ridge, the four-hundred-foot-high garrison along a six-mile front. Two-thousand-foot-high Lookout Mountain was south of the ridge and contained a substantial number of Confederates as well. General Grant understood the suicidal nature of a direct frontal assault on the Confederate positions. General Braxton Bragg's Confederate forces, 45,000 in number, occupied Missionary Ridge east of the city and had artillery field pieces on the top of Lookout Mountain which commanded approaches to the city from the east and the west. Grant, who had been placed in charge of all Union military departments between the Mississippi and the Appalachians by President Lincoln in October 1863, had 77,000 troops. Grant personally went to Chattanooga after placing General George Thomas in command of the Army of the Cumberland.

Grant's strategy was to prepare a three-pronged attack: General Joseph Hooker and his three divisions were sent to outflank the Confederates from the south, come over and around Lookout Mountain, cross the intervening valley, and attack Missionary Ridge on the left flank; General William Tecumseh Sherman and his four divisions were to attack the northern end of Missionary Ridge; and General George Thomas was assigned the command of the center in order to prevent the Confederates from reinforcing their positions. When the plan was finally implemented on November 24, Hooker successfully advanced; however, Sherman was soon bogged down. Grant then ordered Thomas to advance up the center and take the Confederate rifle positions at the foot of Missionary Ridge. Instead, Thomas's men, much to the surprise of the Union command, advanced all the way to the top of Missionary Ridge, sending Bragg's men in flight. The battle, which included some of the heaviest combat of the war, was marked by skirmishes in heavy fog, broken-down chains of command on both sides, impromptu orders and advances, and substantial slaughter. Nonetheless, in the end, Grant could claim a victory which propelled him to supreme commander of all Union forces in March 1864. The battle, along with Union victories at

Vicksburg and Gettysburg in the same year, contributed immensely toward the North's victory in the Civil War.[47]

On November 18, 1863, Parker wrote a revealing letter to his brother Nicholson from Grant's headquarters near Chattanooga, an area which he referred to as a "God forsaken country." Accurately predicting a major battle, Parker insisted that General Bragg's Confederates, the "flower and bulk of the Southern Army" would be wise to flee before the Union forces thrash them and push them out of the region. He added that the enemy was "here within speaking distance in one front." The Seneca officer told his brother that Nicholson and others in the North "who are out of the reach of the noise, excitement, and hardships" of army life "cannot begin to realize what war is." War was two armies face to face whose "whole study and object is to destroy one another" with scouting parties, heavy cannonade and deadly missiles scattering in every direction. He admitted that he was no longer afraid since he had been numbed by the entire experience and that he could go to "regular battle as calmly as I would go to my meal when hungry." Though he specified his will and his intentions about the distribution of his property if he fell in battle, he had every plan "to come home and settle down once more upon my farm, and go to work as all honest men do."[48]

His letter of November 18 also tells us much about his career success in the army. Well-respected, with the rank of captain, Parker turned down an offer by General William Smith to remain on Smith's engineering staff. Parker indicated his loyalty to and admiration for Grant and Parker's goal of providing "services desirable to the best Generals in the Army."[49] "As for the common soldier, he does his duty and pays respect to my shoulder straps." Although James Harrison Wilson, the Union army's inspector general, has left his own writings with racist sentiments toward Parker, the Seneca officer suggested that common soldiers deferred to him and that racial prejudice did not affect his relationship with his troops. Parker had become, in effect, "Grant's Indian."[50]

Although as a Seneca Indian he faced prejudice throughout much of his life, Parker was hardly open-minded when it came to Southerners, especially African Americans, reflecting a bias typical of many Union soldiers. In a letter to his sister Caroline, Parker focused on the war's impact on the South as well as his own perceptions of the region and its peoples. He suggested that rural Southerners "do not live as well or as comfortable as the Tonawanda Indians," not really a surprise after three bloody years of conflict. He insisted that "the negroes, once slaves, of course are all with us and are our servants to pay." He then went on to describe the local Southerners' round log country houses, mostly deserted at the time, claiming that "any Indian house is better and more comfortable and cleaner." Parker noted that prewar textiles manufactured in the North were no longer available and that Southern women were wearing "coarse homespun dresses very much like our old-fashioned flannel." The Seneca officer then bemoaned the fate of the South, while chiding Confederate leaders such as General Bragg at every turn: "O Carrie! This is a most desolate country, and no human being can realize or comprehend the dreadful devastation and horrors created by war, until they have been in its track." The ruins of war were nearly everywhere. He added that just one hundred miles from Louisville, all you see are "lone chimneys standing where once may have been a fine mansion." Only about one acre out of one hundred was still being cultivated in this region and weeds were dominating the landscape.[51]

In and around Chattanooga, the Seneca sachem found "only poor 'white trash'|" who were "so poor that they can hardly speak the English language" and who have a "blind infatuation" for the Confederate cause. He observed that in other areas of the South blacks were now occupying great Southern mansions and had stripped these homes of their fine mahogany and rosewood furniture to furnish their own cabins. Fine dresses "that white ladies once bedecked themselves with, now hang shabbily upon the ungainly figure of some huge, dilapidated Negro wench." Parker, a man of limited wealth who was frequently in debt, identified more with the white planter class of the South whose lifeways were being shattered by the American Civil War than either the lower classes of whites, who composed much of the Confederate armies, or blacks.[52]

Parker's keen interest in Native American history was also revealed in his letter of November 21. Chattanooga, although a Creek
village in the sixteenth-century, had long-established roots in Cherokee history. Cherokee Chief John Ross's boyhood home
(1797–1808) was at the base of the northern end of the Lookout
Mountain range at present-day Chattanooga. At the death of his
mother, Ross moved to the Lookout Mountain Valley, in an area
which became known as Rossville. Later, in 1838, five groups of
Cherokees were removed westward from Ross's Landing in present-
day Chattanooga in the Trail of Tears.[53] Parker informed his sister
that we "are here in the ancient homes of the Cherokees, and our
present quarters are only about 12 miles from John Ross' old home."
To Parker, a Seneca Indian who had resisted emigration west under
the Treaty of Buffalo Creek and who had fought so fervently to win
back the Tonawanda lands, Ross, the head of the Cherokee antiremoval party, was a living legend and his homestead was a shrine,
worthy of pilgrimage.[54]

With no time to write during the intensity of the battle, Parker delayed corresponding to his sister until December 2. One week after
the Union victory, Parker wrote: "We have had a big fight here,
which commenced on the 23rd ult. and lasted 5 days." He then recounted the Chattanooga campaign in infinite detail. Parker vividly
described the intensity of the fighting:

> It was a most terrific battle. The cannonading was like continuous
> thunder and the rattle and crash of musketry was deafening and any
> thing but pleasant—You may have heard of the music of the spheres,
> which to those who have heard it may be exceedingly pleasant and
> harmonious, but the music of the screaming shell and the sharp whiz
> of the bullet are sounds and agreeable or harmonious to a civilized ear.
> It was the latter kind of music that we listened to the live long day—
> until long after the shades of night had spread her pall over the bloody
> battle field.[55]

As for the rebels' last stand and the eventual victory of Union
forces, Parker wrote:

Long before we reached him, the booming of cannon and the rattle of musketry informed us that he was fighting. The enemy had gone through the village and taken a position beyond it; our folks occupied the village, and the enemy were throwing shell, shot and bullets into the village in a perfect storm. We rode through the principal street and almost through the town before we halted. It was very interesting to one's feelings to have the shrill scream of the fearful shell pass near him or to see it explode in his immediate vicinity—The worst of all [of the] shooting is to hear the spark, quick and momentous whiz of the bullets as they pass in showers all around you. It is no use to attempt to come the dodge upon them [sic], for the very act of dodging might cost you your life. The best way is to pay no attention to them, but turning neither to the right or left, we proceed to discharge our duties as soldiers. Our men were severely handled here, but we again drove the enemy and remained over night masters of the field.[56]

In a subsequent letter to his brother Nicholson written from Nashville on January 25, Parker revealed further details about his illness, the Battle of Chattanooga, his impressions about the South, and his admiration for John Ross. His illness nearly resulted in his death since "my pulse apparently died out and my extremities began growing cold." After recovering, he spent four days during the Battle of Chattanooga constantly on horseback, which ultimately led to a major "relapse of the shakes." Consequently, Parker was also "greatly reduced in flesh" as a result of this unidentified but debilitating illness; however, he insisted that he had finally recovered and apparently he was not beset by any further major health problems during the war.[57]

After the Battle of Chattanooga, Grant's reputation soon took a meteoric rise. In March 1864, he assumed command of the entire Union army. Several weeks later, Ely S. Parker was transferred to Grant's headquarters, serving mostly in the capacity as the general's military secretary until the end of the war. From City Point in May 1864 to Appomattox Court House, Parker worked side by side with the man he had first met and befriended in 1860 while the Seneca Indian was employed as an engineer during the designing and building of the federal customs house in Galena, Illinois. In the Civil War, their friendship was revived. Grant frequently praised Parker's abilities and recommended the Seneca for promotion. When Grant needed a staff member to write a congratulatory order to the army after the victory at Chattanooga, he ordered Parker to draft it because he was "good at that sort of thing."[58]

On April 9, 1865, at Appomattox Court House, Grant's faith in the abilities of his Indian military secretary was clear. Grant ordered Parker to serve as the scribe for Lee's surrender. According to General Horace Porter, a leading member of Grant's staff, Parker was chosen to write the draft because his "handwriting presented a better appearance than that of any one else on the staff."[59] In his detailed description of Lee's surrender of his Army of Northern Virginia, Porter described how startled the Confederate general was at seeing and being introduced to the Seneca Indian:

> [Lee] did not exhibit the slightest change of features during this ceremony until Colonel Parker of our staff was presented to him. Parker was a full-blooded Indian, and the reigning Chief of the Six Nations. When Lee saw his swarthy features he looked at him with evident surprise, and his eyes rested on him for several seconds. What was passing in his mind probably no one ever knew, but the natural surmise was that he at first mistook Parker for a negro, and was struck with astonishment to find that the commander of the Union armies had one of that race on his personal staff.[60]

Ely S. Parker's life dramatically changed as a result of the Civil War. Remaining in military service, he parlayed his military fame at Appomattox and his close association with Grant into a successful postwar career. Grant served as best man at Parker's wedding to Minnie Sackett, a white woman, in 1867. Two years later, President Grant appointed Parker commissioner of Indian affairs, the first Native American to hold that position. At the time of Grant's peace policy, Parker had unremitting faith in the American military. He favored the unsuccessful attempt to transfer the Bureau of Indian Affairs to the War Department, which antagonized the newly created United

States Board of Indian Commissioners, headed by William Welsh, a leading Philadelphia Friend.[61]

Parker soon became caught up in the allegations of corruption that characterized the Grant administration. Parker was accused of and tried for illegally signing private contracts for about four million pounds of beef and large amounts of flour; wasting funds for unnecessary materials, excessive freight rates, and improper tribal allocations; bypassing the Board of Indian Commissioners and violating laws on accounting, advertising, and notification of purchases.[62] In the spring of 1871, the House Committee on Appropriations acquitted Parker, finding "no evidence of any pecuniary or personal advantage." Although Parker acknowledged mistakes of judgment, he vehemently denied official wrongdoings and fraud.[63]

Privately blaming Grant for his troubles, Parker left office in disgrace in June 1871. Although he made a significant fortune in business in Connecticut, he lost much of it in the Panic of 1873 and its aftermath. He died two decades later in Fairfield, Connecticut, "an obscure disabled pensioner with a low-paying minor job in the New York City Police Department," surviving in his later years largely through favors and handouts from former military colleagues on General Grant's staff.[64]

10

Endeavor to Persevere

IN THE CLASSIC 1976 WESTERN "THE OUTLAW JOSEY WALES," LONE
Watie, a Cherokee Indian played by Chief Dan George, recounts his
experiences as a "civilized Indian." He tells Josey Wales, played by
Clint Eastwood, about his tragic life, from the time of the Trail of
Tears where he lost his wife and two sons to his "civilized" existence
in Indian Territory. With just the right measure of sarcasm, Lone
Watie reflects on what it means to be "civilized," why he wears a
Lincolnesque stovepipe hat, and what he learned on his visits to
Washington, D.C. He tells Wales how every time the Indians attempted to make appeals to Washington, government officials, as
well as the popular press, would hail their "progress," insisting that
all the Indians needed was to "endeavor to persevere." Lone Watie
turns to him and states that when he got tired of hearing that expression, he, John Jumper, Chilly McIntosh, and others joined up with
the Confederacy.

Although American Indian participation in the Civil War was
more complex than Phil Kaufman's marvelous script would indicate,
there is much truth in that scene. Many American Indians joined the
war effort on both sides out of frustration and because they hoped to

open non-Indian officials' eyes and ears to their concerns. Indeed, there were many individual and community reasons for Indian involvement in this largely non-Indian conflict.

Indian removal, as the scene from "Josey Wales" reveals, was the backdrop to American Indian involvement in the war as much as slavery was for African Americans. As we have shown, American Indian felt much more patriotic to their own nations than to the Stars and Stripes or to the Stars and Bars. Maintaining homeland was and remains a constant in Indian country. Nearly all Indians who participated in the war—North, South, and Trans-Mississippi West—hoped to preserve themselves and their communities from further land loss and removal.

Although there were numerous reasons for Native American involvement in the Civil War, Chief George's brilliant portrayal depicts a very real aspect of American Indian participation. Frustrated with Washington and bitter after the tragedy of removal, some saw the Confederate cause as their own, in part because of their agreement on the slave issue. Still others in the Trans-Mississippi West saw this route as the only way out of most difficult circumstances, especially when the Union abandoned Indian Territory and deserted their Indian allies. All American Indians—in the North, South, and Trans-Mississippi West—were increasingly surrounded and dependent on their white neighbors and caught between two fires. Faced with a precarious existence, American Indians in all three regions saw military involvement as their only chance, the last desperate hope of obtaining a larger and more secure landbase.

Union and Confederate armies were significantly affected by the presence of American Indian troops. At Vicksburg, Indians in the Fourteenth Wisconsin, serving as Union sharpshooters, camouflaged themselves with leaves, crawled on their bellies to get into position, and then silenced the "rebel cannon in front [of their position] almost entirely."[1] A year later, Seneca soldiers of the Fourteenth New York Heavy Artillery replicated the Wisconsin Indians' action when they camouflaged themselves and captured a nest of rebel snipers at the Battle of Spotsylvania.[2] Others such as the Ioway and their Otoe and Omaha relatives served the Union in important but less dramatic ways.[3]

American Indians also had an important impact on Union regimental life. Especially noteworthy were the Oneida Indians of the Fourteenth Wisconsin. They were resourceful in securing food and, even more, in preparing it. Private Elisha Stockwell described how one of the F Company Indians, armed with his Belgian rifle, went squirrel shooting and came back to camp "with all the squirrels he could handily carry, all shot in the head." Squirrel soup, a favorite of the Oneida and other Iroquois Indians', was a welcome substitute for stale hardtack.[4] Lieutenant James K. Newton of De Pere, commander of Company F, who lived adjacent to the Oneida Indian Reservation, made reference to a culinary delight "discovered" by his regiment's recruits:

> You would not believe how many ways we can cook our corn so as to have a variety. We have parched corn, boiled Do. [sic] mush, corn coffee etc. but the latest invention to make it go down good is to half parch it, and then grind it coarse like hominy and then boil it with a small piece of pork to season it. If you have to live on corn altogether, by reason of this war's continuing for a great length of time longer I advise you to cook it in the way I last mentioned.[5]

Parched hominy seasoned with salt pork is a typical Iroquois recipe, "Onon'daat." It has been described as an Indian dish since earliest European contact and is often referred to as sagamite, sapaen, or suppawn.[6]

Confederate forces also benefited significantly by American Indian presence as volunteer-warriors. In a letter to his wife, a Union officer in the Ninth Pennsylvania cavalry described the success of two companies of Confederate Indians at the Battle of Thompson's Station, Tennessee. Although first mistaken for African Americans, these troops were later identified as rebel Indians: "They charged on our valley with a wild yell. I heard it but did not know who it was. They were from Arkansas."[7] After major losses at the Battle of Old Fort Wayne in 1862 and the Battle of Honey Springs in 1863, Confederate Indians led by Colonel Tandy Walker, a Choctaw, with his First Regiment of Choctaw and Chickasaw Mounted Rifles, inflicted a major defeat on Union forces at the Battle of Poison Springs near Camden, Arkansas on April 18, 1864. Walker's Choctaw and Chickasaw, as Confederate General Samuel B. Maxey wrote in his report of the operation, performed "nobly, gallantly, gloriously."[8] Indeed, Walker's forces, along with several Chickasaw units—the First Chickasaw Infantry, Shecoe's Chickasaw Battalion, and the First Battalion of Chickasaw Cavalry—provided valuable service to the South for much of the war.[9]

To admit all this is not to deny that ugly incidents were perpetrated by Indians. Charges of scalping, as we have seen, were not just war propaganda used to rouse hatred against the other side. Scalping by American Indians did occur, perpetrated by the Thomas Legion as well as by Indians at the Battle of Pea Ridge in 1862.[10] At Worcester, Massachusetts, after "misguided citizens" passed liquor through the windows of railroad cars, two Indians attacked a Union sergeant of the Twenty-first Pennsylvania, who tried to empty their canteens of spirits and was saved only by "a guard in the aisle who used his musket-butt to good effect."[11] In another account, a Columbia, South Carolina woman indicated she and her property were threatened by an intoxicated Indian during Sherman's burning of the city; in her case, a Union private in an Iowa regiment came to her rescue, knocking the drunken Indian unconscious.[12]

The postwar impact of the Civil War was especially noticeable in small tight knit American Indian communities. As participants in the bloodiest fighting from the Napoleonic Wars to World War I, many veterans came back disabled. Amputees and psychologically scarred veterans were a common feature of every community in the United States after the bloodshed ended. The war also created a disproportionate number of widows and orphans, leading to further Indian dependence and poverty and to the establishment of numerous orphanages and asylums in Indian country.[13]

There were no winners for the Indian veterans and their communities. In some cases, most notably the Catawba and the eastern and western Cherokee, examples chosen for study in this book, the Indians allied themselves with the losing Confederate side. But the Indian nations who chose the North—the Delaware, the Ottawa and Ojibwa, the Lumbee, the Pamunkey, the Seneca—ended up losing too. In the peace that followed, their existence remained tenuous at best right through the contemporary period of American history.

Unlike their black counterparts who gained emancipation, overcame slavery, and theoretically had legal standing after the Thirteenth, Fourteenth, and Fifteenth Amendments to the Constitution were passed during Reconstruction, American Indians remained "domestic dependent nations," and the newly strengthened federal government accelerated its campaign against them. In the Fourteenth Amendment, adopted in 1868, the Congress inserted the following: "Representatives shall be apportioned among the several states according to their respective numbers, counting the whole number of persons in each state, excluding 'Indians not taxed.'|" Previously set apart by "civilized" and "savage" labels, now American Indians achieved a new category of legal limbo.[14]

Out of the halls of the Capitol, wars of conquest spread to every part of the region and weapons and strategy perfected in four years of Civil War were now directed against American Indians such as Captain Jack, Crazy Horse, Geronimo, and Quanah Parker. National heroes of the Civil War, Philip Sheridan and William Tecumseh Sherman, ran the frontier army, while Ulysses S. Grant served eight ignominious years in the White House. In 1882, the *New York Times* reported that in the previous decade, the Indians were the only "excuse" for the United States to maintain its armed forces since 80 percent of the War Department budget and 73 percent of its personnel were used to pacify the Indians on the frontier.[15]

In 1884, the United States Supreme Court handed down one of its most ludicrous decisions affecting American Indians in *Elk v. Wilkins*. Justice Horace Gray declared Indian tribes to be "alien nations" since an Indian owed immediate allegiance to his tribe and not to the people of the United States. To Gray, an American Indian could not become a United States citizen unless the federal government consented to it by treaty or naturalization.[16] Since federal–Indian treaty making had ended in 1871, the Indian had only the route of naturalization opened to him if he desired to be a United States citizen. In the twilight zone of Indian existence, the Elk decision literally made the Indian a legal alien in his native land.

The United States Supreme Court did more than deal with United States citizenship for American Indians. They built on their earlier decision in the *Cherokee Tobacco* case, defining the primacy of Congress in Indian affairs. A year before *Elk v. Wilkins*, the court decided a case, *Ex Parte Crow Dog*, that set in motion the development of the doctrine of plenary power. Crow Dog, a Brulé Sioux Indian, had been sentenced to death by a Dakota territorial court for murdering Chief Spotted Tail; nevertheless, the United States Supreme Court ordered Crow Dog's release because the Court claimed the United States had no jurisdiction over Indian crimes on a reservation. In response to what the non-Indian world considered to be a "state of lawlessness" on Indian reservations, the Congress in 1885 passed the Seven Major Crimes Act, extending federal jurisdiction to specific crimes—murder, manslaughter, rape, assault with intent to kill, arson, burglary, and larceny "within any territory of the United States, and either within or without an Indian reservation. . . ."[17] The act for the first time extended federal jurisdiction "over strictly internal crimes of Indians against Indians, a major blow at the integrity of the Indian tribes and a fundamental readjustment in relations between the American Indians and the United States government."[18]

In 1886, in *United States v. Kagama*, a case involving the murder of one Indian by another within the limits of the Hoopa Valley Reservation in California, the court held that "Indian tribes are wards of the nation. They are communities dependent on the United States. Dependent largely for their daily food. Dependent for their political rights. They owe no allegiance to the States, and receive from them no protection."[19] Although the Hoopa had been under Mexican domination until 1848 and did not have a treaty relationship with the United States, the Treaty of Guadalupe Hidalgo between Mexico and the United States ceded California, which, according to the Court, brought them under American jurisdiction.

The doctrine of plenary power was firmly established by 1903. In that year, the United States Supreme Court in *Lone Wolf v. Hitchcock* gave the doctrine its most extensive definition, one that has affected the status of American Indian nations and their treaty rights ever since. Under the Treaty of Medicine Lodge Creek of 1867, no part of the Kiowa and Comanche Reservation could be ceded without approval of three-fourths of the adult males; nevertheless, a three-man federal commission headed by David Jerome arranged an agreement for the allotment of tribal lands and the opening up of "surplus" reservation lands to non-Indians. The Jerome Commission failed to obtain three-fourths approval. On June 6, 1900, Congress nevertheless confirmed the agreement. Lone Wolf, a prominent Kiowa, then sued the secretary of the interior, the commissioner of Indian affairs, and the commissioner of the General Land Office, attempting to enjoin the implementation of the allotments. Despite support from the Indian Rights Association, Lone Wolf lost the case. On January 5, 1903, the United States Supreme Court held that the plaintiff's contention "in effect ignores the status of the contracting Indians and the relation of dependency they bore and continue to bear toward the government of the United States."[20]

The Court, misreading history, stated its view on Congress's authority over Indian affairs: "Plenary authority over the tribal relations of the Indians has been exercised by Congress from the beginning, and the power has always been deemed a political one, not subject to be controlled by the judicial department of the government." Although the Court indicated that the breaking of a federal treaty should occur only when it is in the interest of the country and the Indians themselves, the decision made it clear how the jurists on the nation's highest court read the past history of Indian-white relations: "When, therefore, treaties were entered into between the United States and a tribe of Indians, it was never doubted that the power to abrogate existed in Congress, and that in a contingency, such power might be availed of from considerations of governmental policy, particularly consistent with the perfect good faith towards the Indians."[21]

The President and Congress played their points in this post-Civil War assault on Indians. From the (Dawes) General Allotment Act of 1887 onward, the Congress consciously tried to break up the Indian land base and attempted to absorb native peoples into the body politic. The act codified as national policy what had been taking place for many years. The President of the United States was given the discretion to allot reservation land to Indians, the title to be held in trust for twenty-five years. American Indians accepting allotment were to be "awarded" United States citizenship. Heads of families were to receive 160 acres with smaller plots going to other Indians. All "surplus" reservation lands after the allotment process was completed would be put up for sale and moneys obtained would be used for Indian education.[22] Between 1887 and 1934, American Indian landholdings in the United States shrank from an estimated 138 million to 52 million acres under the misworkings of the allotment policies, including outright murder, guardianship frauds, and tax foreclosures, all of which separated the allottee from his lands.[23]

For American Indians and their communities, the Civil War became another sad event in their tragic history since European colonization. This major milestone in American history, as we have seen, was also a watershed in American Indian history. Yet, as was true of their involvement in past conflicts, American Indians did not just "grin and bear it." They did not just "endeavor to persevere." Caught between two fires, they chose sides. Their heroism—the actions of Black Beaver, the Gravaraets, the Harris and Parker brothers, and Stand Watie—are a hidden history of the war that should not be ignored in the annals of this Herculean conflict. America's two great national epics—"the winning of the West" and "the Blue and the Gray"—intersected between 1861 and 1865. Unfortunately, where they did, the greatest victims were American Indians.

Notes

NCDAH	North Carolina Department of Archives and History
NYSA	New York State Archives
NYSL, MD	New York State Library, Manuscript Division
OIA	Office of Indian Affairs
Op. A.G.	*Opinions* of the United States Attorney General
OQG	Office of the Quartermaster General
OR	United States War Department, Comp. *The War of the Rebellion: A Compilation of the Official Records of the Union and Confederate Armies.* Washington, D.C.: U.S.G.P.O., 1880–1901. 128 vols.
PL, DU	Perkins Library, Duke University
RG	Record Group
SCDAH	South Carolina Department of Archives and History, Columbia, S.C.
SI	Smithsonian Institution
SINM	Seneca-Iroquois National Museum
Stat.	*United States Statutes at Large*
USACC	United States Army Continental Command
U.S.C.T.	United States Colored Troops
U.S.G.P.O.	United States Government Printing Office

Chapter 1. Not Ten Years of Peace

1. *ARCIA*, 1867: p. 145.
2. Alexis de Tocqueville, *Democracy in America* (1831; paperback reprint, New York: Vintage, 1954), I, 353–354.
3. 7 Stat. 156 (1817); 7 Stat. 195 (1819).
4. 7 Stat. 333 (1830).
5. Arthur DeRosier, Jr., *The Removal of the Choctaw Indians* (Knoxville: University of Tennessee Press, 1970), pp. 123–132.
6. James H. Kettner, *The Development of American Citizenship, 1608–1870* (Chapel Hill: University of North Carolina Press, 1978), p. 293.
7. 10 Stat. 1159 (1855); 12 Stat. 1237 (1862).
8. *Goodell v. Jackson*, 20 Johns. Rep. 693, 712 (N.Y., 1823).

9. *State ex. rel. Marsh v. Managers of Elections for District of York*, 1 Bailey 215, 216 (S.C., 1829).

10. See Chapter 4 of this book as well as Gerald M. Sider, *Lumbee Indian Histories: Race, Ethnicity, and Indian Identity in the Southern United States* (New York: Cambridge University Press, 1993), pp. 19–23; Karen I. Blue, *The Lumbee Problem: The Making of an American Indian People* (London: Cambridge University Press, 1980), pp. 46–50; John Hope Franklin, *The Free Negro in North Carolina, 1790–1860* (Chapel Hill: University of North Carolina Press, 1943), pp. 63–81. For the humiliating treatment perpetrated on Virginia's Indians, see Helen C. Rountree, "The Indians of Virginia: A Third Race in a Biracial State," in *Southeastern Indians Since the Removal Era*, Walter L. Williams, Ed. (Athens: University of Georgia Press, 1979), pp. 40–45; and especially her *Pocahontas People: The Powhatan Indians of Virginia Through Four Centuries* (Norman: University of Oklahoma Press, 1990), pp. 219–235.

11. *Cherokee Nation v. Georgia*, 5 Pet. 1 (U.S., 1831).

12. *Worcester v. Georgia*, 6 Pet. 515 (U.S., 1832).

13. Kettner, *The Development of American Citizenship*, pp. 299–300.

14. 7 Op. A.G. (1856). R. Alton Lee, "Indian Citizenship and the Fourteenth Amendment," *South Dakota History* 4 (1974): 204–206.

15. Felix S. Cohen, *Handbook of Federal Indian Law* (Washington, D.C.: U.S.G.P.O., 1942; reprint Albuquerque: University of New Mexico Press, 1971), pp. 153–154.

16. 4 Stat., 411–412 (1830).

17. Anthony F. C. Wallace, *The Long Bitter Trail: Andrew Jackson and the Indians* (New York: Hill and Wang, 1993), p 49. For the best analysis of Jacksonian Indian policies, see Ronald N. Satz, *American Indian Policy in the Jacksonian Era* (Lincoln: University of Nebraska Press, 1975).

18. Wallace, *The Long Bitter Trail*, p. 94.

19. Russell Thornton, *The Cherokees: A Population History* (Lincoln: University of Nebraska Press, 1990), p. 76.

20. Wallace, *The Long Bitter Trail*, p. 101. For a recent analysis of the Second Seminole War, see James W. Covington, *The Seminoles of Florida* (Gainesville, Fla.: University Press of Florida, 1993), pp. 50–109.

21. William T. Hagan, *American Indians*, 1st ed. (Chicago: University of Chicago Press, 1961), p. 77.

22. James D. Richardson, Ed., *A Compilation of the Messages and Papers of the Presidents, 1789–1897*, (Washington, D.C.: U.S.G.P.O., 1900), II: 457–458.

23. Wallace, *The Long Bitter Trail*, pp. 102–120; Robert M. Utley, *The Indian Frontier of the American West, 1846–1890* (Albuquerque: University of New Mexico Press, 1984), p. 4.

24. Hubert H. Bancroft, *The Works of Hubert H. Bancroft* (San Francisco: The History Co., 1890), XXV, 561 passim. I should like to thank Dr. Jack Campisi of Wellesley College for allowing me access to his rich research files on the Indians of northern California.

25. Edward D. Castillo, "The Impact of Euro-American Exploration and Settlement," *Handbook of North American Indians*, Vol. VIII: *California*, Robert F. Heizer, Ed. (Washington, D.C.: Smithsonian Institution, 1978), p. 118. Russell Thornton, *American Indian Holocaust and Survival: A Population History Since 1492* (Norman: University of Oklahoma Press, 1987). pp. 104–113; Alfred L. Kroeber, "The California Indian Population About 1910," in *Ethnographic Interpretations*, 1–6. University of California Publications in American Archaeology and Ethnology, 47 (2) (Berkeley: University of California Press, 1976), pp. 69–71; Robert F. Heizer, "Historical Demography," in *Handbook of North American Indians*, VIII: 91.

26. United States Congress. *Senate Document No. 131: Memorial of the Northern California Indian Association Praying that Lands Be Allotted to the Landless Indians of the Northern Part of the State of California*, Jan. 21, 1904, 58th Cong., 2d sess. (Washington, D.C., 1904), p. 1.

27. Frederick Law Olmsted, *The Papers of Frederick Law Olmsted*. Vol. V: *The California Frontier, 1863–1865*, Victoria Post Ranney, Ed. (Baltimore: Johns Hopkins University Press, 1983), p. 688.

28. A summary of the depredations can be found in *ARCIA*, 1862: p. 191. See also Sherburne Cook, *The Conflict Between California Indians and White Civilization* (Berkeley: University of California Press, 1976), pp. 255–361; Robert F. Heizer and Alan A. Almquist, *The Other Californians: Prejudice and Discrimination Under Spain, Mexico and the United*

States to 1920 (Berkeley: University of California Press, 1971), pp. 23–91; Robert F. Heizer, Ed., *The Destruction of the California Indians* (Salt Lake City, Utah: Peregrine Smith, 1974); and Heizer's *Ishi, The Last Yahi: A Documentary History* (Berkeley: University of California Press, 1979).

29. Heizer, *The Destruction of the California Indians*, vi–ix.
30. J. Y. McDuffie to A.B. Greenwood [Commissioner of Indian Affairs], Sept. 4, 1859, in United States Congress. Senate. *Executive Document No. 46: Report to the Secretary of the Interior, Communicating, in Compliance with a Resolution of the Senate, the Correspondence Between the Indian Office and the Present Superintendents and Agents in California, and J. Ross Browne, Esq.*, 36th Cong., 1st sess. (Dec. 5, 1859–June 25, 1860), Congressional Serial Set 1033, XI, 30.
31. Albert L. Hurtado, *Indian Survival on the California Frontier* (New Haven, Conn.: Yale University Press, 1988), pp. 130, 180–187.
32. *ARCIA*, 1862, p. 459.
33. Lynwood Carranco and Estle Beard, *Genocide and Vendetta: The Round Valley Wars of Northern California* (Norman: University of Oklahoma Press, 1981), p. 94.
34. J. Ross Browne to A. B. Greenwood, Oct. 18, 1859, in United States Congress, House of Representatives, *Ex. Doc. 46*, 36th Cong., 1st sess., Congressional Serial Set 1033, XI, 15.
35. Ibid.
36. Ibid., p. 14. Castillo quotes another report by Browne which describes a massacre of sixty Indian men, women, and children at Humboldt who "lay weltering in their own blood." Browne described that "girls and boys lay here and there with their throats cut from ear to ear." "The Impact of Euro-American Exploration and Settlement," p. 108.
37. Ethan Allen Hitchcock to Colonel S. Cooper [adjutant general of the United States], March 31, 1853. In United States Congress, House of Representatives, *Executive Document No. 76: Message from the President of the United States. Transmitting Report in Regard to Indian Affairs on the Pacific*, 34th Cong., 3rd sess. (Dec. 1, 1856–March 3, 1857), Congressional Serial Set 906, IX, 78.

38. Castillo, "The Impact of Euro-American Exploration and Settlement," pp. 110–112.

39. *ARCIA*, 1861: pp. 639–640.

40. Hurtado, *Indian Survival on the California Frontier*, pp. 144–151; Castillo, "The Impact of Euro-American Exploration and Settlement," pp. 110–112.

41. Thomas J. Henley to Captain H. M. Judah, Dec. 29, 1855. In United States Congress, House of Representatives, *Executive Document No. 76*, 34th Cong., 3rd sess., Congressional Serial Set 906, IX, 107–108.

42. Hurtado, *Indian Survival on the California Frontier*, p. 145; Castillo, "The Impact of Euro-American Exploration and Settlement," pp. 110–112.

43. United States Congress, House of Representatives, *Executive Document No. 76*, 34th Cong., 3rd sess., Congressional Serial Set 906, IX, pp. 102, 106–108, 110.

44. General John E. Wool to United States Senator [from California] John B. Weller, Oct. 5, 1856. In United States Congress, House of Representatives, *Executive Document No. 76*, 34th Cong., 3rd sess., Congressional Serial Set 906, IX, p. 141.

45. Hurtado, *Indian Survival on the California Frontier*, p. 147; Castillo, "The Impact of Euro-American Exploration and Settlement," p. 108.

46. George E. Baker, Ed., *The Works of William H. Seward* (Boston: Houghton, Mifflin and Co., 1853–1884), IV: 363.

47. David A. Nichols, *Lincoln and the Indians: Civil War Policy and Politics* (Columbia: University of Missouri Press, 1978), pp. 2–4. For more on Lincoln and his Indian policies, see Edmund J. Danziger, Jr., *Indians and Bureaucrats: Administering the Reservation Policy During the Civil War* (Urbana: University of Illinois Press, 1974).

48. Jefferson Davis, *The Papers of Jefferson Davis*, Linda L. Crist et al., Eds. (Baton Rouge, La.: Louisiana State University Press, 1971), IV, 91.

49. For more on Davis' relationship with the Indians, see Clement Eaton, *Jefferson Davis* (New York: The Free Press, 1977), pp. 16–19, 82–83. Eaton claims that Black Hawk praised Davis for his kindness when the Indian leader was transported as a prisoner of war to St. Louis (p. 17). Among Davis's ancestors was the Powhatan Indian chieftain

Opechancanough. Davis, *The Papers of Jefferson Davis*, James T. McIntosh, Ed., I, 488–489. For Davis's years as Secretary of War, see *The Papers of Jefferson Davis*, Crist et al., Eds., V.

Chapter 2. Union Scouts and Home Guards:
The Delaware of the Western Border

1. The most comprehensive history of these Indians is C. A. Weslager, *The Delaware Indians: A History* (New Brunswick, N.J.: Rutgers University Press, 1972; paperback reprint, 1989). For their westward removal and migrations, see C. A. Weslager, *The Delaware Indian Westward Migration* (Wallingford, Pa.: Middle Atlantic Press, 1978); also see Richard C. Adams, *A Brief History of the Delaware Indians*, in United States Congress, Senate Document No. 501, 59th Cong., 1st sess. (Washington, D.C., 1906). Information about the Delaware can also be found in Herbert C. Kraft, *The Lenape: Archaeology, History and Ethnography* (Newark: New Jersey Historical Society, 1986); Laurence M. Hauptman and Jack Campisi, Eds., *Neighbors and Intruders: An Ethnohistorical Exploration of the Indians of Hudson's River* (Ottawa: National Museum of Man, Canadian Ethnology Service Paper No. 39, 1978); Anthony F. C. Wallace, *King of the Delawares: Teedyuscung, 1700–1763* (Philadelphia: University of Pennsylvania Press, 1949; paperback reprint, Syracuse, N.Y.: Syracuse University Press, 1991); and Ives Goddard, "Delaware," in Bruce Trigger, Ed., *Handbook of North American Indians. XV: The Northeast* (Washington, D.C.: Smithsonian Institution, 1978), pp. 213–239.

2. For Delaware opposition to American expansion, see Richard White, *The Middle Ground: Indians, Empires, and Republic in the Great Lakes Region, 1650–1815* (New York: Cambridge University Press, 1991), pp. 277–295; Gregory Evans Dowd, *A Spiritual Resistance: The North American Indian Struggle for Unity, 1745–1815* (Baltimore: Johns Hopkins University Press, 1992), pp. 29–40.

3. Jeanne and James Ronda, "As They Were Faithful: Chief Aupaumat and the Struggle for Stockbridge Survival, 1757–1830," *American Indian Culture and Research Journal* 3 (1979): 43–55. For White Eyes, see

White, *The Middle Ground*, pp. 359–385. For George Washington's commendations of the Delaware, see George Washington, *The Writings of George Washington*, John C. Fitzpatrick, Ed. (Washington, D.C.: U.S.G.P.O., 1937), XX, 44–45. For Delaware participation on the American side in the Second Seminole War, see Grant Foreman, *The Last Trek of the Indians* (Norman: University of Oklahoma Press, 1946; reprint, New York: Russell and Russell, 1972), pp. 183, 199–200 n 7.

4. Foreman, *The Last Trek of the Indians*, p. 183.

5. Weslager, *The Delaware Indians*, pp. 353, 359–398, 430–432; Goddard, "Delaware," pp. 213–239.

6. For the two treaties with the Delaware in Missouri in 1829, see Charles J. Kappler, Comp., *Indian Affairs: Laws and Treaties* (Washington, D.C.: U.S.G.P.O., 1904–1941), II: 303–305.

7. Weslager, *The Delaware Indians*, pp. 359–428; Foreman, *The Last Trek of the Indians*, pp. 182–190; H. Craig Miner and William E. Unrau, *The End of Indian Kansas: A Study of Cultural Revolution, 1854–1871* (Lawrence: Regents Press of Kansas, 1978), pp. 1–24; Adams, *A Brief History of the Delaware Indians*, pp. 40–49.

8. Matthew Page Andrews to Mother, June 4, 1857, Charles Wesley Andrews Papers, Letters, 1853–1857, PL, DU. Miner and Unrau, *The End of Indian Kansas*, pp. 12–17; Albert Castel, *A Frontier State at War: Kansas, 1861–1865* (Ithaca, N.Y.: Cornell University Press, 1958), pp. 8–10.

9. Weslager, *The Delaware Indians*, pp. 405–407; Miner and Unrau, *The End of Indian Kansas*, pp. 114–115.

10. Delaware Petition to President James Buchanan, Oct. 26, 1858, OIA, LR, Delaware Agency, M234, MR275, RG75, NA. See also Joseph Killbuck, Frederick Samuel, et al. to James Buchanan, Feb. 12, 1858; Alson C. Davis to Major B. F. Robinson, Dec. 6, 1858; Davis to Jacob Thompson, Dec. 10, 1858, OIA, LR, Delaware Agency, M234, MR275, RG75, NA.

11. See Miner and Unrau, *The End of Indian Kansas*, pp. 28–40, 82–85; Castel, *A Frontier State at War*, pp. 219–224; Paul Wallace Gates, *Fifty Million Acres: Conflicts Over Kansas Land Policy, 1854–1890* (Ithaca, N.Y.: Cornell University Press, 1954), pp. 54–67, 116–123, 140–142; Annie H. Abel, "Indian Reservations in Kansas and the Extinguish-

ment of Their Title," *Transactions* of the Kansas State Historical Society, 8 (1904): 72–109.

12. For a portrait of Delaware religious practices and beliefs in this period, see Leslie A. White, Ed., *Lewis Henry Morgan: The Indian Journals, 1859–1862* (Ann Arbor: University of Michigan Press, 1959), pp. 49–58.

13. Kappler, Charles J., Comp., *Indian Affairs: Laws of Treaties* (Washington, D.C.: U.S.G.P.O., 1903–1941), II: 614–618 (Treaty of May 6, 1854), 803–807 (Treaty of May 30, 1860), 814–824 (Supplemental Treaty of July 2, 1861).

14. Miner and Unrau, *The End of Indian Kansas*, pp. 37, 98; Castel, *A Frontier State at War*, pp. 219–220; Gates, *Fifty Million Acres*, pp. 116–124, 141–142; Weslager, *The Delaware Indians*, pp. 407–416. For the early history of the remarkably powerful Ewing family traders, see Robert A. Trennert, Jr., *Indian Traders on the Middle Border: The House of Ewing, 1827–1854* (Lincoln: University of Nebraska Press, 1981). Their interest in Kansas Indian matters continued through the Civil War. See George Ewing to Thomas Ewing, Jr., April 11, 1861, May 28, 1862, Ewing Family MSS., LC.

15. *ARCIA*, 1861/1862, p. 23.

16. Ibid., p. 99. For favorable evaluations of Delaware military service to the Union, see *ARCIA*, 1862/1863, pp. 235, 238; *ARCIA*, 1863/1864, pp. 34, 37–38.

17. Carolyn T. Foreman, "Black Beaver," *Chronicles of Oklahoma* 24 (1946): 269–270.

18. Randolph B. Marcy, *Thirty Years of Army Life on the Border* (New York: Harper & Bros., 1866), p. 59.

19. Black Beaver, Compiled Military Service Record, Beaver's Spy Co., Indians, Texas Mtd. Vols., Mexican War, Records of the AGO, RG94, NA; Black Beaver Scout Contract, 1854, Records of the OQG, RG92, NA. Annie H. Abel, *The American Indian as Slaveholder and Secessionist* (Cleveland: Arthur H. Clark Company, 1915; paperback reprint, Lincoln: University of Nebraska Press, 1992), p. 101 n. 153; Foreman, "Black Beaver," 270; Adams, *A Brief History of the Delaware*, p. 37; Weslager, *The Delaware Indians*, p. 417; Thomas W. Dunlay,

Wolves for the Blue Soldiers: Indian Scouts and Auxiliaries with the United States Army, 1860–1890 (Lincoln: University of Nebraska Press, 1982), p. 18.

20. Randolph Marcy quoted in Grant Foreman, *Advancing the Frontier, 1830–1860* (Norman: University of Oklahoma Press, 1933), p. 276.

21. Marcy, *Thirty Years of Army Life on the Border*, pp. 59–65. In Marcy's handbook for overland expeditions, he also wrote extensively about Black Beaver: *The Prairie Traveler* (New York: Harper & Bros., 1859), pp. 188–196.

22. Marcy, *Thirty Years of Army Life on the Border*, p. 57.

23. Marcy, *The Prairie Traveler*, p. 196.

24. Adams, *A Brief History of the Delaware Indians*, p. 37.

25. These facts are well treated in Abel, *The American Indian as Slaveholder and Secessionist*, pp. 57–125.

26. Quoted in Foreman, "Black Beaver," p. 279.

27. Abel, *The American Indian as Slaveholder and Secessionist*, p. 101 n. 153.

28. Emory quoted in Adams, *A Brief History of the Delaware Indians*, p. 38.

29. Ibid., pp. 37–39; Foreman, "Black Beaver," 279–280; Abel, *The American Indian as Slaveholder and Secessionist*, p. 101 n. 153.

30. Abel, *The American Indian as Slaveholder and Secessionist*, pp. 129–134; Robert L. Duncan, *Reluctant General: The Life and Times of Albert Pike* (New York: E. P. Dutton, 1961), pp. 168–183; Alvin M. Josephy, Jr., *The Civil War in the American West*, (New York: Alfred A. Knopf, 1991) pp. 323–361; Walter L. Brown, "Albert Pike, 1809–1891" (Ph.D. diss., University of Texas, 1955), p. 553; M. K. McNeil, "Confederate Treaties with the Tribes of Indian Territory," *Chronicles of Oklahoma* 42 (Winter 1964–65): 408–420.

31. Abel, *The American Indian as Slaveholder and Secessionist*, pp. 99, 180–181 n. 326; Arrell M. Gibson, "Confederates on the Plains: The Pike Mission to the Wichita Agency," *Great Plains Journal* 4 (Fall 1964): 7–16.

32. *OR*, Ser. IV, 1:1, pp. 542–554.

33. Ibid., Ser. I, 8:1, p. 26.

34. Ibid., Ser. I, 22:2, p. 1021; Ser. I, 24:2, p. 735. Even beyond Black Beaver's great influence, the Delaware allied themselves with other

Unionist Indians. See John Connor [Head Chief] et al., to Opothleyahola, Jan. 4, 1862 (misdated 1861), OIA, LR, Delaware Agency,
M234, MR276, NA.

35. Frank Johnson, Delaware Indian Agent Report in "The Victory in
Northern Texas," *New York Times*, Feb. 15, 1863, p. 1.

36. *OR*, Ser. IV, 2:2, pp. 352–357.

37. Annie H. Abel, *The American Indian as Participant in the Civil War,
1862–1865* (Cleveland: Arthur H. Clark, 1919; paperback reprint,
Lincoln: University of Nebraska Press, 1992, with new title: *The
American Indian in the Civil War, 1862–1865*), pp. 183–184.

38. Ibid.; Arrell M. Gibson, *The Kickapoos: Lords of the Middle Border* (Norman: University of Oklahoma Press, 1963), pp. 195–200; W. W. Newcomb, Jr., *The Indians of Texas: From Prehistoric to Modern* (Austin: University of Texas Press, 1961), pp. 358–359; "The Victory in Northern
Texas," *New York Times*, Feb. 15, 1863.

39. According to Frank Johnson, the Delaware's Indian Agent, Ben
Simon was a "loyal and a true friend of the government," even
though Johnson feared his being "controlled by Mormon influence."
Frank Johnson to William P. Dole, March 7, 1863, OIA, LR,
Delaware Agency, M234, MR276, RG75, NA. For more on Simon,
see Frank Johnson to Commissioner Dole, March 7, 1863; Ben
Simon et al. to the Department of the Interior, Feb. 3, 20, 1864;
Simon et al. to Commissioner Dole, May 9, 1864, OIA, LR,
Delaware Agency, M234, MR276, NA.

40. See, for example, Moses et al. to Secretary of the Interior, Feb. 3,
1864, OIA, LR, Delaware Agency, M234, MR276, RG75, NA.

41. See note 38.

42. *OR*, Ser. IV, 2:2, p. 355.

43. Gibson, *The Kickapoos*, pp. 199–200.

44. Fall Leaf to Commissioner of Indian Affairs, Dec. 4, 1863; Falleaf et
al. to Commissioner of Indian Affairs, Aug. 24, 1863; Falleaf et al. to
William P. Dole, Sept. 15, 1863; John Moses et al. to Secretary of the
Interior, Feb. 3, 1864; Ben Simon, Captain Fall Leave [sic] et al. to
Commissioner Dole, May 9, 1864; Capt. Fall Leaf to Indian Com-
missioner, May 10, 1864, OIA, LR, Delaware Agency, M234, MR276,

RG75, NA. For Falleaf and his family's conservatism, see Weslager, *The Delaware Indians*, pp. 417–418, 418 (photograph), 442–443, 449 (photograph). See also note 42.

45. Fall Leaf to Commissioner of Indian Affairs, Dec. 4, 1863; Adams, *A Brief History of the Delaware Indians*, pp. 33–35, 39–40.

46. Fall Leaf et al. to Commissioner of Indian Affairs, Aug. 24, 1863.

47. Falleaf et al. to William P. Dole, Sept. 15, 1863.

48. *OR*, Ser. I, 13:1, pp. 434–522.

49. Abel, *The American Indian in the Civil War*, pp. 91–123; Josephy, *The Civil War in the American West*, pp. 354–359; Wiley Britton, *The Union Indian Brigade in the Civil War* (Kansas City, Mo., Franklin Hudson, 1922), pp. 58–79; Gary Heath, "The First Federal Invasion of Indian Territory, *Chronicles of Oklahoma* 44 (Winter 1966–67): 409–419.

50. Muster Rolls, Co. D, Second Kansas Indian Home Guards, Records of the AGO, RG94, NA.

51. Moses wrote the Secretary of the Interior that Captain Falleaf "has the confidence of all." John Moses et al. to Secretary of the Interior, Feb. 3, 1864, OIA, LR, Delaware Agency, M234, MR276, NA. Jim Ned, Compiled Military Service Record, CW, Records of the AGO, RG94, NA.

52. Marcy, *Thirty Years of Army Life on the Border*, pp. 69–71.

53. Quoted in Abel, *The American Indian as Slaveholder and Secessionist*, pp. 303, 330, 341.

54. Abel, *The American Indian in the Civil War, 1862–1865*, pp. 273–274 n. 785.

55. W. Craig Gaines, *The Confederate Cherokees: John Drew's Regiment of Mounted Rifles* (Baton Rouge, La.: Louisiana State University Press, 1989), pp. 104–122.

56. Fall Leaf to Commissioner of Indian Affairs, Dec. 4, 1863.

57. *OR*, Ser. I, 13:1, pp. 277–278.

58. Abel, *The American Indian in the Civil War, 1862–1865*, p. 197.

59. Fall Leaf to Commissioner of Indian Affairs, Dec. 4, 1863; Frank Johnson to Commissioner of Indian Affairs, Sept. 20, 1863, OIA, Delaware Agency, M234, MR276, NA; Muster Roll of Co. M, 6th Kansas Cavalry, Records of the AGO, RG94, NA.

60. Fall Leaf to Commissioner of Indian Affairs, Dec. 4, 1863.

61. Edmund J. Danziger, Jr., "The Office of Indian Affairs and the Problem of Civil War Refugees in Kansas," *Kansas Historical Quarterly* 35 (Autumn 1969): 257–275. See also Danziger, *Indians and Bureaucrats*, pp. 133–136; Nichols, *Lincoln and the Indians*, pp. 34–63; and Dean Banks, "Civil War Refugees from Indian Territory in the North, 1861–1864, *Chronicles of Oklahoma* 41 (Autumn 1963): 286–298.

62. Castel, *A Frontier State at War*, pp. 110–157; Richard S. Brownlee, *Gray Ghosts of the Confederacy: Guerrilla Warfare in the West, 1861–1865* (Baton Rouge: Louisiana State University Press, 1958), chapter 7; Michael Fellman, *Inside War: The Guerrilla Conflict in Missouri During the American Civil War* (New York: Oxford University Press, 1989), pp. 25, 41, 53, 206–207, 254; Jay Monaghan, *Civil War on the Western Border, 1854–1865* (Boston: Little, Brown, 1955), pp. 274–285. For White Turkey's action against Quantrill, see Farley, *The Delaware Indians in Kansas*, p. 14.

63. *ARCIA*, 1862/1863, p. 238.

64. "Property Damages of 124 Delawares, 1863 . . . by white men," OIA, LR, Delaware Agency, M234, MR276, RG75, NA.

65. Castel, *A Frontier State at War*, pp. 216–217.

66. Muster Rolls, Regimental Books, M Company, Sixth Kansas Cavalry, Records of the AGO, RG94, NA.

67. *ARCIA*, 1865/1866, pp. 15, 247.

68. John Connor to William Dole, Feb. 9, April 15, 1864; Captain Sarcoxie, Robert J. E. Journeycake to Dole, May 10, 1864; Captain Falleaf to Indian Commissioner, May 10, 1864; Ben Simon, Captail Fall Leave [sic] to Commissioner Dole, May 9, 1864, OIA, LR, Delaware Agency, M234, MR276, RG75, NA.

69. Every annual report of the Commissioner of Indian Affairs from 1860 to 1865 had recommended the removal of the Delaware and the other Indians from Kansas. For negotiations with the Cherokee, see John Ross et al. to William P. Dole, May 25, 1864; Ross et al. to James Steele, June 8, 1864, in Gary Moulton, Ed., *The Papers of Chief John Ross* (Norman: University of Oklahoma Press, 1985), II: 580, 585–588.

70. Kappler, Comp., *Indian Affairs: Laws and Treaties*, II: 937–942; Weslager, *The Delaware Indians*, pp. 421–429.

71. Foreman, "Black Beaver," pp. 282–292; Weslager, *The Delaware Indians*, p. 443.

Chapter 3. The General: The Western Cherokee and the Lost Cause

1. There are many writings on Stand Watie; however, the best treatment is Kenny A. Franks, *Stand Watie and the Agony of the Cherokee Nation* (Memphis, Tenn.: Memphis State University Press, 1979). See also Edward Everett Dale and Gaston Litton, Eds., *Cherokee Cavaliers: Forty Years of Cherokee History as Told in the Correspondence of the Ridge-Watie-Boudinot Family* (Norman: University of Oklahoma Press, 1939). Other book-length treatments include Mabel W. Anderson, *The Life of General Stand Watie*, 2nd ed. rev. (Pryor, Okla.: privately published, 1931), and, more recently, Wilfred Knight, *Red Fox: Stand Watie and the Confederate Indian Nations During the Civil War Years in Indian Territory* (Glendale, Calif.: Arthur H. Clark, 1988). Historians have frequently claimed that Watie was the last Confederate general to surrender. Some Confederates never did abandon the "Lost Cause" such as General Jo Shelby and over 2,000 rebel soldiers who went into Mexico after the war rather than surrender to the "Yankee." See Daniel O'Flaherty, *General Jo Shelby: Undefeated Rebel* (Chapel Hill, N.C.: University of North Carolina Press, 1954). Confederate General Douglas H. Cooper surrendered five days *after* Stand Watie. Four ex-Confederate governors (Allen, Clark, Moore, and Reynolds) and five ex-Confederate generals (Hawes, Cadmus, Wilcox, Magruder, and Price), and later at least three other ex-Confederate generals (Bee, Hindman, and Slaughter) joined Shelby in Mexico. Robert L. Kerby, *Kirby Smith's Confederacy: The Trans-Mississippi South, 1863–1865* (New York: Columbia University Press, 1972).

2. Thornton, *The Cherokees: A Population History*, pp. 90–96.

3. Ibid.; Morris Wardell, *A Political History of the Cherokee Nation, 1838–1907* (1938; paperback reprint edition, Norman: University of Oklahoma Press, 1977), pp. 175–176.

4. Franks, *Stand Watie*, pp. 1–13.
5. For more on Schermerhorn, see Laurence M. Hauptman, *Tribes and Tribulations: Misconceptions About American Indians and Their Histories* (Albuquerque: University of New Mexico Press, 1995), Chapter 4.
6. The best treatment of the Ridge family in this period is Thurman Wilkins, *Cherokee Tragedy: The Ridge Family and the Decimation of a People*, rev. ed. (Norman: University of Oklahoma Press, 1986).
7. Franks, *Stand Watie*, pp. 14–94; Gary Moulton, *John Ross: Cherokee Chief* (Athens: University of Georgia, 1978), pp. 72–126; Wardell, *A Political History of the Cherokee Nation*, pp. 16–75.
8. Grace Steele Woodward, *The Cherokees* (Norman: University of Oklahoma Press, 1963), pp. 223–234.
9. Wardell, *A Political History of the Cherokee Nation*, pp. 71–73; James K. Polk, *The Diary of James K. Polk During His Presidency, 1845 to 1849*, Milo M. Quaife, Ed. (Chicago: A. C. McClurg, 1910), II: 80–81; Richardson, Comp., *A Compilation of the Messages and Papers of the Presidents, 1789–1902*, II: 458–459.
10. Wardell, *A Political History of the Cherokee Nation*, pp. 116–117. For Cherokee slavery, see Theda Perdue, *Slavery and the Evolution of Cherokee Society, 1540–1866* (Knoxville: University of Tennessee Press, 1979).
11. Raymond D. Fogelson, "Who Were the Ani-Kutani? An Excursion into Cherokee Historical Thought," *Ethnohistory* 31 (1984): 255–263. For slaveholding and abolitionist forces within the Cherokee Nation during the Civil War, see Perdue, *Slavery and the Evolution of Cherokee Society*, pp. 119–140.
12. James Mooney, *Myths of the Cherokee 19th Annual Report of the Bureau of American Ethnology*, Part I (Washington, D.C.: Bureau of American Ethnology, Smithsonian Institution, 1900), p. 225.
13. Ibid.; Charles C. Royce, *The Cherokee Nation of Indians* (Washington, D.C.: U.S.G.P.O., 1887; reprint, Chicago: Aldine Publishers, 1965), pp. 225–226; William G. McLoughlin, *The Cherokee Ghost Dance: Essays on the Southeastern Indians, 1789–1861* (Macon, Ga.: Mercer University Press, 1984), pp. 467–468; Wardell, *A Political History of the Cherokee Nation*, pp. 121–122; Perdue, *Slavery and the Evolution of Cherokee Society*, pp. 129–130.

14. Wardell, *A Political History of the Cherokee Nation*, pp. 122–123; Perdue, *Slavery and the Evolution of Cherokee Society*, pp. 129–130.

15. Franks, *Stand Watie*, pp. 115–116. See Chapter 1 of this book for Pike's efforts. For Arkansas efforts to recruit Stand Watie for the Confederacy, see Wardell, *A Political History of the Cherokee Nation*, p. 127.

16. *OR*, Ser. I, 13, pp. 691–692. For McCulloch's recruitment of Watie, see Stephen B. Oates, *Confederate Cavalry West of the River* (Austin: University of Texas Press, 1962; paperback reprint, 1992), pp. 18–19.

17. *OR*, Ser. I, 3, pp. 690–691; Moulton, *John Ross*, pp. 168–174; Wardell, *A Political History of the Cherokee Nation*, pp. 154–156. Moulton also insisted that Ross was influenced by Pike's success among other Indian nations of Indian Territory as well as the fact that a significant number of Confederate troops were "ominously near the Cherokee Nation" (p. 171).

18. *OR*, Ser. IV, 1, pp. 669–687. See also Kenny A. Franks, "An Analysis of Confederate Treaties with the Five Civilized Tribes," *Chronicles of Oklahoma* 50 (Winter 1972–73): 458–473; and Kenneth McNeal, "Confederate Treaties with the Tribes of Indian Territory," pp. 408–420; William H. Graves, "Indian Soldiers for the Gray Army: Confederate Recruitment in Indian Territory," *Chronicles of Oklahoma* 60 (Summer 1991): 134–145.

19. Oates, *Confederate Cavalry West of the River*, pp. 19–20, 167–169; Gaines, *The Confederate Cherokees: John Drew's Regiment of Mounted Rifles* (Baton Rouge: Louisiana State University Press, 1989), pp. 43–61, 74–125.

20. *OR*, Ser. I, 8: pp. 12–13, 22–33. See also Arthur Shoemaker, "The Battle of Chustenahlah," *Chronicles of Oklahoma* 38 (Summer 1960): 180–184; and LeRoy Fisher and Kenny A. Franks, "Confederate Victory at Chusto-Talasah," *Chronicles of Oklahoma* 44 (Winter 1971–72): 452–476; Franks, *Stand Watie*, pp. 120–123.

21. Moulton, *John Ross*, pp. 165–175.

22. Dale and Litton, Eds., *Cherokee Cavaliers*, pp. 146–147; Franks, *Stand Watie*, p. 137.

23. Dale and Litton, Eds., *Cherokee Cavaliers*, pp. 144–147; Franks, *Stand Watie*, pp. 135–153.

24. Dale and Litton, Eds., *Cherokee Cavaliers*, pp. 155–156, 156 n.

25. Ibid., p. 156.

26. Quoted in Franks, *Stand Watie*, pp. 136–137.

27. For the failure of the Confederacy to live up to its treaties with the Indians, see Kenny A. Franks, "The Implementation of the Confederate Treaties with the Five Civilized Tribes," *Chronicles of Oklahoma* 51 (Spring 1973): 21–33; and his "The Confederate States and the Five Civilized Tribes: A Breakdown of Relations," *Journal of the West* 12 (July 1973): 439–454.

28. *OR*, Ser. I, 13:2, pp. 1104–1105.

29. Ibid., pp. 1105–1106.

30. Dale and Litton, Eds., *Cherokee Cavaliers*, pp. 137.

31. *OR*, Ser. I, 13, pp. 94–95.

32. Ibid., Ser. I, 34:1, pp. 1011–1013; James D. Morrison, "Capture of the J. R. Williams," *Chronicles of Oklahoma* 43 (Summer 1964): 105–108; Lee Keun Sang, "The Capture of the J. R. Williams," *Chronicles of Oklahoma* 55 (Spring 1982): 22–33.

33. *OR*, Ser. I, 41:1, p. 778.

34. The battle can be traced in Ibid., pp. 777–794.

35. Ibid. See also Kerby, *Kirby Smith's Confederacy*, pp. 352–355; Monaghan, *Civil War on the Western Border, 1854–1865*, pp. 307–310; Alvin M. Josephy, *The Civil War in the American West* (New York: Alfred A. Knopf, 1991), p. 377; Marvin J. Hancock, "The Second Battle of Cabin Creek, 1864," *Chronicles of Oklahoma* 41 (Winter 1963–64): 414–426; Fred Hood, "Twilight of the Confederacy in the Indian Territory," *Chronicles of Oklahoma* 41 (Winter 1963–64): 414–426.

36. Kerby, *Kirby Smith's Confederacy*, pp. 352–355.

37. *OR*, Ser. I, 41:1, pp. 777–794.

38. W. David Baird, Ed., *A Creek Warrior for the Confederacy: The Autobiography of Chief G. W. Grayson* (Norman: University of Oklahoma Press, 1988), p. 102.

39. *OR*, Ser. I, 41:1, pp. 786–787. For another Indian account of the battle, see Baird, Ed., *A Creek Warrior for the Confederacy*, pp. 95–107.

40. *OR*, Ser. I, 41:1, pp. 777–794; Franks, *Stand Watie*, pp. 170–174.

41. Kerby, *Kirby Smith's Confederacy*, p. 355; Monaghan, *Civil War on the Western Border*, p. 308. Muster rolls of the Second Kansas Indian Home Guard, Records of the AGO, RG94, NA.

42. Oates, *Confederate Cavalry West of the River*, pp. 159–161.

43. *OR*, Ser. I, 47:3, pp. 1100–1101.

44. Franks, *Stand Watie*, p. 182.

45. Ibid., p. 183; Wardell, *A Political History of the Cherokee Nation*, pp. 183–184.

46. *ARCIA*, 1865: 298, 304–307, 338, 343–347. For this remarkable setting, see Edward C. Bearss and Arrell M. Gibson, *Fort Smith: Little Gibraltar on the Arkansas* (Norman: University of Oklahoma Press, 1969). See also Annie H. Abel, *The American Indian Under Reconstruction* (Cleveland: Arthur H. Clark, 1925), pp. 183–186.

47. For Cooley's report on the Fort Smith conference, see *ARCIA*, 1865, 480–537.

48. Wardell, *A Political History of the Cherokee Nation*, pp. 193–207.

49. Franks, *Stand Watie*, pp. 190–196. Dale and Litton, Eds., *Cherokee Cavaliers*, pp. 247–270.

50. Franks, *Stand Watie*, p. 196 and passim.

51. 78 U.S. 616 (1870); see also Robert K. Heimann, "The Cherokee Tobacco Case," *Chronicles of Oklahoma* 41 (Autumn 1963): 299–322. For *Lonewolf v. Hitchcock*, see 187 U.S. 553 (1903).

52. Franks, *Stand Watie*, pp. 208.

53. For an analysis of this family feud, see Gerald A. Reed, "The Ross-Watie Conflict: Factionalism in the Cherokee Nation, 1839–1865" (Ph.D. dissertation, Norman: University of Oklahoma, 1967).

Chapter 4. River Pilots and Swamp Guerrillas:
Pamunkey and Lumbee Unionists

1. Rountree, *Pocahontas' People*, pp. 98, 164, 172, 203. For the Powhatan, see also Rountree, *The Powhatan Indians: Their Traditional History* (Norman: University of Oklahoma Press, 1989); Rountree, "The Indians of Virginia: A Third Race in a Biracial State," pp. 27–48; Rountree, "Ethnicity Among the 'Citizen' Indians of Tidewater Virginia, 1800–1930," in Frank Porter, Ed., *Strategies for Survival: American Indians in the Eastern United States* (Westport, Conn.: Greenwood Press, 1986), pp. 172–209; Theodore Stern, "Chickahominy: The Changing

Culture of a Virginia Indian Community," *Proceedings* of the American Philosophical Society 96 (April 21, 1952): 157–225; Christian F. Feest, "Virginia Algonquians," in Bruce G. Trigger, Ed., *Handbook of North American Indians*, XV: 253–270; James Axtell, "The Rise and Fall of the Powhatan Empire," in *After Columbus: Essays in the Ethnohistory of Colonial North America* (New York: Oxford University Press, 1988), pp. 182–221.

2. Rountree, *Pocahontas' People*, pp. 179–185.

3. Ibid., pp. 191–193.

4. Ibid., pp. 194–198.

5. James Mooney, "The Powhatan Confederacy: Past and Present," *American Anthropologist* 9 (1907): 145. For Mooney's work among the Pamunkey, see L. George Moses, *The Indian Man: A Biography of James Mooney* (Urbana: University of Illinois Press, 1984), pp. 41–42, 162.

6. The writings on the Peninsula Campaign are extensive. For the most comprehensive account, see Stephen W. Sears, *To the Gates of Richmond: The Peninsula Campaign* (New York: Ticknor and Fields, 1992).

7. *OR*, Ser. I, 11:1, pp. 614–617, 137–138, 276.

8. George Alfred Townsend, *Rustics in Rebellion: A Yankee Reporter on the Road to Richmond, 1861–1865* (Chapel Hill: University of North Carolina Press, 1950), p. 53; *OR*, Ser. I, 11:1, pp. 162–163; George B. McClellan, *The Civil War Papers of George McClellan: Selected Correspondence, 1860–1865*, Stephen W. Sears, Ed. (New York: Ticknor and Fields, 1989), p. 262.

9. Rountree, *Pocahontas' People*, p. 198.

10. Ibid.; Stern, "Chickahominy," p. 206. Because of property damage during the Peninsula Campaign, the Pamunkey received monetary compensation after the war.

11. Townsend, *Rustics in Rebellion*, pp. 58–60.

12. Ibid.

13. For the 57th Pennsylvania Volunteer Infantry, see *OR*, Ser. 3, 1:161 and Samuel P. Bates, Comp., *History of the Pennsylvania Volunteers*, 2 vols. (Harrisburg, Pa.: B. Singerly, 1869), II: 246–284. Company K also had the following Iroquois Indians on its muster rolls: Ira Bucktooth, Chauncey Jemison (Jimison), Thompson Jemison (Jimison), Wilson

Pierce, Martin Redeye, Thomas Shongo, Jonas Snow, and Joseph White. "Commencement list," Regimental Books, Company K, 57th Pennsylvania Volunteer Infantry, Records of the AGO, RG94, NA.

14. Cornelius Plummer to Wilson Pierce, March 5, April 1, 1862, Civil War Letters, SINM, Salamanca, N.Y.

15. Levi Turkey Williams to father of Cornelius Plummer, June 1, 1862, SINM. Levi Turkey Williams, compiled military service records, CW, Records of the AGO, RG94, NA.

16. Willet Pierce to his father, June 5, 1862, SINM.

17. Regimental Books, Company K, 57th Pennsylvania Volunteer Infantry, Records of the AGO, RG94, NA. The records suggest that Pierce was accused of desertion. Fidelia Pierce memorandum to Congressman E. B. Vreeland, undated [early 1900s?], SINM.

18. Rountree, *Pocahontas' People*, pp. 16, 33, 36, 98, 103, 130, 131, 145, 175, 203, 216.

19. For Weisiger, see ibid., p. 192. Most of the Powhatans served as civilian land and river pilots.

20. Terrill Bradby disability statement, April 18, 1888; increase in pension Affidavit, Dec. 19, 1894, general affidavit, April 19, 1892; original pension claim, March 14, 1888; Riley Bradby [Neighbor's] general affidavit, Feb. 17, 1888, June 20, 1895; Terrill Bradby invalid claim, March 25, 1892; [William] Terrell Bradby pension file, Certificate No. 19281, invalid Pension, CW, CWPR, NA.

21. James Mooney Pamunkey fieldnotes, MSS. 2218, James Mooney Papers, NAA, SI.

22. See note 18. Bradby's Civil War pension was held up and even denied by military blunders in misspelling his first and last names. See L.N. Buford [auditor] to J.C. Black [commissioner of pensions], Jan. 18, 1888; John S. Williams [auditor] memorandum of Aug. 20, 1888; John R. Lynch [auditor] to Commissioner of Pensions, Sept. 7, 1889; Terrill Bradby to Commissioner of Pensions, Sept. 23, 1892, with attached corroborating signatures of Pamunkey, Sept. 26, 1892: W. A. Bradby [acting chief], Riley Bradby, E. R. Allmond, J. T. Dennis, C. S. Bradby; Terrill Bradby to James H. Vermilya, May 29, 1888, April 16, 1892; Thomas M. Reynolds [acting secretary of the interior] to

Commissioner of Pensions, June 10, 1895; S. S. Ninson [pension agent] to William Lochser [commissioner of pensions], June 15, 1895. [William] Terrill Bradby pension file, Certificate No. 19281, invalid pension, Civil War, CWPR, NA.

23. See notes 20 and 22.

24. Ibid.

25. Mooney fieldnotes, MSS. 2218, Mooney papers, NAA, SI.

26. King William Co., Va., Ended Chancery Cases, File 32. The proceedings of the trial do not appear to be extant. There is a vague reference in the Mooney fieldnotes to this incident.

27. See notes 18 and 20.

28. Mooney, "The Powhatan Confederacy," p. 147.

29. Albert S. Gatschet, Pamunkey Fieldnotes, MSS 2197, Pamunkey Notebook Post 1893, NAA, SI. For more on Bradby in this period, see the news clippings from Washington, D.C. and Richmond newspapers which date from the period 1890 to 1894 in Gatschet's Pamunkey Notebook.

30. Rountree, *Pocahontas' People*, pp. 208–210.

31. For the history of the Indians of Robeson County, North Carolina, see W. McKee Evans, *To Die Game: The Story of the Lowry Band, Indian Guerrillas of Reconstruction* (Baton Rouge: Louisiana State University Press, 1971); Sider, *Lumbee Indian Histories*; Blu, *The Lumbee Problem*. For a uniquely Lumbee perspective of their history, see Adolph L. Dial and David K. Eliades, *The Only Land I Know: A History of the Lumbee Indians* (San Francisco: The Indian Historian Press, 1975).

32. Eric Hobsbawm, *Bandits* (New York: Delacorte Press, 1971), pp. 13–23.

33. Dial and Eliades, *The Only Land I Know*, p. 86.

34. Franklin, *The Free Negro in North Carolina, 1790–1860*, pp. 63–82.

35. John R. Finger, *The Eastern Band of Cherokees, 1819–1900* (Knoxville: University of Tennessee Press, 1984), pp. 82–100, 150, 155–156. For the Thomas Legion, see Stanley Godbold, Jr. and Mattie U. Russell, *Confederate Colonel and Cherokee Chief: The Life of William Holland Thomas* (Knoxville: University of Tennessee Press, 1990).

36. *State v. Locklear*, 44 N.C. 205.

37. Dial and Eliades, *The Only Land I Know*, p. 45.

38. Evans, *To Die Game*, p. 33.

39. W. McKee Evans, "The North Carolina Lumbees from Assimilation to Revitalization," in Williams, Ed., *Southeastern Indians Since the Removal Era*, p. 51.

40. Ibid.; Sider, *Lumbee Indian Histories*, p. 158.

41. Rowena Reed, *Combined Operations in the Civil War* (Annapolis, Md.: Naval Institute Press, 1978), pp. 329–335; John G. Barrett, *The Civil War in North Carolina* (Chapel Hill: University of North Carolina Press, 1963), pp. 262–264. See also Rod Gragg, *Confederate Goliath: The Battle of Fort Fisher* (New York: Harper Collins, 1991).

42. John C. Gorman Recollections, AGO, 1871–1876, Henry Berry Lowry papers, Robeson County, N.C., NCDAH.

43. Evans, *To Die Game*, pp. 35–36.

44. Hauptman, *The Iroquois in the Civil War* (Syracuse, N.Y.: Syracuse University Press, 1993), p. 80; Marion Brunson Lucas, *Sherman and the Burning of Columbia* (College Station: Texas A&M University Press, 1976), pp. 115–117.

45. For Sherman's march through the Carolinas, see Joseph T. Glatthaar, *The March to the Sea and Beyond: Sherman's Troops in the Savannah and Carolinas Campaigns* (New York: New York University Press, 1985); John G. Barrett, *Sherman's March Through the Carolinas* (Chapel Hill: University of North Carolina Press, 1956); and Barrett's *The Civil War in North Carolina*, Chapter XIV.

46. Gorman recollections; Thomas A. Noment affidavit, Dec. 8, 1865, Superior Court [of N.C.] Records: Criminal action papers concerning Henry Berry Lowry, Robeson County, 1862–1865, File: Miscellaneous papers, 1865, NCDAH. N. M. Keyes, Solicitor, affidavit, 1866; murder warrant for Henry Berry Lowry, Sept. 10, 1870, Superior Court Records: Criminal action papers concerning Henry Berry Lowry, Robeson County, 1862–1875, File: Barnes murder, 1864, NCDAH.

47. Evans, *To Die Game*, pp. 38–39.

48. Ibid., pp. 39–41.

49. Washington Sandford Chaffin diary, Feb. 25, 28, March 1, 1865, PL, DU.

50. Dispositions of Calvin Lowry, Oct. 14, 1867; George Dial, Oct. 19, 1867; Robert McKenzie, May 29, 1867, Sinclair Lowry, June 1, 1867; Elias Carlile, Aug. 23, 1867; Jack Carlile, Aug. 23, 1867; Reverend J.H. Coble and L. McKinnon, June 8, 1867. Records of the USACC, 1821–1920, Second Military District, LR, Box 9, RG393, NA. For more firsthand accounts of the Lowry Band, see United States Congress, Senate, *Report No. 41, Report of the Joint Select Committee to Inquire into the Condition of Affairs in the Late Insurrectionary States* ... , 42nd Cong., 2d sess. (Washington, D.C.: U.S.G.P.O., 1872), II: 283–298.
51. Deposition of George Dial, Oct. 19, 1867.
52. Deposition of Calvin Lowry, Oct. 14, 1867.
53. Evans, *To Die Game*, p. 18.
54. William Tecumseh Sherman quoted in Barrett, *Sherman's March Through the Carolinas*, p. 123.
55. Deposition of Elias Carlile, Aug. 23, 1867.
56. *OR*, Ser. I, 47:1, pp. 231–232.
57. Evans, *To Die Game*, pp. 45–49.
58. Solomon Oxendine quoted in Ibid., p. 48.
59. Barrett, *Sherman's March Through the Carolinas*, p. 124.
60. Chaffin Diary, March 9, 1865, PL, DU.
61. Evans, *To Die Game*, pp. 50–51.
62. Sider, *Lumbee Indian Histories*, p. 158.
63. Dial and Eliades, *The Only Land I Know*, pp. 86–87; Sider, *Lumbee Indian Histories*, p. 158.

Chapter 5. Infantrymen in the Army of Northern Virginia: The Catawba

1. W. R. Browne to Thomas J. Portis, April 13, 1863; John A. Davis to Major Memminger, April 12, 1863; Special Order No. 112, May 9, 1863; J. N. Pierce to Secretary of War, May 22, 1863 with notation of June 17, 1863; J. L. Carter to Colonel E. E. Ewell, July 28, 1863, War Department Confederate Records: Muster and Pay Rolls, Box 227, Folder: 1st Choctaw Battalion, Mississippi Cavalry, Pierce, J. W., Records of the CSA, RG109, NA. *OR*, Ser. II, 5, pp. 734, 742, 752–755. A. J. Brown, *History of Newton County, Mississippi, from*

1834–1894 (Jackson, Miss.: Clarion-Ledger Co., 1894), p. 96. See also Ronald N. Satz, "The Mississippi Choctaw: From the Removal Treaty to Federal Agency." In Samuel J. Wells and Roseanna Tubby, Eds., *After Removal: The Choctaw in Mississippi* (Jackson: University Press of Mississippi, 1986), pp. 3–32. Some Choctaw in Louisiana under Chief Greenwood LeFlore joined the Union.

2. Charles M. Hudson, *The Catawba Nation* (Athens: University of Georgia Press, 1970), p. 110.

3. Wilbur R. Jacobs, Ed., *Indians of the Southern Frontier: The Edmond Atkin Report and Plan of 1755* (Columbia, S.C.: University of South Carolina Press, 1954), p. 47.

4. Samuel Cole Williams, Ed., [James] *Adair's History of the American Indian* (Johnson City, Tenn.: Wautaga Press, 1930), p. 235.

5. James H. Merrell, *The Indians' New World: Catawbas and Their Neighbors from European Contact Through the Era of Removal* (New York: W. W. Norton, 1989), p. 207. Catawba racism toward blacks clearly was an acquired characteristic. See James H. Merrell, "The Racial Education of the Catawba Indians," *Journal of Southern History* 50 (August 1984): 363–384.

6. Quoted in Hudson, *The Catawba Nation*, p. 58.

7. Ibid., pp. 48–52; Merrell, *The Indians' New World*, pp. 216–217.

8. Charles H. Hudson, "The Catawba Indians of South Carolina: A Question of Ethnic Survival" In Walter L. Williams, Ed., *Southeastern Indians Since the Removal Era*, (Athens: University of Georgia Press), p. 114; Hudson, *The Catawba Nation*, pp. 63–64; Merrell, *The Indians' New World*, p. 244.

9. Merrell, *The Indians' New World*, p. 245; Douglas Summers Brown, *The Catawba Indians: The People of the River* (Columbia: University of South Carolina Press, 1966), p. 319.

10. Brown, *The Catawba Indians*, pp. 305–318; Merrell, *The Indians' New World*, pp. 245–246.

11. Thomas Cooper and D. J. McCord, Eds., *The Statutes at Large of South Carolina* (Columbia, S.C., 1836–1841), V, 678–679.

12. Merrell states that Cherokee had tribal names "Catawba-Killer" in their ranks in the 1840s, making it awkward if not impossible for the

South Carolina Indians to live comfortably with their North Carolina neighbors. Hudson insists that only about a dozen Catawba still lived among the Cherokee by 1852. Merrell, *The Indians' New World*, p. 252; Hudson, *The Catawba Nation*, p. 66. Hudson's conclusions are largely drawn from James Mooney, *Myths of the Cherokee, 19th Annual Report of the Bureau of American Ethnology* (Washington, D.C.: U.S.G.P.O., 1900), Pt. 1, p. 165.

13. Merrell, *The Indians' New World*, pp. 254–257; Brown, *The Catawba Indians*, pp. 319–322.

14. Brown, *The Catawba Indians*, pp. 326–329.

15. Hudson, *The Catawba Nation*, p. 66; Merrell, *The Indians' New World*, pp. 256–257; Brown, *The Catawba Indians*, p. 329.

16. Brown, *The Catawba Indians*, p. 330.

17. James H. Merrell, " | 'Their Very Bones Shall Fight": The Catawba-Iroquois Wars." In Daniel K. Richter and James H. Merrell, Eds., *Beyond the Covenant Chain: The Iroquois and Their Neighbors, 1600–1800* (Syracuse, N.Y.: Syracuse University Press, 1987), pp. 115–134.

18. Merrell, *The Indians' New World*, p. 121.

19. Ibid., pp. 121–122.

20. Brown, *The Catawba Indians*, p. 330.

21. Hudson, *The Catawba Indians*, p. 67.

22. Ibid., pp. 51–68, 110–111.

23. "Whoop!" [Editorial], *New York Times*, January 26, 1861.

24. Brown, *The Catawba Indians*, p. 330; Thomas J. Blumer, Comp., *Bibliography of the Catawba* (Metuchen, N.J.: Scarecrow Press, 1987), p. xx.

25. This figure was calculated from the compiled military service records of the Catawba men who served. Compiled Military Service Records, Records of the CSA, RG109, NA.

26. Blumer, *Bibliography of the Catawba*, p. xx. According to the Catawba Indian agent, by 1864, five Indians had been killed, two disabled, two severely wounded, one crippled for life, and three taken as prisoners of war. John R. Patton, *Annual Report of November, 1864*, General Assembly of South Carolina—Misc. Communications, 1864, no. 10, SCDAH.

27. Brown, *The Catawba Indians*, p. 330. For more on this company and the commitment of the whites and Indians of York County to the

Confederate cause, see Douglas Summers Brown, *A City Without Cobwebs: A History of Rock Hill, South Carolina* (Columbia: University of South Carolina Press, 1953), pp. 92–102; 300–307.

28. *OR*, Ser. I, 6, pp. 7, 11, 66–68, 73–74.

29. *OR*, Ser. I, 11:2, pp. 853, 865–866.

30. For the Second Battle of Bull Run, see the magnificent work by John J. Hennessy, *Return to Bull Run: The Campaign and Battle of Second Manassas* (New York: Simon and Schuster, 1993).

31. Ibid., p. 206.

32. Ibid., p. 216.

33. Ibid., pp. 245–258.

34. Edward McCrady, "Gregg's Brigade of South Carolinians in the Second Battle of Manassas," *Southern Historical Society Papers*, 12 (1885), 29–30.

35. Quoted in Ibid., p. 34.

36. Hennessy, *Return to Bull Run*, pp. 279–286.

37. *OR*, Ser. I, 12:2, pp. 692–693.

38. For Gregg's Brigade at Antietam, see J. F. L. Caldwell, *The History of a Brigade of South Carolinians Known First as "Gregg's" and Subsequently as "McGowan's Brigade"* (Philadelphia: King and Baird, 1866), pp. 45 and passim.

39. John Michael Priest, *Antietam: The Soldiers Battle* (1989; paperback reprint, New York: Oxford University Press, 1993), pp. 271–273.

40. Ibid.

41. For the best account of the battle and its significance, see Stephen W. Sears, *Landscape Turned Red: The Battle of Antietam* (New York: Ticknor & Fields, 1983).

42. John Harris and James Harris, compiled military service records, Records of the CSA, RG109, NA.

43. "Indian Warriors," *Rock Hill Herald*, Dec. 10, 1885, p. 3.

44. "Monument at Fort Mill," *Rock Hill Herald*, May 19, 1900, p. 2; "Dedication of Catawba Indian Monument, Fort Mill, S.C.," *Rock Hill Herald*, Aug. 4, 1900, p. 2; "Catawba Indian Monument—Fort Mill," *Rock Hill Journal*, Aug. 21, 1903, p. 2.

45. "Catawba Indian Monument—Fort Mill," *Rock Hill Herald*.

46. George Nelson and William Canty, compiled military service records, RG109, Records of the CSA, NA.

47. W. H. Edwards, *A Condensed History of Seventeenth Regiment S.C.V. C.S.A.: From Its Organization to the Close of the War* (Columbia, S.C.: R.L. Bryan Co., 1908), pp. 4–5, 17–32.

48. Ibid., pp. 46–47. For Elliott's Brigade at the Battle of the Crater, see F. W. McMaster, "The Battle of the Crater, July 30, 1864," Papers of the Southern Historical Society 10 (1882): 119–130. See Chapter 8 of this book for an analysis of the Battle of the Crater.

49. Jefferson Ayers, compiled military service record, RG109, Records of the CSA, RG109, NA.

50. Alexander Timms [Tims] and Robert Marsh [Mush], compiled military service records, Records of the CSA, RG109, NA.

51. John Scott, compiled military service record, Records of the CSA, RG109, NA.

52. Robert Crawford, Peter Harris, and Robert Head, compiled military service records, Records of the CSA, RG109, NA.

Chapter 6. Confederate Rangers of the Smokies:
Wil-Usdi's Eastern Band of Cherokee

1. For the best treatments of the Thomas Legion, see Godbold and Russell, *Confederate Colonel and Cherokee Chief*, pp. 90–128; Finger, *The Eastern Band of Cherokees, 1819–1900*, pp. 82–100; and Vernon H. Crow, *Storm in the Mountains: Thomas' Confederate Legion of Cherokee Indians and Mountaineers* (Cherokee, N.C.: Museum of the Cherokee Indian, 1982).

2. Godbold and Russell, *Confederate Colonel and Cherokee Chief*, pp. 1–9.

3. Duane H. King, "The Origin of the Eastern Cherokees as a Social and Political Entity." In Duane H. King, Ed., *The Cherokee Indian Nation: A Troubled History* (Knoxville: University of Tennessee Press, 1979), pp. 164–180.

4. Godbold and Russell, *Confederate Colonel and Cherokee Chief*, pp. 9–77.

5. For recent analyses of this genre, see note 66.

6. Godbold and Russell, *Confederate Colonel and Cherokee Chief*, p. 22. Ac-

cording to Godbold and Russell, "Thomas was unconcerned about the majority of the eastern Cherokee, but he was devoted to the small group in North Carolina with whom he had contracted" (p. 22).

7. Kappler, Comp., *Indian Affairs, Laws and Treaties*, II: pp. 443–444.

8. For Thomas's legal efforts on behalf of the Cherokee, see Richard W. Iobst, "William Holland Thomas and the Cherokee Claims." In King, ed., *The Cherokee Indian Nation: A Troubled History*, pp. 181–201.

9. King, "The Origin of the Eastern Cherokee," p. 180.

10. Finger, *The Eastern Band of Cherokee*, pp. 24–28.

11. Ibid., p. 67; Godbold and Russell, *Confederate Colonel and Cherokee Chief*, pp. 36–55.

12. Godbold and Russell, *Confederate Colonel and Cherokee Chief*, pp. 56–89.

13. See, for example, Ibid., p. 90.

14. Ibid., pp. 90–91.

15. William Holland Thomas to Sarah (wife), Jan. 1, 1861, WHT papers, microfilm, PL, DU.

16. William Holland Thomas to wife, June 17, 1861, WHT correspondence, 1861–1865, PL, DU.

17. Godbold and Russell, *Confederate Colonel and Cherokee Chief*, pp. 92–93.

18. *OR*, Ser. I, 51:2, p. 304; William Holland Thomas to Governor William T. Clark, April 13, 1862, March 14, April 13, May 25, Oct. 8, and Oct. 15, 1862, governor's papers, 155, 157–158, NCDAH, Raleigh, N.C.

19. Thomas to Colonel James Love, April 27, 1863; Thomas to General Bainbridge, April 27, 1864; Colonel John B. Palmer to Thomas, March 11, 1864; WHT correspondence, PL, DU.

20. For the rolls of the Thomas Legion, see Crow, *Storm in the Mountains*, appendices.

21. Mooney, *Myths of the Cherokee*, p. 169.

22. James Mooney, *Historical Sketch of the Cherokee* (Chicago: Aldine Publishing and Smithsonian Institution Press, 1975), pp. 175–176.

23. Crow, *Storm in the Mountains*, p. 59.

24. W. W. Stringfield, "Sketches and Stories and Family Matters," W. W. Stringfield notebook, 109.1, NCDAH, Raleigh. See also Stringfield, "Sixty-Ninth Regiment," in Walter Clark, Ed., *Histories of the Several*

Regiments and Battalions from North Carolina in the Great War 1861–'65 Written by Members of the Respective Companies, (Goldsboro: Nash Brothers Book and Job Printers for The State of North Carolina, 1901), III, pp. 758–759. Stringfield insisted that the Cherokee "were loyal to us to the last" (p. 759). For studies of desertion, see Richard Bardolph, "Inconstant Rebels: Desertion of North Carolina Troops in the Civil War," *North Carolina Historical Review*, 41 (April 1964): 163–189; and the classic treatments of desertion: Ella Lonn, *Desertion During the Civil War* (New York: Century Company, 1928; reprint, Gloucester Mass.: Peter Smith, 1966); and Georgia Lee Tatum, *Disloyalty in the Confederacy* (Chapel Hill: University of North Carolina Press, 1934).

25. Thomas to Clark, Oct. 8, 1861.

26. Thomas to Clark, Oct. 17, 1861.

27. William Holland Thomas notebook, 1862–1865, WHT papers, NCDAH, Raleigh.

28. Thomas to Clark, March 14, 1862.

29. J. G. Martin to William Holland Thomas, April 15, 1862, records of the North Carolina Adjutant General's Office, letterbook, 1861–1862, pp. 606–607, NCDAH, Raleigh.

30. *OR*, Ser. I, 51:2, p. 304.

31. Zebulon Baird Vance, *The Papers of Zebulon Baird Vance*, Frontis W. Johnson, Ed. (Raleigh: North Carolina Department of Archives and History, 1963), I: 385–386.

32. Finger, *The Eastern Band of Cherokee*, p. 84; Crow, *Storm in the Mountains*, p. 4.

33. Mooney, *Myths of the Cherokee*, p. 170. For the close relationship between lacrosse and war in Cherokee culture, see Thomas Vennum, *American Indian Lacrosse: Little Brother of War* (Washington, D.C.: Smithsonian Institution, 1994), pp. 213–235; Raymond Fogelson, "The Cherokee Ball Game: A Study in Southeastern Ethnology," (Ph.D. dissertation, Philadelphia: University of Pennsylvania, 1962), pp. 16–18, 35, 127–137, 232–236.

34. Quoted in Jack Frederick and Anna Gritts Kilpatrick, Trans. and Ed., *The Shadow of Sequoyah: Social Documents of the Cherokees, 1862–1964* (Norman: University of Oklahoma Press, 1965), pp. 7–9.

35. Ibid., pp. 11–15.
36. R. A. Aiken, "Eightieth Regiment (Walker's Regiment of Thomas Legion)." In Walter Clark, Ed., *Histories of the Several Regiments and Battalions from North Carolina in the Great War 1861–'65 Written by Members of the Respective Companies* (Goldsboro: The State of North Carolina and Nash Brothers, Book and Job Printers, 1901), IV: 121, 123.
37. Ibid., pp. 126–127.
38. Finger, *The Eastern Band of Cherokees*, pp. 85–86.
39. Thomas to wife, June 25, 1862, WHT correspondence, PL, DU.
40. Godbold and Russell, *Confederate Colonel and Cherokee Chief*, p. 103; Finger, *The Eastern Band of Cherokees*, p. 86.
41. W.W. Stringfield, "Sixty-Ninth Regiment," p. 736.
42. Crow, *Storm in the Mountains*, p. 16; Finger, *The Eastern Band of Cherokees*, pp. 90–93. Even well after the war, Northern veterans wrote of alleged atrocities by the Cherokee. See the photographic plate reproduced in this book from Daniel Ellis, *Thrilling Adventures of Daniel Ellis, the Great Union Guide of East Tennessee* . . . (New York: Harper and Bros., 1867). See also Samuel W. Scott and Samuel P. Angel, *History of the Thirteenth Regiment Tennessee Volunteer Cavalry U.S.A.* (Philadelphia: P.W. Ziegler, 1903), p. 321.
43. Quoted in Finger, *The Eastern Band of Cherokees*, p. 93. See also Barrett, *The Civil War in North Carolina*, p. 197n; Crow, *Storm in the Mountains*, p. 16.
44. Finger, *The Eastern Band of Cherokees*, p. 93.
45. Crow, *Storm in the Mountains*, pp. 16–17.
46. Finger, *The Eastern Band of Cherokees*, p. 90; Stringfield, "Sixty-Ninth Regiment," pp. 733–736.
47. *OR*, Ser. I, 18, pp. 810–811.
48. *OR*, Ser.I, 31:1, p. 235; W. H. Parker to Thomas, April 17, 1864, WHT correspondence, PL, DU; Barrett, *The Civil War in North Carolina*, p. 199.
49. *OR*, Ser. I, 30:3, p. 501; Godbold and Russell, *Confederate Colonel and Cherokee Chief*, p. 117.
50. Charles H. Kirk, Ed. and Comp., *History of the Fifteenth Pennsylvania Volunteer Cavalry* (Philadelphia: Historical Committee of the Fifteenth

Pennsylvania Cavalry, 1906), pp. 346–347.

51. *OR*, Ser. I, 32:1, p. 137.

52. Ibid., pp. 137–138, 159; Ibid., Ser. I, 32: 2, p. 749. See also Finger, *The Eastern Band of Cherokees*, pp. 95–96.

53. Crow, *Storm in the Mountains*, p. 59.

54. Ibid., pp. 56, 59.

55. Ibid., p. 59; Godbold and Russell, *Confederate Colonel and Cherokee Chief*, p. 113.

56. Thomas to Bainbridge, April 27, 1864.

57. Thomas to A.T. Davidson, Jan. 22, 1864, WHT correspondence, PL, DU. For the Thomas-Vance confrontation, see Godbold and Russell, *Confederate Colonel and Cherokee Chief*, pp. 118–125.

58. Thomas to General [Jackson], July 8, 1864, WHT correspondence, PL, DU.

59. For the best analysis of Thomas's court-martial, see Godbold and Russell, *Confederate Colonel and Cherokee Chief*, pp. 121–126.

60. *OR*, Ser. I, 49:2, pp. 1005–1006, 1013. Crow, *Storm in the Mountains*, pp. 104–106; Barrett, *The Civil War in North Carolina*, pp. 233–237.

61. Finger, *The Eastern Band of Cherokees*, p. 97.

62. For the surrender at Waynesville, see *OR*, Ser. I, 49:2, pp. 754–755; William Cicero Allen, *The Annals of Haywood County, North Carolina* . . . (n.p., n.p., 1935), pp. 60–61, 84–85, 90–92; W.W. Stringfield, "Incidents of the Last Surrender," W. W. Stringfield Papers, Vol. I, PL, DU; Stringfield, "North Carolina Cherokee Indians," North Carolina booklet [DAR], 3 (June, 1903): 22; and Stringfield, "Sixty-Ninth Regiment," pp. 760–761.

63. Stringfield, "Sixty-Ninth Regiment," p. 761; and Stringfield's account in Allen, *The Annals of Haywood County*, p. 91.

64. Allen, *The Annals of Haywood County*, p. 61.

65. Godbold and Russell, *Confederate Colonel and Cherokee Chief*, pp. 128, 145, 181 n. 55.

66. Ibid., pp. 3–8. For the genre of captivity literature, see Kathryn Zabelle Derounian-Strodola and James Arthur Levernier, *The Indian Captivity Narrative, 1550–1900* (New York: Twayne Publishers, 1993); and James Axtell, "The White Indians of Colonial America," *William*

and Mary Quarterly 32 (1975): 55–88. Axtell indicated that children were more easily adopted into Indian communities to "maximize the chances of acculturating them to Indian life" (p. 61).

67. Finger, *The Eastern Band of Cherokees*, p. 62.

68. Crow, *Storm in the Mountains*, p. 141.

69. Finger, *The Eastern Band of Cherokees*, pp. 101–103.

70. North Carolina General Assembly, *Public Laws of the State of North Carolina Passed by the General Assembly at the Session of 1866* (Raleigh, N.C., 1866), p. 120.

71. 15 *U.S. Statutes* 228 (July 27, 1868).

72. For an excellent treatment of the problems the Cherokee faced and their efforts to protect themselves in the post-Civil War period, see Finger, *The Eastern Band of Cherokees*, pp. 106–178.

73. Godbold and Russell, *Confederate Colonel and Cherokee Chief*, pp. 132–150.

74. Finger, *The Eastern Band of Cherokees*, p. 171.

Chapter 7. Sharpshooters in the Army of the Potomac: The Ottawa

1. Company K, First Michigan Sharpshooters Muster Rolls, A.G.O., RG94, NA; and Michigan Adjutant General's Office, *Record of Service of Michigan Volunteers in the Civil War, 1861–1865, XLIV: Record First Michigan Sharpshooters First and Second U.S. Sharpshooters* (Kalamazoo, Mich.: Ihling Bros. & Everard, 1905), pp. 1–100. The author plotted birth and resident information found in these sources with maps and text compiled by Helen Tanner to determine tribal affiliation. See the monumental work by Tanner, *Atlas of Great Lakes Indian History* (Norman: University of Oklahoma Press, 1987).

2. Garrett A. Gravaraet compiled military service record, records of the AGO, RG94, NA; Mother's (Sophie Gravaraet) pension application, application #230334, certificate #177583, Civil War pension record of Garrett A. Gravaraet, NA.

3. For the U.S. Sharpshooters, see Roy M. Marcot, *Civil War Sharpshooter: Hiram Berdan, Military Commander and Firearms Inventor* (Irvine, Calif.: Northwood Heritage Press, 1989), pp. 31, 133–136, 354. See

also Rudolf Aschmann, *Memoirs of a Swiss Officer in the American Civil War* (Heinz K. Meier, Ed.) (Bern, Switzerland: Herbert Lang, 1972).

4. *ARCIA*, 1862, p. 344. For the best work on the Michigan Ottawa, see James M. McClurken, *Gah-Baeh-Jhagwah-Buk: The Way It Happened—A Visual Culture History of the Little Traverse Bay Bands of Odawa* (East Lansing: Michigan State University Museum, 1991); and Mc-Clurken's "We Wish to Be Civilized: Ottawa-American Political Contests on the Michigan Frontier." (Ph.D. dissertation, East Lansing: Michigan State University, 1988).

5. D. C. L. [probably D.C. Leach, Michigan Indian Agent], "Lieut. Garrett A. Gravaraet," obituary newsclipping from the *Advertiser and Tribune*, undated, Garrett A. Gravaraet CWPR, NA.

6. Charles E. Cleland, *Rites of Conquest: The History and Culture of Michigan's Native Americans* (Ann Arbor: University of Michigan Press, 1992), pp. 1–38, 35 n.; Jacqueline Peterson, "Many Roads to Red River: Métis Genesis in the Great Lakes Region, 1680–1815." In Jacqueline Peterson and Jennifer S. H. Brown, Eds., *The New Peoples: Being and Becoming Métis in North America*, (Lincoln: University of Nebraska Press in cooperation with the University of Manitoba Press, 1985), p. 67 n. 19.

7. Peterson, "Many Roads to Red River," p. 45; Cleland, *Rites of Conquest*, pp. 74–127; Joanna E. Feest and Christian F. Feest, "Ottawa." In Bruce G. Trigger, Ed., *Handbook of North American Indians*, XV: *Indians of the Northeast* (Washington, D.C.: Smithsonian Institution, 1978), pp. 772–774.

8. Cleland, *Rites of Conquest*, p. 103.

9. Tanner, *Atlas of Great Lakes Indian History*, p. 6 n.

10. James M. McClurken, "Augustin Hamlin, Jr.: Ottawa Identity and the Politics of Persistence." In James A. Clifton, Ed., *Being and Becoming Indian: Biographical Studies of North American Frontiers* (Chicago: Dorsey Press, 1989), p. 86.

11. Garrett A. Gravaraet to mother and sister, June 22, 1864, Garrett A. Gravaraet CWPR, NA.

12. For another portrait of an Ottawa cultural mediator in the same period, see McClurken, "Augustin Hamlin, Jr.," pp. 82–111.

13. Company K, First Michigan Sharpshooters Muster Rolls, Records of the AGO, RG94, NA.

14. Garrett A. Gravaraet to mother and sister, June 22, 1864, Garrett A. Gravaraet CWPR, NA.

15. *ARCIA*, 1862, p. 345; *ARCIA*, 1863/1864, pp. 447, 451; *ARCIA*, 1864/1865, pp. 452–453. Andrew J. Blackbird, *History of the Ottawa and Chippewa Indians of Michigan* (Ypsilanti, Mich.: Ypsilanti Job Printing House, 1887), p. 70. For the Copperheads, see James M. McPherson, *Battle Cry of Freedom: The Civil War Era* (New York: Oxford University Press, 1988), pp. 782–784.

16. McClurken, "We Wish to Be Civilized," pp. 55–70; Cleland, *Rites of Conquest*, pp. 134–136; Gregory Evans Dowd, *A Spirited Resistance*, pp. 32–45, 127–144; White, *The Middle Ground*, pp. 269–314, 486–492, 507–508.

17. McClurken, "We Wish to Be Civilized," pp. 83–84, 156–160; Cleland, *Rites of Conquest*, maps opposite pp. 148–149; Feest and Feest, "Ottawa," pp. 777–778.

18. For Ottawa in the removal era, see McClurken, "Ottawa Adaptive Strategies to Removal," *Michigan Historical Review* 12 (1986): 26–55. See also McClurken, "Strangers in Their Own Land," *Grand River Valley Review* 6 (1985), 2–25; and McClurken's "We Wish to Be Civilized," chapters 4–6. See also Cleland, *Rites of Conquest*, pp. 225–233.

19. For provisions of the Treaty of Washington (1836), see Kappler, Comp., *Indian Affairs: Laws and Treaties*, II: pp. 453–455.

20. McClurken, "August in Hamlin, Jr.," pp. 98–106.

21. McClurken, *Gah-Baeh-Jhagwah-Buk*, pp. 73–79.

22. Company K, First Michigan Sharpshooters, muster rolls, records of the AGO, RG94, NA.

23. Kappler, Comp., *Indian Affairs: Laws and Treaties*, II: 725–731.

24. McClurken, *Gah-Baeh-Jhagwah-Buk*, pp. 78–79. These complaints were also leveled by Ojibwa leaders. They petitioned that they "had not made adequate provisions for our own young men and women to have any land when they should be of age." They suggested that they take their payment of $18,800 in land "and so guard ourselves and our children from being scattered again." Chiefs and Headmen of the

Chippewa Indians of Saginaw, Swan Creek, and Black River to the President of the United States, Feb. 15, 1864, Records of the Mackinac Agency, 1862–1864, OIA, LR, M234, MR407, NA. The Ottawa appear to have had a similar concern: *ARCIA*, 1862/1863, p. 378.

25. L. M. Hartwick and W. H. Tuller, *Oceana County: Pioneers and Business-men of Today* (Pentwater, Mich.: Pentwater News Steam Print, 1890), pp. 45–46. For the interpreter's Civil War career, see Louis Genereau, Jr., compiled military service record, CW Records of the AGO, RG94, NA; invalid pension record, Louis Genereau, Jr., application #103,131, certificate #72,070, Louis Genereau, Jr., CWPR, NA.

26. Antoine Scott, Compiled Military Service Record, CW Records of the AGO, RG94, NA. In his file, Scott is described as a "civilized Indian." For Scott's heroism, see also Minnie D. Millbrook, "Indian Sharpshooters." In Minnie D. Millbrook, Comp., *Twice Told Tales of Michigan and Her Soldiers in the Civil War* (Ann Arbor: Michigan Civil War Centennial Observance Commission, 1966), p. 48. For more on Scott, see mother's [Elizabeth or We-qua-becomind] application #415,546, Antoine Scott, CWPR, NA.

27. John Robertson, Comp., *Michigan in the War*. Rev. ed. (Lansing: W. S. George and Co., 1882), pp. 543–544.

28. George Harry Weston diary, p. 36, Sept. 27, 1863. PL, DU.

29. Jeremiah Stuart to aunt, Jeremiah Stuart Papers, 1862–1865, PL, DU.

30. Constant C. Hanks to sister, July 24, 1864, Constant C. Hanks Papers, PL, DU.

31. Shelby Foote, *The Civil War: A Narrative* (New York: Random House), III: 154–188.

32. Ibid., III, pp. 189–235.

33. *OR*, Ser. I, 36: 1, pp. 972–974.

34. Henry G. Gravaraet Compiled Military Service Record, CW, Records of the AGO, RG94, NA; widow's [Sophie Gravaraet] pension record, Henry G. Gravaraet, found in Garrett A. Gravaraet's Civil War pension record, NA.

35. *OR*, Ser. I, 36:1, p. 974.

36. Quoted in Robertson, *Michigan in the War*, p. 545.

37. Foote, *The Civil War*, III: 280–316.

38. Ibid., III: 427–446.

39. Robertson, *Michigan in the War*, pp. 546–547.

40. Muster Rolls, Company K, First Michigan Sharpshooters, Records of the AGO, RG94, NA.

41. Garrett A. Gravaraet, Medical File, Company K, First Michigan Sharpshooters, Records of the AGO, RG94, NA; Garrett A. Gravaraet Compiled Military Service Record, CW, Records of the AGO, RG94, NA.

42. Ibid.

43. D. C. L., "Lieut. Garrett A. Gravaraet."

44. George W. Adams, *Doctors in Blue: The Medical History of the Union Army in the Civil War* (New York: Henry Schuman, 1955), pp. 104–105, 155; Gerald F. Linderman, *Embattled Courage: The Experience of Combat in the American Civil War* (New York: The Free Press), pp. 128–129; Paul E. Steiner, *Disease in the Civil War: Natural Biological Warfare in 1861–1865* (Springfield, Ill.: Charles C. Thomas, 1968), pp. 9–16.

45. William Williams Keen, "Military Surgery in 1861 and 1918," *Annals of the American Academy of Political and Social Science*, 80 (1918): 14–15.

46. Garrett A. Gravaraet to mother and sister, June 22, 1864, Garrett A. Gravaraet CWPR, NA.

47. Joseph Finch to Mrs. Gravaraet, July 26, 1864, Garrett A. Gravaraet CWPR, NA.

48. Richard Cooper to D. M. Best, July 25, 1864, Garrett A. Gravaraet, Compiled Military Service Record, CW, Records of the AGO, RG94, NA.

49. Hanks to sister, July 24, 1864.

50. Michael A. Cavanaugh and William Marvel, *The Petersburg Campaign: The Battle of the Crater "The Horrid Pit" June 25–August 6, 1864* (Lynchburg, Va.: H. E. Howard, 1989), pp. 51, 91, 95, 99.

51. Quoted in George S. Bernard, Comp., *War Talks of Confederate Veterans* (Petersburg, Va.: Fenn & Owen, 1892), p. 163. For a fine analysis of western Great Lakes religious practices, including attitudes toward and rituals of death, see Christopher Vecsey, *Traditional Ojibwa Religion and Its Historical Changes* (Philadelphia: American Philosophical Society, 1983).

52. Muster Rolls, Company K, First Michigan Sharpshooters, Records of the AGO, RG94, NA.

53. *ARCIA*, 1864/1865, pp. 452–453. Gravaraet's reputation and that of the sharpshooters are part of Michigan folklore and history. See Charles Moore, *History of Michigan* (Chicago: Lewis Publishing Co., 1915), pp. 431–432; and Philip P. Mason and Paul J. Pentecost, *From Bull Run to Appomattox: Michigan's Role in the Civil War* (Detroit: Wayne State University Press, 1961), pp. 19–20.

Chapter 8. Among the United States Colored Troops: The Pequot

1. The two other Indians in Civil War service from the Ledyard–North Stonington area were Amasa Lawrence and Noyes J. Hoxie (John Noyes Hoxie), both of the Twenty-ninth Connecticut Colored Volunteer Infantry. Hoxie served from August 8, 1864 to October 24, 1865. Amasa Lawrence (Mashantucket Pequot) enlisted August 9, 1864 and served until September 26, 1864. Lawrence was a substitute for John D. Brewster of Ledyard; however, because of his advanced age—he was at least fifty-five years of age and maybe as old as seventy-four—he was discharged at Petersburg, Virginia because he was unable to perform his duties as a soldier as well as for misrepresenting his age! Amasa Lawrence and Noyes J. Hoxie, Compiled Military Service Records, CW, Records of the AGO, RG94, NA. Lawrence is mentioned in Pequot petitions and overseers' reports from 1858 to 1878. Summary of Accounts with Pequots for one year ending April 1, 1878, RG6, Box 15, Conn. S.A., Hartford. See also Jack Campisi, "The Emergence of the Mashantucket Pequot Tribe, 1637–1975," in Laurence M. Hauptman and James Wherry, Eds., *The Pequot Indians in Southern New England: The Fall and Rise of an American Indian Nation*, (Norman: University of Oklahoma Press, 1990), p. 129. In a petition of 1858, Lawrence's age is given as sixty-six years. Both Lawrence and Hoxie are listed as Indians in Barbara W. Brown and James M. Rose, Comps., *Black Roots in Southeastern Connecticut, 1650–1900* (Detroit: Gale Research Company, 1980), pp. 189, 226. Despite its title, the Brown and Rose book also focuses on Native American genealogy.

2. The literature on the United States Colored Infantry is extensive. Joseph T. Glathaar, in his splendid book on these units, never mentions the presence of Native American troops. *Forged in Battle: The Civil War Alliance of Black Soldiers and White Officers* (New York: The Free Press, 1990). See also William A. Gladstone, *The United States Colored Troops, 1863–1867* (Gettysburg, Pa.: Thomas Publications, 1990).

3. Mashantucket Pequot overseer's reports, 1860–1873, Mashantucket Pequot legal papers, Mashantucket Pequot Ethnohistory Project, Mashantucket Pequot Reservation, Ledyard. Mohegan Indian Land Distribution, Report of Commissioners on Distribution of Lands of Mohegan Indians, July 2, 1861 (contains Mohegan tribal roll), Secretary of State Papers, RG6, Box 15, Conn. S.A.

4. Austin George, Recruits' Muster and Descriptive Roll, "Enlisted for the 29th [sic] Regt Conn Vols from the Third Cong./District of Conn.," Records of the CNG, Twenty-ninth, Thirtieth and Thirty-first Colored Volunteer Regiments, Box 6, RG13: 169A, Conn. S.A.

5. Surgeon's certificate in case of George Austin, application for increase, certificate no. 75324, July 30, 1889, Austin George's CWPR, NA.

6. Surgeon's certificate in the case of George Austin, application for increase, Sept. 16, 1891, Austin George's CWPR, NA.

7. This composite portrait is taken from Descriptive Muster Rolls, 31 U.S.C.T., Co. F, Records of the AGO, RG94, NA; Austin George, Recruits' Muster and Descriptive Roll, CNG, CW, "Colored Volunteer Regiments," RG13: 169A, Box 6, RG13, 169A, Conn. S.A. affidavit of Amasa Mcllain, March 1, 1888; declaration for original invalid pension, June 22, 1887, Austin George's CWPR, NA. George-Nedson marriage record, John H. Peckham witness, C. Newton Registrar, Aug. 1, 1851, legal papers, Mashantucket Pequot Ethnohistory Project, Mashantucket Pequot Reservation, Ledyard. Brown and Rose, *Black Roots in Southwestern Connecticut*, p. 189. Frances Caulkins states that in 1850 there were seven families totaling thirty persons living on the Mashantucket Pequot Reservation at Ledyard, including two families of Eastern Pequots; on the Pawcatuck Pequot Reservation at North Stonington there were fifteen to twenty residents. Caulkins claimed that the George family were "of mixed origin," suggesting to me that

they were Pequot Indians with some Mohegan ancestry. *History of New London County* (New London, Conn.: p.p., 1860), pp. 604–605. According to John W. De Forest, there were twenty-eight Mashantucket Pequots in 1848, "of whom twenty reside in Ledyard, while one is in New Haven, one with the Mohegans, two in Windham, and three are gone on whaling voyages." *History of the Indians of Connecticut: From the Earliest Known Period to 1850* (1851; reprint, Hamden, Conn.: Archon Books, Shoe String Press, 1964), pp. 144–145.

8. For analyses of the war, see Francis Jennings, *The Invasion of America: Indians, Colonialism and the Cant of Conquest* (Chapel Hill: University of North Carolina Press, 1975); Neal Salisbury, *Manitou and Providence: Indians, Europeans, and the Making of New England, 1500–1643* (New York: Oxford University Press, 1982); and Alden T. Vaughan, "Pequots and Puritans: The Causes of the War of 1637," *William and Mary Quarterly* 21 (April 1964): 256–269; and Vaughan's *New England Frontier, Puritans and Indians, 1620–1675* (Boston: Little, Brown & Co., 1965; rev. ed., New York: W. W. Norton, 1979). Vaughan has produced three major interpretations of the Pequot War, modifying, revising, and refining his conclusions each time. Recently, Alfred A. Cave has modified some of Jenning's conclusions. See his "The Pequot Invasion of Southern New England: A Reassessment of the Evidence," *New England Quarterly* 27 (March 1989): 27–44; and his "Who Killed John Stone? A Note on the Origins of the Pequot War," *William and Mary Quarterly* 44 (July 1992): 509–521. The four contemporary seventeenth-century accounts of the war written by Lion Gardiner, John Mason, John Underhill, and Philip Vincent are conveniently found together in Charles Orr, Ed., *History of the Pequot War* (Cleveland: Helman-Taylor Co., 1897).

9. James Kendall Hosmer, Ed., *Winthrop's Journal: "History of New England," 1630–1649* (New York: Charles Scribner's Sons, 1908), I: 222.

10. Kevin A. McBride, "The Historical Archaeology of the Mashantucket Pequots, 1637–1900: A Preliminary Analysis." In Hauptman and Wherry, Eds., *The Pequots of Southern New England*, p. 104.

11. Ibid., p. 97; Jack Campisi, "The Emergence of the Mashantucket Pequot Tribe," pp. 117–118; Salisbury, *Manitou and Providence*, pp.

222–224; Jennings, *Invasion of America*, pp. 220–227; Vaughan, *New England Frontier* (1979 ed.), pp. 144–152. For the enslavement of Pequots and dispersal to Bermuda, see Ethel Boissevain, "Whatever Became of the New England Indians Shipped to Bermuda to Be Sold as Slaves," *Man in the Northeast* 11 (Spring 1981): 103–114. Sherburne F. Cook in "Interracial Warfare and Population Decline Among the New England Indians," *Ethnohistory* 20 (Winter 1973): 6–9, insists that 180 Pequot prisoners were distributed as slaves to Indian and non-Indian alike. See also Carolyn T. Foreman, *Indians Abroad, 1493–1938* (Norman: University of Oklahoma Press, 1943), p. 29.

12. Alden T. Vaughan, Ed., *The Puritan Tradition in America, 1620–1730* (New York: Harper and Row, 1972), p. 66. For the Puritans' perception of the Indians, see the excellent article by William S. Simmons, "Cultural Bias in the New England Puritans' Perceptions of Indians," *William and Mary Quarterly*, 3rd ser., 38 (Jan. 1981): 56–72.

13. Cotton Mather, *Magnolia Christi Americana: or, The Ecclesiastic History of New England* (1702; reprint, New York: Russell and Russell, 1967), II: 558.

14. Laurence M. Hauptman, "The Pequot War and Its Legacies." In Hauptman and Wherry, Eds., *The Pequots in Southern New England*, pp. 69–90.

15. Connecticut Adjutant General's Office, Comp., *Record of Service of Connecticut Men in the Army and Navy of the United States During the War of the Rebellion* (Hartford, Conn.: Case, Lockwood and Brainard, 1889), pp. 882–891; *OR*, Ser. III, 4:1, p. 55. William Seraile, "The Struggle to Raise Black Regiments in New York State," *New-York Historical Society Quarterly*, 58 (July 1974): 215–233.

16. This statistical profile is based on an analysis of the descriptive muster rolls, 31st U.S.C.T., Co. F, Records of the AGO, RG94, NA.

17. Robert O. Decker, *The Whaling City: A History of New London* (Chester, Conn.: The Pequod Press, 1976), p. 121. New London's whaling fleet was second only to New Bedford's.

18. James P. Baughman, *The Mallorys of Mystic: Six Generations in American Maritime Enterprise* (Middletown, Conn.: Wesleyan University Press,

1972), pp. 100–120; John Niven, *Connecticut for the Union: The Role of the State in the Civil War* (New Haven, Conn.: Yale University Press, 1965), pp. 387–395.

19. Niven, *Connecticut for the Union*, pp. 349–406.

20. Brown and Rose, Comp., *Black Roots in Southeastern Connecticut*, p. 189.

21. Ledyard Town Meeting Records, 1862–1864, Conn. S.A.; W.A. Croffut and John M. Morris, *The Military and Civil History of Connecticut During the War of 1861–1865* . . . (New York: Ledyard Bill, 1868), p. 460. For the Civil War recruitment system and its abuses, see James W. Geary, *We Need Men: The Union Draft in the Civil War* (DeKalb: Northern Illinois Press, 1991); and three books by Eugene C. Murdock: *Ohio's Bounty System in the Civil War* (Columbus: Ohio State University Press, 1963); *One Million Men: The Civil War Draft in the North* (Madison: State Historical Society of Wisconsin, 1971); and *Patriotism Limited, 1862–1865: The Civil War Draft and the Bounty System* (Kent, Ohio: Kent State University Press, 1967).

22. Horatio T. Strother, *The Underground Railroad in Connecticut* (Middletown, Conn.: Wesleyan University Press, 1962), map opposite p. 118, pp. 128–132.

23. *OR*, Ser. III, 3:1, pp. 567–568.

24. Austin George, Compiled Military Service Record, CW, Records of the AGO, RG94, NA. Eight percent (10,000) of the sailors in the Union navy were African American. David L. Valuska, "The Negro in the Union Navy, 1861–1865" (Ph.D. dissertation, Lehigh, Pa.: Lehigh University, 1973). For a first-rate analysis of the U.S.C.T., see Glatthaar, *Forged in Battle*, pp. 169–200. For the raising of U.S.C.T. units, see *OR*, Ser. II, 5:1, pp. 654–662. The noted writer-historian John William De Forest, the author of *The History of Indians of Connecticut* (1851) and an officer in the Twelfth Connecticut Volunteer Infantry, considered applying for the "colonelcy" of a "colored regiment." He was convinced otherwise because of "the nature of the service that will be assigned" to these troops, namely their use "to garrison unhealthy positions," "for fatigue duty, such as making roads, building bridges and draining marshes; they will be seldom put into battle, and will afford small chance of distinction." *A Volunteer's Ad-*

ventures: A Union Captain's Record of the Civil War, James H. Croushore, Ed. (New Haven, Conn.: Yale University Press, 1946), pp. 50–51.

25. For the best secondary accounts on the siege at Petersburg, see Cavanaugh and Marvel, *The Petersburg Campaign: The Battle of the Crater*.

26. Quoted in Gerald F. Linderman, *Embattled Courage: The Experience of Combat in the American Civil War* (New York, 1987; New York: The Free Press Paperback, 1989), p. 140.

27. *Ibid.*, pp. 146–155; Stephen M. Weld, *War Diary and Letters of Stephen Minot Weld, 1861–1865*, 2nd ed. (Boston: Massachusetts Historical Society, 1979), p. 343.

28. Cavanaugh and Marvel, *The Petersburg Campaign: The Battle of the Crater*, pp. 4–20, 39–45. See Chapter 4 of this book.

29. For Burnside's role, see *OR*, Ser. I, 40:1, pp. 58–70, 128. See William Marvel, *Burnside* (Chapel Hill: University of North Carolina Press, 1991), pp. 390–418 for an excellent analysis of Burnside's role. For Meade, see his testimony: *OR*, Ser. I, 40:1, pp. 44–57. For Grant, see *Personal Memoirs of Ulysses S. Grant* (New York: Charles L. Webster and Co., 1886): I: 310–316; Horace Porter, *Campaigning with Grant* (New York: Century, 1897; paperback reprint, New York: Da Capo, 1986), pp. 258–270; Sylvanus Cadwalader, *Three Years with Grant* (New York: Alfred A. Knopf, 1956), pp. 242–245.

30. Cavanaugh and Marvel, *The Petersburg Campaign: The Battle of the Crater*, pp. 21, 23, 115–119. For the official War Department inquiry on the Battle of the Crater, see *OR*, Ser. I, 40:1. See also William H. Powell, "The Battle of the Petersburg Crater." In Clarence C. Buel and Robert U. Johnson, Eds., *Battles and Leaders of the Civil War* (New York: Century Co., 1888; reprint, New York: Thomas Yoseloff, 1956), IV: 545–560; Henry G. Thomas, "The Colored Troops at Petersburg," in Buel and Johnson, Eds., *Battles and Leaders of the Civil War*, IV: 563–567.

31. John Y. Simon, Ed., *The Papers of Ulysses S. Grant* (Carbondale: Southern Illinois University Press, 1991), XI: 361.

32. Cavanaugh and Marvel, *The Petersburg Campaign: The Battle of the Crater*, p. 41.

33. Houghton, "In the Crater," p. 562.

34. Cavanaugh and Marvel, *The Petersburg Campaign: The Battle of the Crater*, pp. 57, 85.

35. Thomas, "The Colored Troops at Petersburg," pp. 563–567.

36. *OR*, Ser. I, 40:1, p. 598.

37. *OR*, Ser. I, 40:1, p. 104.

38. Thomas, "The Colored Troops at Petersburg," p. 567.

39. Mitchell, *Civil War Soldiers*, p. 6. See also Bernard, *War Talks of Confederate Veterans*, pp. 159–160.

40. Governeur K. Warren to Major General Humphrey, July 31, 1864, Governeur K. Warren MSS, Letterbook, July 31–Aug. 16, 1864, NYSL, MD, Albany.

41. Noah Andre Trudeau, *The Last Citadel: Petersburg, Virginia, June 1864–April 1865* (Boston: Little Brown and Co., 1991), p. 125.

42. *OR*, Ser. I, 40:1, pp. 246–251; Muster Rolls, Regimental Books, F Company, 31st U.S.C.T., Records of the AGO, RG94, NA; Clinton Mountpleasant Compiled Military Service Record, Records of the AGO, RG94, NA. Connecticut Adjutant-General, *Record of Service of Connecticut Men in the Army and Navy*, p. 882. Dudley T. Cornish, *The Sable Army: Negro Troops in the Union Army 1861–1865* (New York: Longmans, Green & Co., 1956), pp. 273–278; Trudeau, *The Last Citadel*, p. 127. Report of George Greenman to General Horace Morse [Conn. adjutant general], Aug. 7, 1864, Reports of Operation [Battle of the Crater, July 30, 1864], Records of the Connecticut AGO, Box 63, RG13, Box 63, Conn. S.A.

43. Austin George [George Austin] Medical File, Thirty-first U.S.C.T., Records of the AGO, RG94, NA.

44. W. C. Williams affidavit, Aug. 14, 1866, Austin George's CWPR, NA.

45. Surgeon's certificate in case of Austin George, Aug. 14, 1866, Austin George's CWPR, NA.

46. Gilbert Billings, neighbor's affidavit, Dec. 14, 1887, Austin George's CWPR, NA.

47. Quoted in Linderman, *Embattled Courage*, p. 128.

48. Ibid., pp. 128–129.

49. Austin George [George Austin] Medical File, Thirty-first U.S.C.T., Records of the AGO, RG94, NA. George W. Adams, *Doctors in Blue*, pp. 104–105.

50. Austin George [George Austin] Medical File, Thirty-first U.S.C.T., Records of the AGO, RG94, NA.

51. Ibid.; declaration for the increase of an invalid pension application, July 18, 1888; application for increase of pension, surgeon's certificate, Sept. 16, 1891, Austin George's CWPR, NA.

52. Steiner, *Disease in the Civil War*, pp. 9–16.

53. Application for increase of pension, surgeon's certificate, Sept. 16, 1891, Austin George's CWPR, NA.

54. Austin George Compiled Military Service Record; Austin George [George Austin] medical files, Records of the AGO, RG94, NA. Lonn, *Desertion During the Civil War*, pp. 205, 234–235.

55. Austin George Compiled Military Service Record; Austin George [George Austin] medical files, records of the AGO, RG94, NA; W. C. Williams affidavit, Dec. 8, 1866; claim for invalid pension, June 22, 1865; increase invalid pension, Feb. 2, 1878 [summarizes pension history], Austin George's CWPR, NA. Trudeau, *The Last Citadel*, p. 126. Eric T. Dean, "|'We Will All Be Lost and Destroyed': Post-Traumatic Stress Disorder and the Civil War," *Civil War History*, 37 (June 1991): 138–151.

56. Muster Rolls of Company F, Thirty-first U.S.C.T., Aug. 31–Dec. 31, 1864; CNG, CW, Conn. "Colored Troops," Box 6, RG16: 169A, Conn. S.A.; Conn. Adjutant General's Office, Comp., *Record of Service of Connecticut Men in the Army and Navy*, p. 882.

57. Claim for invalid pension, June 22, 1865; increase invalid pension, Feb. 2, 1878; duplicate surgeon's certificate, Sept. 5, 1877; Examining surgeon report in the case of an applicant for increase of pension, Jan. 19, 1878; increase of invalid pension application, July 3, 1889; invalid pension, dropped from rolls, pensioner dead, Dec. 31, 1895, Austin George's CWPR, NA. Austin George's tombstone, Mashantucket Pequot Reservation.

58. Affidavit of Austin George, March 1, 1888, Austin George's CWPR, NA.

Chapter 9. Union Officers: Two Seneca Brothers from
New Bern to Appomattox

1. Hauptman, *The Iroquois in the Civil War*, chapters 1–3.
2. For an excellent biography of Ely S. Parker, see William H. Armstrong, *Warrior in Two Camps: Ely S. Parker, Union General and Seneca Chief* (Syracuse, N.Y.: Syracuse University Press, 1978).
3. Ibid., pp. 7–17. M. Stagers and Co. to Newton Parker, Jan. 8, 1857; Ely S. Parker to Caroline Parker, July 19, 1850; Newton Parker to Ely S. Parker, Dec. 16, 1850, June 31, 1851, Oct. 15, 30, 1852; Caroline Parker to Ely S. Parker, May 29, 1850, ESP MSS, APS.
4. Elisabeth Tooker, "On the Development of the Handsome Lake Religion," *Proceedings* of the American Philosophical Society 133 (March 1989): 44–45; Henry S. Manley, "Buying Buffalo from the Indian," *New York History* 28 (July 1947): 313–329; Armstrong, *Warrior in Two Camps*, pp. 10–35, 64–67; 77–78. Isaac Newton Parker to Sara Jemison Parker, Aug. 17, 1862. During the American Civil War, Iroquois leaders asked Washington officials to nominate Martindale to negotiate and resolve their Kansas claims. Peter Wilson, Maris Pierce, et al. to William P. Dole, April 28, 1864, Records of the New York Agency, OIA, LR, M234, MR590, RG75, NA. For Ely S. Parker's efforts to overturn the treaty of 1838, see Ely S. Parker and Isaac Shanks [Seneca delegates] to Commissioner of Indian Affairs William Medill, Jan. 20, 1848, OIA, LR, M234, MR587, RG75, NA. Kappler, Comp., *Indian Affairs: Laws and Treaties* II: 502–516.
5. Lewis Henry Morgan, *The League of the Ho-de-no-sau-nee, or Iroquois* (Rochester, NY, 1851; paperback reprint, New York: Corinth Books, 1962). Lewis Henry Morgan to Newton Parker, Dec. 19, 1849, Nov. 4, 1851; Caroline Parker to Ely S. Parker, July 5, 1853, ESP MSS, APS. Lewis Henry Morgan to General Benjamin Butler, Dec. 14, 1863, found in Compiled Military Service Record of Isaac Newton Parker, CW, Records of the AGO, RG94, NA. See also notes 44 and 45 and Thomas R. Trautmann, *Lewis Henry Morgan and the Invention of Kinship* (Berkeley: University of California Press, 1987), pp. 36–57.

6. Arthur C. Parker, *The Life of General Ely S. Parker, Last Grand Sachem of the Iroquois and General Grant's Military Secretary* (Buffalo, N.Y.: Publications of the Buffalo Historical Society no. 23, 1919), pp. 100, 189. For Newt Parker's escapades, also see Armstrong, *Warrior in Two Camps*, pp. 56–57, 139; Newton Parker to Caroline Parker, Aug. 7, 1853; Caroline Parker to Ely S. Parker, Feb. 15, 1855, April 5, 1859; Chauncey C. Jemison to Caroline Parker, Nov. 30, 1854; Theron Seymour to Ely S. Parker, Dec. 11, 1854, ESP MSS, APS.

7. See note 3.

8. Isaac Newton Parker enlistment papers, June 18, 1862; "of Description of Isaac Newton Parker, 'Third Sergeant of Co. D. 132nd Reg't N.Y.S.V.' from the Descriptive Roll Book of Co. D 132 Regiment N.Y. Vol. Infantry, P. J. Claassen, Col. Commanding . . ., Sept. 15, 1862," both found in INP MSS, BECHS.

9. Isaac Newton Parker to Sara Jemison, March 1, Nov. 1, 1860, Jan. 25, Sept. 3, 1861, INP MSS, BECHS; Caroline [Carrie] Parker to Sarah Jemison, April 7, 1855, March 20, 1858, INP MSS, BECHS.

10. Isaac Newton Parker to Sara Jemison, Nov. 28, 1859, Jan. 25, Oct. 17, 1860, Jan. 3, Feb. 6, 18, 26, March 1, 1861, INP MSS, BECHS. Please note that Newt Parker spelled his wife's first name with and without the letter "h."

11. Isaac Newton Parker to Sara Jemison, Jan. 31, Feb. 18, Oct. 17, 1860, Jan. 25, 31, Feb. 26, 1861; Isaac Newton Parker, April 29, June 13, Sept. 3, 1861; Sara Jemison to Isaac Newton Parker, Jan. 31, 1860, INP MSS, BECHS.

12. Isaac Newton Parker to Sara Jemison Parker, Feb. 26, March 1, Dec. 28, 1861, May 7, 1864, INP MSS, BECHS.

13. Descriptive muster rolls, regimental books, D Company, 132nd NYS Volunteer Infantry, records of the AGO, RG94, NA.

14. Isaac Newton Parker to Sara Jemison Parker, Oct. 9, 1861, INP MSS, BECHS. Hauptman, *The Iroquois and the Civil War*, Chapter 1; Armstrong, *Warrior in Two Camps*, pp. 80–83. It should be noted that both the "federal government and the State of New York initially displayed either indifference or hostility or both to the suggestion of using

black volunteers to fight the South." Seraile, "The Struggle to Raise Black Regiments in New York State," p. 215.

15. Hugh Hastings, Comp., "One Hundred and Thirty Second Regiment of Infantry," GAR Collection, Box 28, Folder 22, NYSL, MD, Albany. Hastings was the New York State Historian and compiled this regimental history based on the notes made by Colonel Claassen and Lieutenant Cusick. Hastings later published some of this material in *Second Annual Report* [of the New York State Historian] (Albany, 1897), Appendix F.

16. For official citations of Iroquois heroism, see *OR*, Ser. 1, 33:1, pp. 60–76; ser. 1, 40:1, p. 814. See also New York State Historian, *Second Annual Report*, Appendix F; and Peter J. Claassen to Whom It May Concern, Jan. 14, 1865, Cornelius C. Cusick's ACP Branch Document File 1888, Box 1168, Records of the AGO, RG94, NA.

17. Hauptman, *The Iroquois in the Civil War*, Chapter 3. For Cusick's own account of the 132nd New York State Volunteers, see his unpublished accounts of the fighting in North Carolina: "Operations of the Confederate Forces Under Major General George E. Pickett, Against New Berne, N.C. February 1–4, 1864. The 132nd N.Y. Interposes" and his "North Carolina[:] the fight near Kinston, N.C. The Rebels badly used up—Our troops march seventy-three miles in thirty-nine hours," Aug. 2, 1896, 132nd New York State Volunteer Infantry, GAR Collection, Box 28, Folder 22, NYSL. For the lobbying effort to secure Iroquois admission to military service, see C. [Chauncey] C. Jemison [Jamison] to Isaac Newton Parker, Aug. 5, 1862, NYSL. Isaac Newton Parker to Sara Jemison Parker, Nov. 12, 1861, INP MSS, BECHS. Ely S. Parker to William P. Dole [Commissioner of Indian Affairs], March 5, 1862, Dole to Parker, March 12, 1862, Records of the New York Agency, OIA, LR, M234, MR590, RG75, NA. Colonel John Fisk to Ely S. Parker, April 4, 1862, ESP MSS, APS. Cornelius C. Cusick to Abraham Lincoln, Jan. 23, 1865, [Cusick's] ACP Branch Document File 1888, Box 1168, Records of the AGO, RG94, NA.

18. Hauptman, *The Iroquois in the Civil War*, Chapter 3. Cornelius C. Cusick to Adjutant General U.S. Army, April 2, 1883, [Cusick's] ACP

Branch Document File, 1888, Box 1168, Records of the AGO, RG94, NA. New York State Historian, *Second Annual Report*, Appendix F. Cornelius C. Cusick, pension record, Lizzie B. Cusick's [wife's] pension application 800,281, certificate 587,550, CWPR, NA. Cusick died on January 3, 1904. Elias Johnson, *Legends, Traditions and Laws, of the Iroquois* or *Six Nations, and History of the Tuscarora Indians* (Lockport, N.Y.: Union Printing and Publishing Co., 1881), pp. 171–172; E. Roy Johnson, *The Tuscaroras: History—Traditions—Culture* (Murfreesboro, N.C.: Johnson Publishing Co., 1968), II, pp. 228–229; Barbara Graymont, Ed., *Fighting Tuscarora: The Autobiography of Chief Clinton Rickard* (Syracuse, N.Y.: Syracuse University Press, 1973). For the accusations against Cusick and Jemison, see the letter reprinted in this collection: C. C. Jemison to Isaac Newton Parker, Aug. 5, 1862, NYSL, MD.

19. Isaac Newton Parker to Sara Jemison Parker, Aug. 17, 1862, INP MSS, BECHS.

20. Gerald E. Wheeler and A. Stuart Pitt, "The 53rd New York: A Zoo-Zoo Tale," *New York History* 37 (Oct. 1956): 415–420. Descriptive Muster Roll, D Company, 132nd NYS Volunteer Infantry; Morning Reports, 1863–1865 (monthly summaries), D Company, 132nd NYS Volunteer Infantry, Records of the AGO, RG75, NA. Isaac Newton Parker to Sara Jemison Parker, Aug. 17, 1862, Dec. 24, 1862, INP MSS, BECHS.

21. Hastings, Comp., "One Hundred and Thirty Second Regiment of Infantry."

22. Ibid.; Isaac Newton Parker, Military Service Record, Records of the AGO, RG94, NA; Isaac Newton Parker to Sara Jemison Parker, Feb. 3, Dec. 27, 1863, INP MSS, BECHS; Isaac Newton Parker to Caroline Parker, June 26, 1864, ESP MSS, APS; Armstrong, *Warrior in Two Camps*, pp. 82, 104–105.

23. Isaac Newton Parker to Sara Jemison Parker, Aug. 17, 1862, Jan. 15, Feb. 3, 26, April 3, May 17, Oct. 5, 18, 1863; Isaac Newton Parker to Martha Hoyt Parker, Aug. 15, 1863, INP MSS, BECHS. After the war, the Indians in the company were falsely accused of scalping Confederates in 1864. Their white comrades-in-arms came to their defense: Dudley A. Beekman to Hugh Hastings, March 21, 1897; A.

Luersen to Hastings, May 23, 1897, GAR Collection, 132nd New York State Volunteer Infantry, Package 14, NYSL.

24. Isaac Newton Parker to Martha Hoyt Parker, April 1, 1864, ESP MSS, APS.

25. Hastings, Comp., One Hundred and Thirty Second Regiment of Infantry." Armstrong, *Warrior in Two Camps*, p. 104. Armstrong maintains that thirty-five soldiers were killed in the explosion of the torpedo mines.

26. Isaac Newton Parker to Sara Jemison Parker, Dec. 1, 1862, Jan. 15, 1863, undated letter, early 1863, Feb. 3, 20, 26, April 3, May 17, Oct. 5, 18, Nov. 4, Dec. 27, 1863; Jan. 3, 1864, INP MSS, BECHS. For the details of the bounty controversy of 1863 and 1864 which involved underage and other Iroquois recruits, see Hauptman, *The Iroquois and the Civil War*, Chapter 8.

27. Isaac Newton Parker to Sara Jemison Parker, Oct. 18, 1863, INP MSS, BECHS.

28. Lewis Henry Morgan to General Benjamin Butler, Dec. 14, 1863.

29. Barrett, *The Civil War in North Carolina*, pp. 203–212.

30. Ibid.

31. Ibid. The battle can be traced in *OR*, Ser. I, 33:1, pp. 60–76.

32. *OR*, ser. I, 33:1, p. 62.

33. Ibid. p. 76.

34. R. Emmett Fiske to Whom It May Concern, Jan. 13, 1865, [Cusick's] ACP branch document, File 1888, Box 1168, records of the AGO, RG94, NA.

35. Isaac Newton Parker map of Union Forces at New Bern and notes of Battle of Batchelder's Creek, Feb. 1, 1864 and other notes, May 10, 1864, ESP MSS, APS. Descriptive muster roll, regimental books, D Company, 132nd NYS Volunteer Infantry, records of the AGO, RG75, NA; pension record of William Kennedy, certificate #308,776, application #519187, "Widow Kennedy, mother of William Kennedy," CWPR, NA.

36. *OR*, Ser. I, 40:1, pp. 814–816.

37. New York State Historian, *Second Annual Report*, Appendix F; Peter J. Claassen to Whom It May Concern, Jan. 14, 1865, [Cusick's]

ACP Branch Document File 1888, Box 1168, Records of the AGO, RG94, NA.

38. Isaac Newton Parker to Asher Wright, April 1, 1865, Foster John Hudson pension records, mother's application (Louisa Johnnyjohn Hudson), CWPR, NA. Asher Wright served the Seneca from 1831 to 1875 and was a major force in education, religious life, and social welfare of the Indians in western New York. For Wright's missionary work among the Seneca, see Thomas S. Abler, "Protestant Missionaries and Native Cultures: Parallel Careers of Asher Wright and Silas T. Rand," *American Indian Quarterly* 16 (Winter 1992): 25–38; and William N. Fenton, "Toward the Gradual Civilization of the Indian Natives: The Missionary and Linguistic Work of Asher Wright (1803–1875) Among the Senecas of Western New York," *Proceedings of the American Philosophical Society* 100 (Dec. 1956): 567–581.

39. See note 13.

40. Quoted in Simon, Ed., *The Papers of Ulysses S. Grant*, XVII: 408.

41. Ibid., pp. 407–408.

42. Armstrong, *Warrior in Two Camps*, p. 139; H. Craig Miner, *The Corporation and the Indian: Tribal Sovereignty and Industrial Civilization in Indian Territory* (Columbia: University of Missouri Press, 1976), pp. 27–28; Foreman, *The Last Trek of the Indians*, p. 339 n. 50; Parker, *The Life of General Ely S. Parker*, p. 189. There is an undated newsclipping in the Lewis Henry Morgan MSS at the University of Rochester Library which mentions the offer of a military commission to Parker at the end of the Civil War.

43. Parker, *The Life of Ely S. Parker*, p. 191.

44. The two best studies of Ely S. Parker are Armstrong, *Warrior in Two Camps*; and Parker, *The Life of General S. Parker*. See also Elisabeth Tooker, "Ely S. Parker: Seneca, ca. 1828–1895." In Margot Liberty, Ed., *American Indian Intellectuals*, (St. Paul, Minn.: West Publishing Co., 1978), pp. 15–30; Henry G. Waltmann, "Ely Samuel Parker (1869–1871)." In Robert Kvasnicka and Herman Viola, Eds., *The Commissioners of Indian Affairs, 1824–1877*, (Lincoln, Neb., 1979), pp. 123–134; and William S. McFeeley, *Grant: A Biography* (New York, W.

W. Norton, 1981; New York: W. W. Norton paperback edition, 1982), pp. 88, 146, 160, 286, 305–318.

45. Armstrong, *Warrior in Two Camps*, pp. 84–107.

46. Ibid., p. 87.

47. For the Battle of Chattanooga, see James Lee McDonough, *Chattanooga: A Death Grip on the Confederacy* (Knoxville: University of Tennessee Press, 1984).

48. Ely S. Parker to Nicholson Parker, Nov. 18, 1863, Ely S. Parker MSS, APS, Philadelphia.

49. Ibid.

50. Ibid.

51. Ely S. Parker to Caroline Parker Mountpleasant, Nov. 21, 1863, Ely S. Parker MSS, APS.

52. Ibid.

53. The sixteenth century Creek town of Chiaha was "on an island near present day Chattanooga." Ronald N. Satz, *Tennessee's Indian Peoples: From White Contact to Removal, 1540–1840* (Knoxville: University of Tennessee Press, 1979), p. 8. Despite writings to the contrary, the word "Chattanooga" is not of Cherokee language origin. Floyd Lounsbury to Laurence M. Hauptman, June 18, 1991, letter in author's possession. Dr. Lounsbury, Professor Emeritus of Anthropology at Yale University, is the foremost linguist of the Iroquoian languages which includes Cherokee. For John Ross and Cherokee presence in late eighteenth and early nineteenth century Chattanooga, see Moulton, *John Ross: Cherokee Chief*, pp. 5–6, 99.

54. Ely S. Parker to Caroline Parker Mountpleasant, Nov. 21. 1863.

55. Ely S. Parker to Caroline Parker Mountpleasant, Dec. 2, 1863, ESP MSS, APS.

56. Ibid.

57. Ely S. Parker to Nicholson Parker, Jan. 25, 1864, ESP MSS, APS.

58. Quoted in Armstrong, *Warrior in Two Camps*, p. 91.

59. Horace Porter, "The Surrender at Appomattox Court House." In Robert U. Johnson and Clarence C. Buel, Eds., *Battles and Leaders of the Civil War* (New York: Century Co., 1882; reprint, New York:

Thomas Yoseloff, 1956), p. 740. For Parker's role at Appomattox, see also "General Ely S. Parker's Narrative" [of General Lee's Surrender at Appomattox], Ulysses S. Grant MSS, Series 8, Box 2, LC; Cadwalader, *Three Years with Grant*, p. 323; Porter, *Campaigning with Grant*, pp. 33–34, 200, 207–208, 476–481; and Simon, *The Papers of Ulysses S. Grant*, 14: 361, 374–378.

60. Porter, "The Surrender at Appomattox Court House," p. 741.

61. Armstrong, *Warrior in Two Camps*, pp. 137–145.

62. Waltmann, "Ely Samuel Parker," pp. 127–131.

63. U.S. Congress, House of Representatives, House Report No. 39: *Investigation into Indian Affairs*, 39th Cong., 3d sess., pp. i–vii, 32–33.

64. Waltmann, "Ely Samuel Parker," p. 131. See also Armstrong, *Warrior in Two Camps*, pp. 162–194.

Chapter 10. Endeavor to Persevere

1. Joseph Stockton Diary quoted in Richard Wheeler, *The Siege of Vicksburg* (1978 paperback reprint; New York: Harper Perennial, 1991), p. 202.

2. James C. Fitzpatrick, "The Ninth Corps," *New York Herald*, June 30, 1861, p. 1; "Chief Silverheels' Capture," *Warren [Pa.] Mail*, Aug. 23, 1887, p. 1.

3. Martha Royce Blaine, *The Ioway Indians* (Norman: University of Oklahoma Press, 1979), pp. 251–253.

4. Elisha Stockwell, Jr., *Private Elisha Stockwell, Jr., Sees the Civil War*, Byron R. Abernethy, Ed. (Norman: University of Oklahoma Press, 1958), pp. 32–33, 74–75, 79–80, 88–89.

5. James K. Newton, *A Wisconsin Boy in Dixie: The Selected Letters of James K. Newton*, Stephen E. Ambrose, Ed. (Madison: University of Wisconsin Press, 1961), pp. 138–139.

6. Arthur C. Parker, *Parker on the Iroquois*, William N. Fenton, Ed. (Syracuse, N.Y.: Syracuse University Press, 1968), pp. 73–74; recipe of Amelia Williams (Tuscarora) in Marlene Johnson, Comp., *Iroquois Cookbook*, 2nd ed. (Tonawanda Indian Reservation: Peter Doctor Memorial Indian Fellowship Foundation, 1989), p. 8.

7. Letter from unknown officer [probably medical officer], Ninth Pa. Cavalry to wife, March 13, 1863, LC.

8. *OR*, Ser. I, 34:1, pp. 841–844.

9. Arrell M. Gibson, *The Chickasaws* (Norman: University of Oklahoma Press, 1971), pp. 259–271.

10. See Chapter 5. At least one of "the federal dead was indeed scalped" at Pea Ridge. Gaines, *The Confederate Cherokees*, p. 90. See also *OR*, Ser. I, 7, pp. 194–195, 206.

11. Journal of Major John Chester White, Oct. 8, 1863, LC.

12. Lucas, *Sherman and the Burning of Columbia*, pp. 115–116.

13. Hauptman, *The Iroquois in the Civil War*, pp. 129–144; Eric T. Dean, "| 'We Will All Be Lost and Destroyed'," pp. 138–151; Phillip S. Paludan, *'A People's Contest': The Union and Civil War, 1861–1865* (New York: Harper and Row, 1988), pp. 316–338.

14. United States Constitution, Amendment XIV, Section 2.

15. "The Great Expense of Keeping the Indian Quiet," *New York Times*, March 9, 1882, p. 1.

16. *Elk v. Wilkins*, 112 U.S. 98 (1884).

17. *Ex Parte Crow Dog*, 109 U.S. 556 (1883).

18. 23 Stat. 362 (1885).

19. *United States v. Kagama*, 118 U.S. 375 (1886).

20. *Lonewolf v. Hitchcock*, 187 U.S. 535 (1903).

21. Ibid.

22. 24 Stat. 388 (1887).

23. See D.S. Otis, *The Dawes Act and the Allotment of Indian Lands*, Francis P. Prucha, Ed. (Norman: University of Oklahoma Press, 1973). For the impact on one Indian nation, the Wisconsin Oneida, see Laurence M. Hauptman, *The Iroquois and the New Deal* (Syracuse, N.Y.: Syracuse University Press, 1981), pp. 70–77.

Bibliography

ARCHIVES/MANUSCRIPT COLLECTIONS

American Philosophical Society, Philadelphia

1. William N. Fenton MSS.
2. Ely S. Parker MSS.
3. Frank Speck MSS.

Buffalo and Erie County Historical Society, Buffalo, N.Y.

1. Arthur C. Parker MSS.
2. Ely S. Parker MSS.
3. Isaac Newton Parker MSS.
4. Maris B. Pierce MSS.
5. Peter B. Porter MSS.
6. Miscellaneous scrapbook dealing with Indians and slavery, 1859–1870.
7. Wilkeson Family MSS (Letters Concerning Indian Volunteers).

Buffalo Civil War Roundtable, Buffalo, N.Y.

List of Iroquois Soldiers in the Civil War.

Connecticut State Archives, Hartford

1. Ledyard town meeting records.
2. Mohegan Land Distribution. Report of Commissioners on Distribution of Lands of Mohegan Indians, July 2, 1861. RG 6.
3. Mohegan and Pequot Overseer's Reports, 1858–1884.
4. Records of the Connecticut Adjutant General's Office. RG 13:169A.
   a. Records of the Connecticut National Guard, 29th, 30th, and 31st Colored Volunteer Regiments, Civil War [6 boxes of descriptive muster rolls and correspondence].
   b. Reports of Operations [Battle of the Crater, July 30, 1864], Aug. 7, 1864.

Duke University, Durham, N.C.

1. Journal of Matthew P. Andrews [Charles Wesley Andrews] MSS.
2. Diaries of Washington Sandford Chaffin.
3. Confederate States of America Archives.
4. Jefferson Davis MSS.
5. Alfred Burton Greenwood MSS.
6. Constant C. Hanks MSS.
7. William Williams Stringfield MSS.
8. Jeremiah Stuart MSS.
9. William Holland Thomas MSS.
10. George Harry Weston MSS.

Haverford College, Quaker Collection, Haverford, Pa.

1. Records of the Philadelphia Yearly Meeting of Friends, Indian Committee.
2. Records of the Baltimore Yearly Meeting. Special Committee on Indian Concerns.

Hauptman, Laurence M.

1. Mashantucket Pequot fieldnotes, 1982–1994.
2. Seneca fieldnotes, 1971–1994.

Library of Congress, Manuscript Division, Washington, D.C.

1. Battle of Thompson's Station, Tenn., March 13, 1863, MSS. [author unknown].
2. George Ewing and Ewing Family MSS.
3. Ulysses S. Grant MSS.
4. Andrew Johnson MSS.
5. Abraham Lincoln MSS.
6. Patrick Ryan diary.
7. Theodore Edgar Saint John MSS.
8. James Wadsworth (and Wadsworth Family) MSS.
9. John Chester White journal.

Mashantucket Pequot Tribe of Connecticut, Ledyard, Conn. Legal Papers

1. Overseers' reports, 1860–1873 [Mashantucket Pequot Ethnohistory Project].
2. Austin George–Sabrina Nedson marriage record, April 1, 1851.

Mountpleasant, Edison, Tuscarora Reservation, Lewiston, N.Y.

List of Tuscarora Soldiers in the Civil War.

National Archives, Washington, D.C.

I. RG29. Records of the Bureau of the Census M704 Population Schedules of the Eight Census, 1860.
II. U.S. Department of the Interior. Records of the Bureau of Indian Affairs. RG75. Correspondence of the Office of Indian Affairs (Central Office) and related records: Letters received, 1824–1881, M234.
  A. California Superintendency, 1849–1880.
  B. Central Superintendency, 1857–1867.
  C. Choctaw Agency, 1860–1866.
  D. Delaware Agency, 1855–1873.
  E. Green Bay Agency, 1838–1867.
  F. Mackinac Agency, 1853–1866.
  G. Neosho Agency, 1831–1867.

    H. New York Agency, 1829–1880.

    I. Seneca Agency in N.Y., 1824–1832.

    J. Six Nations Agency, 1824–1834.

    K. Southern Superintendency, 1857–1865.

    L. Wichita Agency, 1857–1866.

III. Records of the U.S. Department of War.

    A. Records of Volunteer Soldiers Who Served During the Mexican War: RG94. Black Beaver's Indian Spy Company.

    B. Records of Volunteer Soldiers Who Served During the Civil War: RG 94.

       1. Appointment, Commissions, and Personnel Branch.

       2. Compiled military service records.

       3. Medical/Hospital records.

       4. Regimental books.

          a. Clothing books.

          b. Morning reports.

          c. Order books.

          d. Letter books.

          e. Regimental description books [Muster Rolls].

The following units were researched at the National Archives:

       1. Union Units: Kansas.

          a. First Kansas Indian Home Guard.

          b. Second Kansas Indian Home Guard.

          c. Third Kansas Indian Home Guard.

          d. Fourth Kansas Indian Home Guard.

          e. Sixth Kansas Cavalry.

          f. Fourteenth Kansas Cavalry.

       2. Union Unit: Michigan.

First Michigan Sharpshooters.

       3. Union Units: New York.

          a. First New York Light Artillery.

          b. Thirteenth New York Heavy Artillery.

          c. Fourteenth New York Heavy Artillery.

      d. Twelfth New York Cavalry.

      e. Twenty-fourth New York Cavalry.

      f. Eighty-sixth New York Volunteer Infantry.

      g. Ninety-eighth New York Volunteer Infantry.

      h. 132nd New York Volunteer Infantry.

      i. 154th New York Volunteer Infantry.

    4. Union Unit: Pennsylvania.

Fifty-seventh Pennsylvania Volunteer Infantry.

    5. Union Unit: Wisconsin.

Fourteenth Wisconsin Volunteer Infantry.

    6. Union Units: United States Colored Troops.

      a. 23rd U.S.C.T.

      b. 31st U.S.C.T.

C. Records relating to service in the regular U.S. military.

    1. Records relating to service in the U.S. Army: RG94, 391, 407.

    2. Records relating to service in the U.S. Navy and U.S. Marine Corps: RG24, 125, 127.

      a. Log books and muster rolls.

        (1) U.S. *Huron*

        (2) U.S. *Onondaga*

        (3) U.S. *Rhode Island*

        (4) U.S. *Schockon*

        (5) U.S. *Daylight* (chartered steamer)

        (6) U.S. *Epsilon* (picket tugboat)

        (7) U.S. *Spuyten Duyvil* (torpedo boat)

D. Records of movements and activities of volunteer union activities: RG94, RG407.

E. Records of Confederate soldiers who served during the Civil War: RG109.

F. Records of Confederate movements and activities: RG109.

The following units were researched at the National Archives:

    1. Confederate Units: Indian Territory.

      a. First Indian Confederate Mounted Rifles.

      b. Second Indian Confederate Mounted Rifles.

2. Confederate Unit: Mississippi.

First Mississippi Choctaw Cavalry Battalion.

3. Confederate Unit: North Carolina.

Thomas Legion.

4. Confederate Units: South Carolina.
   a. Fifth South Carolina Volunteer Infantry.
   b. Twelfth South Carolina Volunteer Infantry.
   c. Seventeenth South Carolina Volunteer Infantry.

G. Veterans' Claims.
   1. Mexican War pension records.
   2. Civil War pension records.

H. Other National Archives Records Series.
   1. Records of the Quartermaster General: RG92.
   2. Records of the U.S. Army Continental Command,: RG393.
   3. Records of the War Department relating to Confederate prisoners of war.
   4. Records of Indian Scouts.

Newberry Library. D'Arcy McNickle Center for the History of the American Indian, Chicago

Iroquois Indians: A Documentary History of the Six Nations and Their League: Francis Jennings et al., Eds. 50 microfilm reels.

New York State Archives, Albany

A. War of 1812 pension record applications.
B. Civil War records:
   1. Abstracts of Civil War muster rolls of New York units.
      a. First New York Light Artillery.
      b. Thirteenth New York Heavy Artillery.
      c. Fourteenth New York Heavy Artillery.
      d. Twelfth New York Cavalry.
      e. Twenty-fourth New York Cavalry.
      f. Eighty-sixth New York Volunteer Infantry.
      g. Ninety-eighth New York Volunteer Infantry.

    h. 132nd New York Volunteer Infantry.

    i. 154th New York Volunteer Infantry.

2. Correspondence and petition files of Adjutant General's Office, 1862–1866.

3. Register of letters received by the Adjutant General's Office, 1862–1866.

4. Town Clerks' registers of officers, soldiers, and seamen.

New York State Library, Manuscript Division, Albany

1. William M. Beauchamp MSS.

2. Bliss Family MSS.

3. Grand Army of the Republic Collection.

4. Franklin B. Hough MSS.

5. Indian census (Schoolcraft) of 1845.

6. Arthur C. Parker MSS.

7. Governeur Warren MSS.

8. John Wool MSS.

New York Yearly Meeting of Friends, Haviland Record Room, New York City

Records of the New York Yearly Meeting of Friends, Joint Indian Committee, 1835–1863.

North Carolina Division of Archives and History, Raleigh

1. Henry Berry Lowry Collection.

    a. North Carolina Adjutant General's Office report [by John C. Gorman], 1871–1876.

    b. North Carolina superior court records, Robeson County, 1862–1865.

2. North Carolina. Adjutant General's Office. Letter book, 1861–1862.

3. North Carolina governors' papers: Henry T. Clark, 1861–1862.

4. William Williams Stringfield Collection.

5. William Holland Thomas notebook, 1861–1862.

Oklahoma Historical Society, Oklahoma City

1. Grant Foreman papers (WPA), Indian–pioneer history.
2. Quapaw agency records.

Oneida Nation of Indians of Wisconsin

1. MSS in Oneida Indian Museum.
   a. List: "The Following Are Civil War Veterans Who Never Came Back to Oneida, Wisconsin."
   b. Jan Malcolm, "Pentagon Report" [on Oneida war veterans].
2. Oneida Language Department.
The Oneida Language and Folklore Project Stories (WPA), 1938–1941.

Onondaga Historical Association, Syracuse, N.Y.

1. Sanford Thayer file.
2. Newsclipping files relative to Onondaga Indians:
   a. Samuel George.
   b. Civil War.
   c. Aunt Dinah John.

Pennsylvania Historical and Museum Commission

1. Merle Deardorff MSS.
2. Department of Military Affairs: Muster rolls and related records of the fifty-seventh Pennsylvania Volunteer Infantry: RG19.

Rochester Museum and Science Center, Rochester, N.Y.

William Jones diary.

Seneca-Iroquois National Museum, Salamanca, N.Y.

Civil War Collection: Letters of Seneca soldiers.

Smithsonian Institution, National Anthropological Archives, Washington, D.C.

1. Albert Gatschet MSS.
2. J. N. B. Hewitt MSS.

3. James Mooney MSS.
4. James W. Terrell MSS.
5. Erminie Wheeler-Voegelin MSS: "The 19th and 20th Century Ethnohistory of Various Groups of Cayuga Indians."

South Carolina Department of Archives and History, Columbia, S.C.

Report of J. R. Patton, Catawba Indian Agent, Oct. 1, 1864. General Assembly of South Carolina—Miscellaneous Communications, 1864, no. 10.

State Historical Society of Wisconsin, Madison

1. Powless, Joseph and John Archiquette diary. Trans. by Oscar Archiquette.
2. Wisconsin Adjutant General, descriptive muster rolls for fourteenth Wisconsin Volunteer Infantry. 2 microfilm reels.

Swarthmore College, Friends Historical Library, Swarthmore, Pa.

1. Elkinton family MSS.
2. Journals of Ebenezer Worth, Sr., 1843–1875.
3. Records of the Baltimore Yearly Meeting, Standing Committee on the Indian Concern.
4. Records of the Philadelphia Yearly Meeting, Indian Committee.

University of Rochester, Rush Rhees Library, Rochester, N.Y.

1. Lewis Henry Morgan MSS.
2. Arthur C. Parker MSS.
3. Ely S. Parker MSS.
4. William Seward MSS.
5. James Wadsworth MSS.

University of South Carolina, South Caroliniana Library

W. K. Bachman Papers.

Western Carolina University, Cullowhee, N.C.

James W. Terrell MSS.

York County Public Library, Rock Hill, S.C.

1. Douglas Summers Brown Collection of Catawba Indian History.
2. Newspaper clippings files.

GOVERNMENT PUBLICATIONS

Adams, Richard C. *A Brief History of the Delaware Indians*. In U.S. Congress, Senate Document No. 501, 59th Cong., 1st sess. Washington, D.C.: U.S. Government Printing Office, 1906.

American State Papers. 38 vols. Washington, D.C.: U.S. Government Printing Office, 1832–1861.

Clark, Walter, Ed. *Histories of the Several Regiments and Battalions from North Carolina in the Great War 1861–'65*. Vols. III and IV. Goldsboro: Nash Bros. Book and Job Printers for the State of North Carolina, 1901.

Cohen, Felix S. *Handbook of Federal Indian Law*. Washington, D.C.: U.S. Government Printing Office, 1942; reprint, Albuquerque: University of New Mexico Press, 1971.

Congressional Globe, 1848–1873.

Connecticut Adjutant General's Office, Comp. *Record of Service of Connecticut Men in the Army and Navy in the Army and Navy of the United States During the War of the Rebellion*. Hartford, Conn.: Case, Lockwood and Brainard, 1889.

Donaldson, Thomas, Comp. *Extra Census Bulletin. The Six Nations of New York*. Prepared for the Eleventh Census, 1890. Washington, D.C.: U.S. Government Printing Office, 1894.

Heizer, Robert F., Ed. *Handbook of North American Indians*. Vol. VIII: *California*. Washington, D.C.: Smithsonian Institution, 1978.

Kappler, Charles J., Comp. *Indian Affairs: Laws and Treaties*. 5 vols. Washington, D.C.: U.S. Government Printing Office, 1903–1941.

Michigan Adjutant General's Office. *Record of Service of Michigan Volunteers in the Civil War, 1861–1865*. Vol. XLIV: *Record of First Michigan Sharp-*

shooters *First and Second U.S. Sharpshooters*. Kalamazoo, Mich.: Ihling Bros. and Everard, 1905.

Mooney, James. *Sacred Formulas of the Cherokee. 7th Annual Report of the Bureau of American Ethnology*. Washington, D.C.: American Bureau of Ethnology, Smithsonian Institution, 1891.

————. *The Siouan Tribes of the East*. Bureau of American Ethnology, Smithsonian Institution. Washington, D.C.: U.S. Government Printing Office, 1894.

————. *Myths of the Cherokee. 19th Annual Report of the Bureau of American Ethnology*, Part I. Washington, D.C.: Bureau of American Ethnology, Smithsonian Institution, Washington, D.C.: U.S. Government Printing Office, 1900.

Moore, John W., Ed. *Roster of North Carolina Troops in the War Between the States*. 4 vols. Raleigh, N.C.: Ashe and Gatling, State Printers, 1882.

New York State. *Census of the State of New York for 1855*. Compiled by Franklin B. Hough. Albany: Charles Van Benthuysen, 1857.

————. *Census of the State of New York for 1865*. Compiled by Franklin B. Hough. Albany: Charles Van Benthuysen and Son, 1867.

————. *Census of the State of New York for 1875*. Compiled by C. W. Seaton. Albany: Weed, Parsons and Co., 1877.

New York State Historian (Hugh Hastings). *2nd Annual Report*. Albany, 1897.

Phisterer, Frederick, Comp. *New York in the War of the Rebellion, 1861 to 1865*, 3rd ed. 6 vols. Albany: J. B. Lyon Co. State Printers, 1912.

Richardson, James D., Ed. *A Compilation of the Messages and Papers of the Presidents, 1789–1897*. Volume II. Washington, D.C.: U.S. Government Printing Office, 1900.

Robertson, John [Michigan Adjutant General's Office], Comp. *Michigan in the War*, rev. ed. Lansing, Mich.: W. S. George, 1882.

Royce, Charles C. *The Cherokee Nation of Indians*. Washington, D.C.: U.S. Government Printing Office, 1887; reprint, Chicago: Aldine Publishers, 1965.

Town of Brant. *Records of Soldiers and Officers in the Military Service*. Brant, N.Y., 1865.

Trigger, Bruce G., Ed. *Handbook of North American Indians*. Vol. 15: *Northeast*. Washington, D.C.: Smithsonian Institution, 1978.

U.S. Bureau of the Census. *Population of the United States in 1860: Eighth Census.* Washington, D.C.: U.S. Government Printing Office, 1864.

—————. *Ninth Census: The Statistics of the Population of the United States.* Washington, D.C.: U.S. Government Printing Office, 1872.

U.S. Congress. House of Representatives. Executive Document No. 76: *Message from the President of the United States Transmitting Report in Regard to Indian Affairs on the Pacific.* Dec. 1, 1856–March 3, 1857. 34th Cong., 3rd sess. Congressional Serial Set 906, IX.

U.S. Congress. Senate. Executive Document No. 46: *Report to the Secretary of the Interior, Communicating, in Compliance with a Resolution of the Senate, The Correspondence Between the Indian Office and the Present Superintendents and Agents in California, and J. Ross Browne, Esq.* 36th Cong., 1st sess. (Dec. 5, 1859–June 25, 1860). Congressional Serial Set 1033, XI.

—————. Report No. 41: *Report of the Joint Select Committee to Inquire Into the Condition of Affairs in the Late Insurrectionary States. . . .* Vol. II. 42nd Cong., 2d sess. Washington, D.C.: U.S. Government Printing Office, 1872.

—————. Document No. 131: *Memorial of the Northern California Indian Association Praying that Lands Be Allotted to the Landless Indians of the Northern Part of the State of California.* Jan. 21, 1904. 58th Cong., 2d sess. Washington, D.C.: U.S. Government Printing Office, 1904.

U.S. Department of the Interior, Commissioner of Indian Affairs, *Annual Reports,* 1856–1875.

U.S. War Department. Provost-General's Bureau. *Statistics, Medical and Anthropological.* Washington, D.C.: U.S. Government Printing Office, 1875.

—————. *The War of the Rebellion: A Compilation of the Official Records of the Union and Confederate Armies.* 128 vols. Washington, D.C.: U.S. Government Printing Office, 1880–1901.

—————. *Atlas to Accompany the Official Records of the Union and Confederate Armies.* Washington, D.C.: U.S. Government Printing Office, 1891–1895.

—————. Navy. *Official Records of the Union and Confederate Navies in the War of the Rebellion.* 30 vols. Washington, D.C.: U.S. Government Printing Office, 1894–1922.

United States. Statutes at Large.

Vance, Zebulon Baird. *The Papers of Zebulon Baird Vance*, Frontis W. Johnson, Ed. Vol I. Raleigh: North Carolina Department of Archives & History, 1963.

Vennum, Thomas. *American Indian Lacrosse: The Little Brother of War.* Washington, D.C.: Smithsonian Institution Press, 1994.

Washington, George. *The Writings of George Washington.* Vol. XX. John C. Fitzpatrick, Ed. Washington, D.C.: U.S. Government Printing Office, 1937.

Wisconsin Adjutant General's Office. *Roster of Wisconsin Volunteers: War of the Rebellion, 1861–1865.* 2 vols. Madison: Democrat Printing Co. State Printers, 1886.

COURT DECISIONS

Cherokee Nation v. Georgia (U.S.), 5 Pet. 1 (1831).

Cherokee Tobacco Case (U.S.), 78 U.S. 616 (1870).

Dred Scott v. Sanford (U.S.), 19 Howard 393 (1857).

Elk v. Wilkins, 112 U.S. 120 (1884).

Ex Parte Crow Dog, 109 U.S. 556 (1883).

Goodell v. Jackson (N.Y.), 20 Johns Rep. 693 (1823).

Lonewolf v. Hitchcock (U.S.), 187 U.S. 553 (1903).

State ex. rel Marsh v. Managers of Elections for District of York (S.C.), 1 Bailey 215.

United States v. Elm, 25 Fed. Cas. 1006 (Case No. 15,048, 1877).

United States v. Kagama, 118 U.S. 375 (1886).

Worcester v. Georgia (U.S.), 6 Pet. 515 (1832).

NEWSPAPERS AND MAGAZINES

Albany [N.Y.] Argus

Charleston [S.C.] Mercury

Cleveland Plain Dealer

Chicago Tribune

Detroit Free Press

Frank Leslie's Illustrated

Harper's Weekly
National Tribune [Grand Army of the Republic]
Niles' National Register [Baltimore]
Newbern [N.C.] Progress
New York Herald
New York Times
Philadelphia Inquirer
Richmond Dispatch
Rock Hill [S.C.] Herald
Warren [Pa.] Mail
Yorkville [S.C.] Enquirer

BOOKS, BOOKLETS, PAMPHLETS

Abel Annie Heloise, *The American Indian as Participant in the Civil War, 1862–1865* (Cleveland: Arthur H. Clark, 1919; paperback reprint, Lincoln: University of Nebraska Press, 1992, with new title: *The American Indian in the Civil War, 1862–1865*).

———. *The American Indian as Slaveholder and Secessionist*. Cleveland: Arthur H. Clark, 1915 paperback reprint, Lincoln: University of Nebraska Press, 1992.

———. *The American Indian Under Reconstruction* (Retitled in 1993 edition: *The American Indian and the End of the Confederacy, 1863–1866*). Cleveland: Arthur H. Clark, 1925; paperback edition, Lincoln: University of Nebraska Press, 1993.

Abrams, George H. J. *The Seneca People*. Phoenix: Indian Tribal Series, 1976.

Adair, James. *Adair's History of the American Indians*. Samuel Cole Williams, Ed. Johnson City, Tenn.: Wantaga Press, 1930.

Adams, George W. *Doctors in Blue: The Medical History of the Union Army in the Civil War*. New York: Henry Schuman, 1955.

Adams, James Truslow. *History of the Town of Southampton* (East of Canoe Place). Bridgehampton, N.Y.: Hampton Press, 1918.

Adams, William. *Historical Gazetteer and Biographical Memorial of Cattaraugus County, N.Y.* Syracuse, N.Y.: Lyman, Horton and Co., 1893.

Alcott, Louisa May. *Hospital Sketches*. Boston: J. Redpath, 1863.

Allen, William Cicero. *The Annals of Haywood County, North Carolina.* . . . 1935; reprint, Spartanburg, S.C.: Reprint Co., 1977.

Anderson, Mabel W. *The Life of General Stand Watie*. 2nd ed. rev. Pryor, Okla.: privately printed, 1931.

Andrews, J. Cutler. *The North Reports the Civil War*. Pittsburgh: University of Pittsburgh Press, 1955.

Andrews, J. Cutler. *The South Reports the Civil War*. Princeton, N.J.: Princeton University Press, 1970.

Anson, Bert. *The Miami Indians*. Norman Oklahoma: University of Oklahoma Press, 1970.

Armstrong, William H. *Warrior in Two Camps: Ely S. Parker, Union General and Seneca Chief*. Syracuse, N.Y.: Syracuse University Press, 1978.

Aschmann, Rudolf. *Memoirs of a Swiss Officer in the American Civil War*. Heinz K. Meier, Ed. Bern, Switzerland: Herbert Lang, 1972.

Avery, John. *History of the Town of Ledyard, 1650–1900*. Norwich, Conn.: Noyes and Davis, 1901.

Axtell, James. *After Columbus: Essays in the Ethnohistory of Colonial North America*. New York: Oxford University Press, 1988.

Bailey, M. Thomas. *Reconstruction in Indian Territory: A Story of Avarice, Discrimination, and Opportunism*. Port Washington, N.Y.: Kennikat Press, 1972.

Baird, W. David. *Peter Pitchlynn: Chief of the Choctaws*. Norman: University of Oklahoma Press, 1972.

———. *The Choctaw People*. Phoenix: Indian Tribal Series, 1973.

———. *The Quapaw Indians: A History of the Downstream People*. Norman, Okla.: University of Oklahoma, 1980.

———, Ed. *A Creek Warrior for the Confederacy: The Autobiography of Chief G. W. Grayson*. Norman: University of Oklahoma Press, 1988.

Baker, George E., Ed. *The Works of William H. Seward*. Volumes I–IV. Boston: Houghton, Mifflin, 1853–1884.

Bancroft, Hubert H. *The Works of Hubert H. Bancroft*. Vol. XXV. San Francisco: The History Co., 1890.

Barnes, David M. *The Draft Riots in New York: July, 1863. The Metropolitan Police: Their Services During Riot Week. Their Honorable Record*. New York: Baker and Woodwin, 1863.

Barrett, John G. *Sherman's March Through the Carolinas*. Chapel Hill: University of North Carolina Press, 1956.

——. *The Civil War in North Carolina*. Chapel Hill: University of North Carolina Press, 1963.

Basler, Roy, Ed. *Collected Works of Abraham Lincoln*. 8 vols. New Brunswick, N.J.: Rutgers University Press, 1953.

Bates, Samuel P., Comp. *History of Pennsylvania Volunteers*. Vol. II Harrisburg, Pa.: B. Singerly, 1869.

Bauer, K. Jack. *Soldiering: The Civil War Diary of Rice C. Bull*. Novato, Calif.: Presidio Press, 1977.

Baughman, James P. *The Mallorys of Mystic: Six Generations in American Maritime Enterprise*. Middletown, Conn.: Wesleyan University Press, 1972.

Bearss, Edward C., and Arrell M. Gibson. *Fort Smith: Little Gibraltar on the Arkansas*. Norman: University of Oklahoma Press, 1969.

Bernard, George S., Comp. *War Talks of Confederate Veterans*. Petersburg, Va.: Fenn and Owen, 1892.

Bernstein, Iver. *The New York City Draft Riots: Their Significance for American Society and Politics in the Age of the Civil War*. New York: Oxford University Press, 1990.

Bettersworth, John K. *Confederate Mississippi: The People and Politics of a Cotton State in Wartime*. Baton Rouge: Louisiana State University Press, 1943.

Bieder, Robert E. *Science Encounters the Indian: The Early Years of American Ethnology*. Norman: University of Oklahoma Press, 1986.

Blackbird, Andrew J. *History of the Ottawa and Chippewa Indians of Michigan*. Ypsilanti, Mich.: Ypsilanti Job Printing House, 1887.

Blaine, Martha Royce. *The Ioway Indians*. Norman: University of Oklahoma Press, 1979.

Blu, Karen I. *The Lumbee Problem: The Making of an American Indian People*. London: Cambridge University Press, 1980.

Blumer, Thomas J., Comp. and Annot. *Bibliography of the Catawba*. Metuchen, N.J.: Scarecrow Press, 1987.

Boatner, Mark M., III. *The Civil War Dictionary*, rev. ed. New York: David McKay Co., 1988.

Britton, Wiley, *The Civil War on the Border*. 2 vols. New York: G. P. Putnam's Sons, 1904.

Britton, Wiley, *The Union Indian Brigade in the Civil War*. Kansas City, Mo.: Franklin Hudson, 1922.

Brown, A. J. *History of Newton County, Mississippi from 1834–1894*. Jackson, Miss.: Clarion-Ledger Co., 1894.

Brown, Barbara W., and James M. Rose, Comps. *Black Roots in Southeastern Connecticut, 1650–1900*. Detroit: Gale Research Company, 1980.

Brown, Douglas Summers. *A City Without Cobwebs: A History of Rock Hill, South Carolina*. Columbia: University of South Carolina Press, 1953.

———. *The Catawba Indians: The People of the River*. Columbia: University of South Carolina Press, 1966.

Brownlee, Richard S. *Gray Ghosts of the Confederacy: Guerrilla Warfare in the West, 1861–1865*. Baton Rouge: Louisiana State University Press, 1958.

Buel, Clarence C., and Robert U. Johnson, Eds. *Battles and Leaders of the Civil War*. 4 vols. New York: Century Co., 1884–1888; reprint, New York: Thomas Yoseloff, 1956.

Cadwalader, Sylvanus. *Three Years with Grant*, Benjamin P. Thomas, Ed. New York: Alfred A. Knopf, 1956.

Caldwell, J. F. L. *The History of a Brigade of South Carolinians Known First as "Gregg's" and Subsequently as "McGowan's" Brigade*. Philadelphia: King and Baird, 1866.

Campisi, Jack, and Laurence M. Hauptman, Eds. *The Oneida Indian Experience: Two Perspectives*. Syracuse, N.Y.: Syracuse University Press, 1988.

Campisi, Jack, Michael Foster, and Marianne Mithun, Eds. *Extending the Rafters: Interdisciplinary Approaches to Iroquoian Studies*. Albany, N.Y.: State University of New York Press, 1984.

Carranco, Lynwood, and Estle Beard. *Genocide and Vendetta: The Round Valley Wars of Northern California*. Norman: University of Oklahoma Press, 1981.

Castel, Albert E. *A Frontier State at War: Kansas, 1861–1865*. Ithaca, N.Y.: Cornell University Press, 1958.

———. *General Sterling Price and the Civil War in the West*. Baton Rouge: Louisiana State University Press, 1968.

———. *Decision in the West: The Atlanta Campaign of 1864*. Lawrence: University Press of Kansas, 1992.

Caulkins, Frances M. *History of New London County*. New London, Conn.: privately printed, 1860.

Cavanaugh, Michael A., and William Marvel. *The Petersburg Campaign: The Battle of the Crater "The Horrid Pit." June 25–August 6, 1864.* Lynchburg, Va.: H. E. Howard, 1989.

Chazanof, William. *Joseph Ellicott and the Holland Land Company of Western New York.* Syracuse, N.Y.: Syracuse University Press, 1970.

Cleland, Charles E. *Rites of Conquest: The History and Culture of Michigan's Native Americans.* Ann Arbor: University of Michigan Press, 1992.

Coggins, Jack. *Arms and Equipment of the Civil War.* Garden City, N.Y.: Doubleday and Co., 1962.

Cook, Adrian. *The Armies of the Streets: The New York City Draft Riots of 1863.* Lexington: University Press of Kentucky, 1974.

Cook, Sherburne. *The Conflict Between the California Indians and White Civilization.* Berkeley: University of California Press, 1976.

Cooper, Alonzo. *In and Out of Rebel Prisons.* Oswego, N.Y.: R. J. Oliphant, 1888.

Cornish, Dudley, T. *The Sable Army: Negro Troops in the Union Army, 1861–1865.* New York: Longman, Green, 1956.

Covington, James W. *The Seminoles of Florida.* Gainesville: University Press of Florida, 1993.

Croffut, W. A., and John M. Morris. *The Military and Civil History of Connecticut During the War of 1861–1865. . . .* New York: Ledyard Bill, 1868.

Crow, Vernon H. *Storm in the Mountains: Thomas' Confederate Indians and Mountaineers.* Cherokee, N.C.: Museum of the Cherokee Indians, 1982.

Crozier, Emmet. *Yankee Reporters, 1861–1865.* New York: Oxford University Press, 1956.

Current, Richard N. *The History of Wisconsin.* Vol. II: *The Civil War Era, 1848–1873.* Madison: State Historical Society of Wisconsin, 1976.

Dale, Edward Everett, and Gaston Litton, Eds. *Cherokee Cavaliers: Forty Years of Cherokee History as Told in Correspondence of the Ridge-Watie-Boudinot Family.* Norman: University of Oklahoma Press, 1939.

Danziger, Edmund J., Jr. *Indians and Bureaucrats: Administering the Reservation Policy During the Civil War.* Urbana: University of Illinois Press, 1974.

Davis, Jefferson. *The Papers of Jefferson Davis.* 7 vols. James T. McIntosh, Linda L. Crist, et al., Eds. Baton Rouge: Louisiana State University Press, 1971–1992.

Davis, William C. *Jefferson Davis: The Man and His Hour*. New York: HarperCollins, 1991.

De Forest, John W. *A Volunteer's Adventures: A Union Captain's Record of the Civil War*, James W. Croushore, Ed. New Haven, Conn.: Yale University Press, 1946.

De Forest, John W. *History of the Indians of Connecticut from the Earliest Known Period to 1850*. Hamden, Conn.: Archon Books, Shoe String Press Reprint of 1851 edition, 1964.

De Rosier, Arthur, Jr. *The Removal of the Choctaw Indians*. Knoxville: University of Tennessee Press, 1970.

Dearing, Mary R. *Veterans in Politics: The Story of the G. A. R.* Baton Rouge: Louisiana State University Press, 1952.

Debo, Angie. *The Rise and Fall of the Choctaw Republic*. Norman: University of Oklahoma Press, 1934.

Decker, Robert O. *The Whaling City: A History of New London*. Chester, Conn.: The Pequod Press, 1976.

Derounian-Strodola, Kathryn Zabelle, and James Arthur Levernier. *The Indian Captivity Narrative, 1550–1900*. New York: Twayne Publishers, 1993.

Dial, Adolph L., and David K. Eliades. *The Only Land I Know: A History of the Lumbee Indians*. San Francisco: The Indian Historian Press, 1975.

Dornbusch, Charles E., Comp. *Military Bibliography of the Civil War*. 4 vols. Cornwallville, N.Y.: Hope Farm Press, 1961–1987.

Dowd, Gregory Evans. *A Spiritual Resistance: The North American Indian Struggle for Unity, 1745–1815*. Baltimore: Johns Hopkins University Press, 1992.

Duncan, Robert L. *Reluctant General: The Life and Times of Albert Pike*. New York: E. P. Dutton, 1961.

Dunlay, Thomas W. *Wolves for the Blue Soldiers: Indian Scouts and Auxiliaries with the United States Army, 1860–1890*. Lincoln: University of Nebraska Press, 1982.

Dyer, Frederick H. *A Compendium of the War of Rebellion*. 3 vols. Des Moines: Dyer Publishing Co., 1908; reprint, New York: Thomas Yoseloff, 1959.

Eaton, Clement. *Jefferson Davis*. New York: The Free Press, 1977.

Edwards, W. H. *A Condensed History of Seventeenth Regiment S. C. V. C. S. A.: From Its Organization to the Close of the War*. Columbia, S.C.: R. L. Bryan Co., 1908.

Edwards, William B. *Civil War Guns*. Harrisburg, Pa.: Stackpole Co., 1962.

Elliott, Charles Pinckney. *Elliott's Brigade: How It Held the Crater and Saved Petersburg*. Savannah, Ga.: Review Print Co., 1900.

Ellis, Daniel. *Thrilling Adventures of Daniel Ellis, the Great Union Guide of East Tennessee. . . .* New York: Harper and Bros., 1867.

Ellis, Richard. *The Union at Risk: Jacksonian Democracy, States' Rights and the Nullification Crisis*. New York: Oxford University Press, 1987.

Evans, W. McKee. *To Die Game: The Story of the Lowry Band, Indian Guerrillas of Reconstruction*. Baton Rouge: Louisiana State University Press, 1971.

Fancher, Isaac A. *Past and Present of Isabella County Michigan*. Indianapolis: B. F. Bowen, 1911.

Fellman, Michael. *Inside War: The Guerrilla Conflict in Missouri During the American Civil War*. New York: Oxford University Press, 1989.

Finger, John R. *The Eastern Band of Cherokees, 1819–1900*. Knoxville: University of Tennessee Press, 1984.

Fischer, LeRoy H., Ed. *The Civil War in Indian Territory*. Los Angeles: Morrison, 1974.

Foote, Shelby. *The Civil War: A Narrative*. 3 vols. New York: Random House, 1958–1974.

Foreman, Carolyn T. *Indians Abroad, 1493–1938*. Norman: University of Oklahoma Press, 1943.

Foreman Grant. *Advancing the Frontier, 1830–1860*. Norman: University of Oklahoma Press, 1933.

———. Foreman, Grant. *The Five Civilized Tribes*. Norman, Okla.: University of Oklahoma Press, 1934.

———. *Indian Removal: The Emigration of the Five Civilized Tribes of Indians*. Norman: University of Oklahoma Press, 1953.

———. *The Last Trek of the Indians*. Norman: University of Oklahoma Press, 1946; reprint, New York: Russell and Russell, 1972.

Fox, William F. *Regimental Losses in the American Civil War, 1861–1865*. Albany, N.Y.: Albany Publishing Co., 1889.

Franklin, John Hope. *The Free Negro in North Carolina, 1790–1860*. Chapel Hill: University of North Carolina Press, 1943.

Franks, Kenny A. *Stand Watie and the Agony of the Cherokee Nation*. Memphis: Memphis State University Press, 1979.

Frassanito, William A. *Grant and Lee: The Virginia Campaigns, 1864–1865*. New York: Charles Scribner's Sons, 1983.

Futch, Ovid. *History of Andersonville Prison*. Gainesville: University Press of Florida, 1968.

Gaines, W. Craig. *The Confederate Cherokees: John Drew's Regiment of Mounted Rifles*. Baton Rouge: Louisiana State University Press, 1989.

Gara, Larry. *The Liberty Line: The Legend of the Underground Railroad*. Lexington: University Press of Kentucky, 1961.

Gates, Paul Wallace. *Fifty Million Acres: Conflicts Over Kansas Land Policy, 1854–1890*. Ithaca, N.Y.: Cornell University Press, 1954.

Geary, James W. *We Need Men: The Union Draft in the Civil War*. DeKalb: Northern Illinois University Press, 1991.

Gibson, Arrell M. *The Kickapoos: Lords of the Middle Border*. Norman: University of Oklahoma Press, 1963.

———. *The Chickasaws*. Norman: University of Oklahoma Press, 1971.

Gibson, Arrell, Ed. *America's Exiles: Indian Colonization in Oklahoma*. Oklahoma City: Oklahoma Historical Society, 1976.

Gladstone, William A. *United States Colored Troops, 1863–1867*. Gettysburg, Pa.: Thomas Publications, 1990.

———. *Men of Color*. Gettysburg, Pa.: Thomas Publications, 1993.

Glatthaar, Joseph T. *The March to the Sea and Beyond: Sherman's Troops in the Savannah and Carolinas Campaign*. New York: New York University Press, 1985.

———. *Forged in Battle: The Civil War Alliance of Black Soldiers and White Officers*. New York: The Free Press, 1990.

Godbold, E. Stanley, Jr. and Mattie U. Russell. *Confederate Colonel and Cherokee Chief: The Life of William Holland Thomas*. Knoxville: University of Tennessee Press, 1990.

Gould, Benjamin A. *Investigations in the Military and Anthropological Statistics of American Soldiers*. Cambridge, Mass.: Hurd and Houghton, 1869.

Gragg, Rod. *Confederate Goliath: The Battle of Fort Fisher*. New York: Harper-Collins, 1991.

Grant, Ulysses S. *Personal Memoirs of Ulysses S. Grant*. 2 vols. New York: Charles L. Webster and Co., 1886.

Gray, Wood. *The Hidden Civil War: The Story of the Copperheads*. New York: Viking Press, 1942.

Graymont, Barbara. *The Iroquois in the American Revolution*. Syracuse, N.Y.: Syracuse University Press, 1972.

————, Ed. *Fighting Tuscarora: The Autobiography of Chief Clinton Rickard*. Syracuse, N.Y.: Syracuse University Press, 1973.

Hagan, William T. *American Indians*, 1st and 3rd editions. Chicago: University of Chicago Press, 1961 and 1993.

Hagerman, Edward. *The American Civil War and the Origins of Modern Warfare: Ideas, Organization and Field Command*. Bloomington: Indiana University Press, 1988.

Haller, John, Jr. *Outcasts From Evolution: Scientific Attitudes of Racial Inferiority, 1859–1900*. Urbana: University of Illinois Press, 1971.

Hartwick, L. M., and W. H. Tuller. *Oceana County: Pioneers and Businessmen of Today*. Pentwater, Mich.: Pentwater News Steam Print, 1890.

Hauptman, Laurence M. *The Iroquois and the New Deal*. Syracuse, N.Y.: Syracuse University Press, 1981.

————. *The Iroquois Struggle for Survival: World War II to Red Power*. Syracuse, N.Y.: Syracuse University Press, 1986.

————. *Formulating American Indian Policy in New York State, 1970–1986*. Albany, N.Y.: State University of New York, 1988.

————. *The Iroquois in the Civil War*. Syracuse, N.Y.: Syracuse University Press, 1993.

————. Hauptman, Laurence M. *Tribes and Tribulations: Misconceptions About American Indians and Their Histories*. Albuquerque: University of New Mexico Press, 1995.

————, Ed. *A Seneca Indian in the Union Army: The Letters of Sergeant Isaac Newton Parker*. Columbia, Md.: White Mane Publishing Co., 1995.

Hauptman, Laurence M., and Jack Campisi, Eds. *Neighbors and Intruders: An Ethnohistorical Exploration of the Indians of Hudson's River*. Ottawa: National Museum of Man, Canadian Ethnology Service Paper No. 39, 1978.

Hauptman, Laurence M. and James D. Wherry, Eds. *The Pequots in Southern New England: The Fall and Rise of an American Indian Nation*. Norman, Okla.: University of Oklahoma Press, 1990.

Heizer, Robert, Ed. *The Destruction of the California Indians*. Salt Lake City, Utah: Peregrine Smith, 1974.

———, Ed. *Ishi, The Last Yahi: A Documentary Record*. Berkeley: University of California Press, 1979.

Heizer, Robert F. and Alan A. Almquist. *The Other Californians: Prejudice and Discrimination Under Spain, New Mexico and the United States to 1920*. Berkeley: University of California Press, 1971.

Hennessy, John J. *Return to Bull Run: The Campaign and Battle of Second Manassas*. New York: Simon and Schuster, 1993.

Hesseltine, William B. *Civil War Prisons: A Study in War Psychology*. Columbus: Ohio State University Press, 1930.

Hitchcock, Ethan Allen. *Fifty Years in Camp and Field: A Diary of Ethan Allen Hitchcock, U.S.A.* W. A. Croffut, Ed. New York: G.P. Putnam's Sons, 1909.

———. *A Traveler in Indian Territory: The Journal of Ethan Allen Hitchcock* . . . Grand Foreman, Ed. Cedar Rapids, Iowa: Torch Press, 1930.

Hobsbawm, Eric. *Bandits*. New York: Delacorte Press, 1969.

Hosmer, James Kendall, Ed. *Winthrop's Journal: "History of New England," 1630–1649*. Vol. I. New York: Charles Scribner's Sons, 1908.

Howard, James H. *Shawnee!* Athens: Ohio State University Press, 1981.

Hudson, Charles M. *The Catawba Nation*. Athens: University of Georgia Press, 1970.

———. *The Southeastern Indians*. Knoxville, Tenn.: University of Tennessee Press, 1976.

Hurtado, Albert L. *Indian Survival on the California Frontier*. New Haven, Conn.: Yale University Press, 1988.

Jacobs, Wilbur R., Ed. *Indians of the Southern Frontier: The Edmond Atkin Report and the Plan of 1755*. Columbia: University of South Carolina Press, 1954.

Jennings, Francis. *The Invasion of America: Indians, Colonialism and the Cant of Conquest*. Chapel Hill: University of North Carolina Press, 1975.

Johnson, Elias. *Legends, Traditions and Laws of the Iroquois, or Six Nations and History of the Tuscarora Indians*. Lockport, N.Y.: Union Printing and Publishing Co., 1881.

Johnson, E. Roy. *The Tuscaroras: History—Traditions—Culture*. 2 vols. Murfreesboro, N.C.: Johnson Publishing Co., 1968.

Johnson, Marlene, Comp. *Iroquois Cookbook*, 2nd ed. Tonawanda Indian Reservation: Peter Doctor Memorial Indian Fellowship Foundation, 1989.

Josephy, Alvin M., Jr. *The Civil War in the American West*. New York: Alfred A. Knopf, 1991.

Keegan, John. *The Face of Battle*. New York: Viking, 1976.

———. *The Mask of Command*. New York: Viking, 1987.

Kelley, Daniel G. *What I Saw and Suffered in Rebel Prisons*. Buffalo: Thomas, Howard and Johnson, 1868.

Kennedy, Francis H., Ed. *The Civil War Battlefield Guide*. Boston: Houghton Mifflin, 1990.

Kerby, Robert L. *Kirby's Smith's Confederacy: The Trans-Mississippi South, 1863–1865*. New York: Columbia University Press, 1972.

Kettner, James H. *The Development of American Citizenship, 1608–1870*. Chapel Hill: University of North Carolina Press, 1978.

Kilpatrick, Jack F., and Anna G. Kirkpatrick Trans. and Eds. *The Shadow of Sequoyah: Social Documents of the Cherokees, 1862–1964*. Norman: University of Oklahoma Press, 1965.

King, Duane H., Ed. *The Cherokee Nation: A Troubled History*. Knoxville: University of Tennessee Press, 1979.

Kirk, Charles H., Ed. and Comp. *History of the Fifteenth Pennsylvania Volunteer Cavalry*. Philadelphia: Historical Committee of the Society of the Fifteenth Pennsylvania Cavalry, 1906.

Kittinger [Joseph] Diary, 1861–1865. Buffalo: Kittinger Co. in cooperation with the Buffalo and Erie County Historical Society, n.d.

Klement, Frank L. *The Copperheads of the Middle West*. Chicago: University of Chicago Press, 1960.

———. *Wisconsin and the Civil War*. Madison: State Historical Society of Wisconsin, 1963.

———. Klement, Frank L. *The Limits of Dissent*. Lexington, Ky.: University Press of Kentucky, 1970.

———. *Dark Lanterns: Secret Political Societies, Conspiracies, and Treason Trials in the Civil War*. Baton Rouge: Louisiana State University Press, 1984.

Knight, Wilfred. *Red Fox: Stand Watie and the Confederate Indian Nations During the Civil War Years in Indian Territory*. Glendale, Calif.: Arthur H. Clark, 1988.

Kraft, Herbert C. *The Lenape: Archaeology, History and Ethnography*. Newark: New Jersey Historical Society, 1986.

Kvasnicka, Robert and Herman Viola, Eds. *The Commissioners of Indian Affairs, 1824–1977*. Lincoln: University of Nebraska Press, 1979.

Latner, Richard B. *The Presidency of Andrew Jackson: White House Politics, 1829–1837*. Lexington: University Press of Kentucky, 1979.

Liberty, Margot, Ed. *American Indian Intellectuals*. St. Paul, Minn.: American Ethnological Society and West Publishing Co., 1978.

Linderman, Gerald F. *Embattled Courage: The Experience of Combat in the American Civil War*. New York: The Free Press, 1987.

Livermore, Thomas. *Numbers and Losses in the Civil War in America, 1861–1865*. 2nd ed. Boston: Houghton Mifflin, 1901.

Long, Everett B. *The Civil War Day by Day: An Almanac, 1861–1865*. Garden City, N.Y.: Doubleday, 1971.

Lonn, Ella. *Desertion During the Civil War*. Boston: Century Company, 1928; reprint, Gloucester, Mass.: Peter Smith, 1966.

Lucas, Marion Brunson. *Sherman and the Burning of Columbia*. College Station: Texas A&M University Press, 1976.

Marcot, Roy M. *Civil War Sharpshooter: Hiram Berdan, Military Commander and Firearms Inventor*. Irvine, Calif.: Northwood Heritage Press, 1989.

Marcy, Randolph B. *The Prairie Traveler*. New York: Harper and Bros., 1859.

———. *Thirty Years of Army Life on the Border*. New York: Harper and Bros., 1866.

Marszalek, John F. *Sherman: A Soldier's Passion for Order*. New York: The Free Press, 1993.

Marvel, William. *Burnside*. Chapel Hill: University of North Carolina Press, 1991.

Mason, Philip P., and Paul J. Pentecost. *From Bull Run to Appomattox: Michigan's Role in the Civil War*. Detroit: Wayne State University Press, 1961.

Mather, Cotton. *Magnolia Christi Americana: or the Ecclesiastical History of New England*. Vol II. 1702; reprint, New York: Russell and Russell, 1967.

Maxwell, William Quentin. *Lincoln's Fifth Wheel: The Political History of the United States Sanitary Commission*. New York: Longmans Green, 1956.

McClellan, George B. *McClellan's Own Story*. New York: Charles L. Webster, 1887.

―――. *The Civil War Papers of George B. McClellan: Selected Correspondence, 1861–1865*. Stephen W. Sears, Ed. New York: Ticknor and Fields, 1989.

McClurken, James M. *Gah-Baeh-Jhagwah-Buk: The Way It Happened—A Visual Culture History of the Little Traverse Bay Bands of Odawa*. East Lansing: Michigan State University Museum, 1991.

McDonough, James Lee. *Chattanooga: A Death Grip on the Confederacy*. Knoxville: University of Tennessee Press, 1984.

McLoughlin, William G. *The Cherokee Ghost Dance: Essays on the Southeastern Indians, 1789–1861*. Macon, Ga.: Mercer University Press, 1984.

McPherson, James M. *The Negro's Civil War*. New York: Pantheon Books, 1965.

―――. *Ordeal by Fire: The Civil War and Reconstruction*. New York: Knopf, 1982.

―――. *Battle Cry of Freedom: The Civil War Era*. New York: Oxford University Press, 1988.

Merrell, James H. *The Indians' New World: Catawbas and Their Neighbors from European Contact Through the Era of Removal*. New York: W. W. Norton, 1989.

Milling, Chapman J. *Red Carolinians*. Chapel Hill: University of North Carolina Press, 1940.

Miner, H. Craig. *The Corporation and the Indian: Tribal Sovereignty and Industrial Civilization in Indian Territory*. Columbia: University of Missouri Press, 1976.

Miner, H. Craig, and William E. Unrau. *The End of Indian Kansas: A Study of Cultural Revolution, 1854–1871*. Lawrence: Regents Press of Kansas, 1978.

Mitchell, Joseph B. *The Badge of Gallantry*. New York: Macmillan Publishing Co., 1968.

Mitchell, Reid. *Civil War Soldiers: Their Expectations and Their Experiences*. New York: Viking Press, 1988.

Monaghan, Jay. *Civil War on the Western Border, 1854–1865*. Boston: Little, Brown and Co., 1955.

Mooney, James. *Historical Sketch of the Cherokee*. Chicago: Aldine Publishing and Smithsonian Institution Press, 1975.

Moore, Charles. *History of Michigan*. Chicago: Lewis Publishing Co., 1915.

Morgan, Lewis Henry. *The League of the Ho-de-no-sau-nee, or Iroquois*. Rochester, N.Y., 1851. Paperback reprint, New York: Corinth Press, 1962.

Moses, L. George. *The Indian Man: A Biography of James Mooney*. Urbana: University of Illinois Press, 1984.

Moulton, Gary E. *John Ross: Cherokee Chief*. Athens: University of Georgia Press, 1978.

———, Ed. *The Papers of Chief John Ross*. 2 vols. Norman: University of Oklahoma Press, 1985.

Murdock, Eugene C. *Ohio's Bounty System in the Civil War*. Columbus: Ohio State University Press, 1963.

———. *Patriotism Limited, 1862–1865: The Civil War Draft and Bounty System*. Kent, Ohio: Kent State University Press, 1967.

———. *One Million Men: The Civil War Draft in the North*. Madison: State Historical Society of Wisconsin, 1971.

Newcomb, W. W., Jr. *The Indians of Texas: From Prehistoric to Modern*. Austin: University of Texas Press, 1961.

Newton, James K. *A Wisconsin Boy in Dixie. The Selected Letters of James K. Newton*. Stephen Ambrose, Ed. Madison: University of Wisconsin Press, 1961.

Nichols, David A. *Lincoln and the Indians: Civil War Policy and Politics*. Columbia: University of Missouri Press, 1978.

Niven, John. *Connecticut for the Union: The Role of the State in the Civil War*. New Haven, Conn.: Yale University Press, 1965.

O'Flaherty, Daniel. *General Jo Shelby: Undefeated Rebel*. Chapel Hill: University of North Carolina Press, 1954.

Oates, Stephen B. *Confederate Cavalry West of the River*. Austin: University of Texas Press, 1962; paperback reprint, Austin: University of Texas Press, 1992.

Olmsted, Frederick Law *The Cotton Kingdom: A Traveler's Observation on Cotton and Slavery in the American Slave States*. Arthur M. Schlesinger, Ed. New York: Alfred A. Knopf, 1953.

————. *A Journey in the Back Country*. New York: Schocken Books, 1970; reprint of 1860 edition.

————. *The Papers of Frederick Law Olmsted*. Vol. V: *The California Frontier, 1863–1865*. Victoria Post Ranney, Ed. Baltimore: Johns Hopkins University Press, 1983.

Orr, Charles, Ed. *History of the Pequot War*. Cleveland: Helman-Taylor Co., 1897.

Otis, D. S. *The Dawes Act and the Allotment of Indian Lands*. Francis Paul Prucha, Ed. Norman: University of Oklahoma Press, 1973.

Paludan, Phillip S. *Victims: A True Story of the Civil War*. Knoxville; University of Tennessee Press, 1981.

————. *"A People's Contest": The Union and the Civil War, 1861–1865*. New York: Harper and Row, 1988.

Pancoast, Charles Edward. *A Quaker Forty-Niner: The Adventures of Charles Edward Pancoast*. Anna Paschall Hannum, Ed. Philadelphia: University of Pennsylvania, 1930.

Parker, Arthur C. *The Life of General Ely S. Parker, Last Grand Sachem of the Iroquois and General Grant's Military Secretary*. Publication 23. Buffalo, N.Y.: Buffalo Historical Society, 1919.

————. *Parker on the Iroquois*. William N. Fenton, Ed. Syracuse, N.Y.: Syracuse University Press, 1968.

Parks, Joseph Howard. *General Edmund Kirby Smith, C. S. A.* Baton Rouge: Louisiana State University Press, 1954.

Perdue, Theda. *Nations Remembered: An Oral History of the Five Civilized Tribes, 1865–1907*. Westport, Conn.: Greenwood Press, 1980.

Perdue, Theda. *Slavery and the Evolution of Cherokee Society, 1540–1866*. Knoxville: University of Tennessee Press, 1979.

Polk, James K. *The Diary of James K. Polk During His Presidency, 1845 to 1849*. Vol. II. Milo M. Quaife, Ed. Chicago: A. C. McClurg, 1910.

Porter, Horace. *Campaigning with Grant*. 1897. Paperback reprint, New York: DeCapo, 1986.

Priest, John Michael. *Antietam: The Soldiers' Battle*. Shippensburg, Pa.: White Mane Publishing Co., 1989; paperback reprint, New York: Oxford University Press, 1993.

Prucha, Francis Paul. *Atlas of American Indian Affairs*. Lincoln: University of Nebraska Press, 1990.

Prucha, Francis Paul. *The Great Father: The United States Government and the American Indians*. 2 vols. Lincoln: University of Nebraska Press, 1984.

Reed, Rowena. *Combined Operations in the Civil War*. Annapolis, Md.: Naval Institute Press, 1978.

Reed, William H. *Hospital Life in the Army of the Potomac*. Boston: William V. Spencer, 1866.

Resek, Carl. *Lewis Henry Morgan: American Scholar*. Chicago: University of Chicago Press, 1960.

Rountree, Helen C. *Pocahontas' People: The Powhatan Indians of Virginia Through Four Centuries*. Norman: University of Oklahoma Press, 1990.

———. *The Powhatan Indians: Their Traditional History*. Norman: University of Oklahoma Press, 1989.

Salisbury, Neal. *Manitou and Providence: Indians, Europeans, and the Making of New England, 1500–1643*. New York: Oxford University Press, 1982.

Sanford, Washington L. *History of Fourteenth Illinois Cavalry and the Brigades to Which It Belonged*. Chicago: R. R. Connelley and Sons, 1898.

Satz, Ronald N. *American Indian Policy in the Jacksonian Era*. Lincoln: University of Nebraska Press, 1975.

Scaife, H. Lewis. *History and Condition of the Catawba Indians of South Carolina*. Philadelphia: Indian Rights Association, 1896.

Scott, Samuel W., and Samuel P. Angel. *The Thirteenth Regiment Tennessee Volunteer Cavalry, U.S.A.* Philadelphia: P. W. Ziegler, 1903.

Sears, Stephen W. *Landscape Turned Red: The Battle of Antietam*. New York: Ticknor and Fields, 1983.

———. *George B. McClellan, the Young Napoleon*. New York: Ticknor and Fields, 1988.

———. *To the Gates of Richmond: The Peninsula Campaign*. New York: Ticknor and Fields, 1992.

Shannon, Fred. *The Organization and Administration of the Union Army*. 2 vols. Cleveland: Arthur H. Clark, 1928.

Sider, Gerald M. *Lumbee Indian Histories: Race, Ethnicity, and Indian Identity in the Southern United States*. New York: Cambridge University Press, 1993.

Siebert, Wilbur H. *The Underground Railroad*. 1898. Reprint, New York: Arno Press and the New York Times, 1968.

Simmons, William S. *Spirit of the New England Tribes: Indian History and Folklore, 1620–1984*. Hanover, N.H.: University Press of New England, 1986.

Simon, John Y., Ed. *The Papers of Ulysses S. Grant*. 15 vols. Carbondale: Southern Illinois University Press, 1967.

Slotkin, Richard. *Gunfighter Nation: The Myth of the Frontier in Twentieth-Century America*. New York: Atheneum, 1992.

Smith, Adelaide W. *Reminiscences of an Army Nurse During the Civil War*. New York: Greaves, 1911.

Sommers, Richard. *Richmond Redeemed: The Siege at Petersburg*. Garden City, N.Y.: Doubleday, 1981.

Steiner, Paul E. *Disease in the Civil War: Natural Biological Warfare in 1861–1865*. Springfield, Ill.: Charles C. Thomas, 1968.

Stockwell, Elisha, Jr. *Private Elisha Stockwell Sees the Civil War*. Byron R. Abernethy, Ed. Norman: University of Oklahoma Press, 1958.

Strother, Horatio T. *The Underground Railroad in Connecticut*. Middletown, Conn.: Wesleyan University Press, 1962.

Tanner, Helen Hornbeck. *Atlas of Great Lakes Indian History*. Norman: University of Oklahoma Press, 1987.

Tatum, Georgia Lee. *Disloyalty in the Confederacy*. Chapel Hill: University of North Carolina Press, 1934.

Thornton, Russell. *American Indian Holocaust and Survival: A Population History Since 1492*. Norman: University of Oklahoma Press, 1987.

———. *The Cherokees: A Population History*. Lincoln: University of Nebraska Press, 1990.

Tocqueville, Alexis de. *Democracy in America*. 2 vols., 1831; New York: Vintage Books, 1954.

Townsend, George A. *Rustics in Rebellion: A Yankee Reporter on the Road to Richmond*. Chapel Hill: University of North Carolina Press, 1950.

Trautman, Thomas R. *Lewis Henry Morgan and the Invention of Kinship*. Berkeley: University of California Press, 1987.

Trennert, Robert A., Jr. *Indian Traders on the Middle Border: The House of Ewing, 1827–1854*. Lincoln: University of Nebraska Press, 1981.

Trudeau, Noah Andre. *Bloody Roads South: The Wilderness to Cold Harbor.* Boston: Little, Brown and Co., 1989.

———. *The Last Citadel: Petersburg, Virginia, June 1864–April 1865.* Boston: Little, Brown and Co., 1991.

Utley, Robert M. *Frontier Regulars: The United States Army and the Indian, 1866–1891.* New York: Macmillan, 1973.

———. *The Indian Frontier of the American West, 1846–1890.* Albuquerque: University of New Mexico Press, 1984.

Vaughan, Alden T. *New England Frontier: Puritans and Indians, 1620–1675.* Boston: Little, Brown, 1964. Rev. ed. New York: W. W. Norton, 1979.

———, Ed. *The Puritan Tradition in America, 1620–1730.* New York: Harper and Row, 1972.

Vecsey, Christopher. *Traditional Ogibwa Religion and Its Historical Changes.* Philadelphia: American Philosophical Society, 1983.

Vecsey, Christopher and William A. Starna, Eds. *Iroquois Land Claims.* Syracuse, N.Y.: Syracuse University Press, 1988.

Vinovskis, Maris A., Ed. *Toward a Social History of the American Civil War: Exploratory Essays.* Cambridge, U.K.: Cambridge University Press, 1990.

Viola, Herman J. *Diplomats in Buckskin: A History of Indian Delegations in Washington City.* Washington, D.C.: Smithsonian Institution Press, 1981.

Wallace, Anthony F. C. *King of the Delawares: Teedyuscung, 1700–1763.* Philadelphia: University of Pennsylvania Press, 1949; paperback reprint, Syracuse, N.Y.: Syracuse University Press, 1991.

———. *The Death and Rebirth of the Seneca.* New York: Knopf, 1970.

———. Wallace, Anthony F. C. *The Long Bitter Trail: Andrew Jackson and the Indians.* New York: Hill and Wang, 1993.

Wardell, Morris. *A Political History of the Cherokee Nation, 1838–1907.* Norman: University of Oklahoma Press, 1938.

Washburn, Wilcomb E., Ed. *The American Indian and the United States: A Documentary History.* 4 vols. Westport, Conn.: Greenwood Press, 1973.

Weighley, Russell. *The American Way of War: A History of United States Military Strategy and Policy.* New York: Macmillan, 1973.

Weisberger, Bernard A. *Reporters for the Union.* Boston: Little, Brown, 1953.

Welcher, Frank J. *The Union Army, 1961–1865: Organization and Operations.* Vol. I: *The Eastern Theatre.* Bloomington: Indiana University Press, 1989.

Weld, Stephen M. *War Diary and Letters of Stephen Minot Weld, 1861–1865*. Boston: Massachusetts Historical Society, 1979.

Wells, Samuel J., and Roseanna Tubby, Eds. *After Removal: The Choctaw in Mississippi*. Jackson: University Press of Mississippi, 1986.

Weslager, C. A. *The Delaware Indians: A History*. New Brunswick, N.J.: Rutgers University Press, 1972.

———. *The Delaware Indian Westward Migration*. Wallingford, Pa.: Middle Atlantic Press, 1978.

———. *The Nanticoke Indians: Past and Present*, 2nd ed. Newark: University of Delaware Press and Associated University Press, 1983.

Wheeler, Richard. *Sword Over Richmond: An Eyewitness History of McClellan's Peninsula Campaign*. New York: Harper and Row, 1986.

Wheeler, Richard. *The Siege of Vicksburg*. New York: Thomas Y. Crowell, 1978; paperback reprint, Harper Perennial, 1991.

White, Leslie A., Ed. *Lewis Henry Morgan: The Indian Journals, 1859–1862*. Ann Arbor: University of Michigan Press, 1959.

White, Richard. *The Middle Ground: Indians, Empires, and Republics in the Great Lakes Region, 1650–1815*. New York: Cambridge University Press, 1991.

Wiley, Bell Irvin. *The Life of Billy Yank: The Common Soldier of the Union*. Indianapolis, Ind.: Bobbs-Merrill, 1952.

Wiley, Bell Irvin. *The Life of Johnny Reb: The Common Soldier of the Confederacy*. Indianapolis: Bobbs-Merrill, 1943.

Wilkins, Thurman. *Cherokee Tragedy: The Ridge Family and the Decimation of a People*. rev. ed. Norman: University of Oklahoma Press, 1986.

Williams, Walter L., Ed. *Southeastern Indians Since the Removal Era*. Athens: University of Georgia Press, 1979.

Winey, Michael J., and Mark H. Dunkelman. *The Hardtack Regiment: An Illustrated History of the 154th Regiment, New York State Infantry Volunteers*. Rutherford, N.J.: Fairleigh Dickinson Press, 1981.

Woodward, Grace Steele. *The Cherokees*. Norman: University of Oklahoma Press, 1963.

Wooster, Robert. *The Military and United States Indian Policy, 1865–1903*. New Haven: Yale University Press, 1988.

Wright, Muriel H., and LeRoy H. Fischer. *Civil War Sites in Oklahoma*.

Oklahoma City: Oklahoma Historical Society, 1967.

Young, Mary E. *Redskins, Ruffleshirts and Rednecks: Indian Allotments in Alabama and Mississippi, 1830–1860*. Norman: University of Oklahoma Press, 1961.

ARTICLES

Abel, Annie H. "Indian Reservations in Kansas and the Extinguishment of Their Title." *Transactions* of the Kansas State Historical Society 8 (1904): 72–109.

Abler, Thomas S. "Friends, Factions, and the Seneca Nation Revolution of 1848." *Niagara Frontier* 21 (Winter 1974): 74–79.

———. "Protestant Missionaries and Native Cultures: Parallel Careers of Asher Wright and Silas T. Rand." *American Indian Quarterly* 16 (Winter 1992): 25–38.

Aiken, R. A. "Eightieth Regiment." (Walker's Regiment of Thomas Legion). In Walter Clark, Ed., *Histories of the Several Regiments and Battalions from North Carolina in the Great War 1861–'65*, Vol. IV. Raleigh, N.C.: Nash Bros. Book and Job Printers for the State of North Carolina, 1901.

Axtell, James. "The White Indians of Colonial America." *William and Mary Quarterly* 32 (1975): 55–88.

Banks, Dean. "Civil War Refugees from Indian Territory in the North, 1861–1864." *Chronicles of Oklahoma* 41 (Autumn 1963): 286–298.

Bardolph, Richard. "Inconstant Rebels: Desertion of North Carolina Troops in the Civil War." *North Carolina Historical Review* 41 (April 1964): 163–189.

Bearss, Edwin C. "The Battle of Pea Ridge." *Arkansas Historical Quarterly* 20 (Spring 1961): 74–94.

———. "The Civil War Comes to Indian Territory: The Flight of Opothleyahola." *Journal of the West* 11 (January 1972): 9–42.

Bieder, Robert E., and Christopher Plant. "Annuity Census as a Source for Historical Research: The 1858 and 1869 Tonawanda Seneca Annuity Censuses." *American Indian Culture and Research Journal* 5, no. 1 (1981): 33–46.

Blassingame, John. "The Union Army as an Educational Institution." *Journal of Negro Education* 34 (Spring 1965): 152–159.

Boissevain, Ethel. "Whatever Became of the New England Indians Shipped to Bermuda to Be Sold as Slaves." *Man in the Northeast* 11 (Spring 1981): 103–114.

Britton, Wiley. "Union and Confederate Indians in the Civil War." In Clarence C. Buel and Robert U. Johnson, Eds., *Battles and Leaders of the Civil War*, vol. I. New York: Century Co., 1884.

Cain, Marvin R. "A 'Face of Battle' Needed: An Assessment of Motives and Men in Civil War Historiography." *Civil War History* 28 (March 1982): 5–27.

Campisi, Jack. "The Emergence of the Mashantucket Pequot Tribe." In Laurence M. Hauptman and Jack Campisi, Eds., *The Pequots in Southern New England: The Fall and Rise of an American Indian Nation*. Norman: University of Oklahoma Press, 1990.

Castel, Albert. "A New View of the Battle of Pea Ridge." *Missouri Historical Review* 62 (January 1968): 136–151.

Castillo, Edward D. "The Impact of Euro-American Exploration and Settlement." In Robert F. Heizer, Ed., *Handbook of North American Indians*. Vol. VIII: *California*. Washington D.C.: Smithsonian Institution, 1978.

Cave, Alfred A. "The Pequot Invasion of Southern New England: A Reassessment of the Evidence." *New England Quarterly* 27 (March 1989): 27–44.

———. "Who Killed John Stone? A Note on the Origins of the Pequot War." *William and Mary Quarterly* 44 (July 1992): 509–521.

Clifford, Roy A. "Indian Regiments in the Battle of Pea Ridge." *Chronicles of Oklahoma* 25 (Winter 1947–1948): 314–322.

Cook, Sherburne F. "Interracial Warfare and Population Decline Among the New England Indians." *Ethnohistory* 20 (Winter 1973): 1–24.

Dale, Edward E. "Some Letters of General Stand Watie." *Chronicles of Oklahoma* 1 (January 1921): 30–59.

Danziger, Edmund J., Jr. "The Office of Indian Affairs and the Problem of Civil War Refugees in Kansas." *Kansas Historical Quarterly* 35 (Autumn 1969): 257–275.

Davies, Wallace E. "The Problem of Race Segregation in the Grand Army of the Republic." *Journal of Southern History* 13 (August 1947): 354–372.

Dean, Eric T. " | 'We Will All Be Lost and Destroyed': Post-Traumatic Stress Disorder and the Civil War." *Civil War History* 37 (June 1991): 138–151.

Elder, Glen H., Jr. "Military Times and Turning Points in Men's Lives." *Developmental Psychology* 22 (March 1986): 233–245.

Evans, W. McKee. "The North Carolina Lumbees from Assimilation to Revitalization." In Walter L. Williams, Ed., *Southeastern Indians Since the Removal Era*. Athens: University of Georgia Press, 1979.

Feest, Christian F. "Virginia Algonquians." In Bruce G. Trigger, Ed., *Handbook of North American Indians*. Vol. XV: *The Northeast*. Washington, D.C.: Smithsonian Institution, 1978.

Feest, Joanna E., and Christian F. Feest. "Ottawa." In Bruce G. Trigger, Ed., *Handbook of North American Indians*. Vol. XV: *The Northeast*. Washington, D.C.: Smithsonian Institution, 1978.

Fenton, William N. "Toward the Gradual Civilization of the Indian Natives: The Missionary and Linguistic Work of Asher Wright (1803–1875) Among the Seneca of Western New York." *Proceedings* of the American Philosophical Society 100 (December 1956): 567–581.

Fenton, William N. "Asher Wright's Seneca Mission." *Proceedings* of the American Philosophical Society 100 (1956): 567–581.

———, Ed. "Seneca Indians by Asher Wright (1859)." *Ethnohistory* 4 (1957): 302–321.

Fisher, LeRoy, and Kenny A. Franks. "Confederate Victory at Chusto-Talasah." *Chronicles of Oklahoma* 44 (Winter 1971–1972): 452–476.

Fogelson, Raymond D. "Who Were the Ani-Kutani? An Excursion into Cherokee Historical Thought." *Ethnohistory* 31 (1984): 255–263.

Foreman, Carolyn T. "Black Beaver." *Chronicles of Oklahoma* 24 (1946): 269–292.

Franks, Kenny A. "An Analysis of the Confederate Treaties with the Five Civilized Tribes." *Chronicles of Oklahoma* 50 (Winter 1972–1973): 458–473.

———. "The Confederate States and the Five Civilized Tribes: A Breakdown of Relations." *Journal of the West* 12 (July 1973): 439–454.

———. "The Implementation of the Confederate Treaties with the Five Civilized Tribes." *Chronicles of Oklahoma* 51 (Spring 1973): 21–33.

Freeman, Charles. "The Battle of Honey Springs." *Chronicles of Oklahoma* 13 (June 1935): 154–168.

Geary, James W. "Civil War Conscription in the North: A Historiographic Review." *Civil War History* 32 (1986): 208–228.

Gibson, Arrell M. "Confederates on the Plains: The Pike Mission to the Wichita Agency." *Great Plains Journal* 4 (Fall 1964): 7–16.

———. "Native Americans and the Civil War." *American Indian Quarterly* 9 (Fall 1985): 385–410.

Goddard, Ives. "Delaware." In Bruce G. Trigger, Ed., *Handbook of North American Indians*. Vol. XV: *The Northeast*. Washington, D.C.: Smithsonian Institution, 1978.

Graves, William H. "Indian Soldiers for the Gray Army: Confederate Recruitment in Indian Territory." *Chronicles of Oklahoma* 60 (Summer 1991): 134–145.

Graymont, Barbara. "New York State Indian Policy After the Revolution." *New York History* 57 (October 1976): 438–474.

Haller, John S. "Civil War Anthropometry: The Making of a Racial Ideology." *Civil War History* 16 (December 1970): 309–324.

Halliburton, R., Jr. "Chief Greenwood LeFlore and His Malmaison Plantation." In Samuel J. Wells and Roseanna Tubby, Eds., *After Removal: The Choctaw in Mississippi*. Jackson: University Press of Mississippi, 1986.

Hallock, Judith Lee. "The Role of the Community in Civil War Desertion." *Civil War History* 29 (June 1983): 123–134.

Hancock, Marvin J. "The Second Battle of Cabin Creek, 1864." *Chronicles of Oklahoma* 41 (Winter 1963–1964): 414–426.

Hauptman, Laurence M. "The Pequot War and Its Legacies." In Laurence M. Hauptman and James D. Wherry, Eds., *The Pequots in Southern New England: The Fall and Rise of an American Indian Nation*. Norman: University of Oklahoma Press, 1990.

———. "Samuel George (1795–1873): A Study of Onondaga Conservatism." *New York History* 70 (January 1989): 4–22.

———. "The Missionary From Hell." In Laurence M. Hauptman, *Tribes and Tribulations: Misconceptions About American Indians and Their Histories.* Albuquerque: University of New Mexico Press, 1995.

Heath, Gary N. "The First Federal Invasion of Indian Territory." *Chronicles of Oklahoma* 44 (Winter 1966/1967): 409–419.

Heimann, Robert K. "The Cherokee Tobacco Case." *Chronicles of Oklahoma* 41 (Autumn 1963): 299–322.

Hoig, Stan. "War for Survival: Wichita Indians During the Civil War." *Chronicles of Oklahoma* 60 (1984): 266–283.

Holmes, Amy E. "'Such Is the Price We Pay': American Widows and the Civil War Pension System." In Maris A. Vinovskis, Ed., *Toward a Social History of the American Civil War: Exploratory Essays.* New York: Cambridge University Press, 1990.

Hood, Fred. "Twilight of the Confederacy in the Indian Territory." *Chronicles of Oklahoma* 41 (Winter 1963–1964): 414–426.

Horsman, Reginald. "The Wisconsin Oneidas in the Preallotment Years." In Jack Campisi and Laurence M. Hauptman, Eds., *The Oneida Experience: Two Perspectives.* Syracuse, N.Y.: Syracuse University Press, 1988.

Houghton, Charles H. "In the Crater." In Clarence C. Buel and Robert U. Underwood, Eds., *Battles and Leaders of the Civil War,* Vol. IV. New York: Century Co., 1887; reprint, New York: Thomas Yoseloff, 1956.

Hudson, Charles M. "The Catawba Indians of South Carolina: A Question of Ethnic Survival." In: *Southeastern Indians Since the Removal Era.* Walter L. Williams, Ed. Athens: University of Georgia Press, 1979.

Keen, William Williams. "Military Surgery in 1861 and 1918." *Annals of the American Academy of Political and Social Science* 80 (November 1918): 11–15.

Kelsey, Harry. "William P. Dole and Mr. Lincoln's Indian Policy." *Journal of the West* 10 (July 1971): 484–492.

———. "Charles Mix." In Robert Kvasnicka and Herman Viola, Eds., *The Commissioners of Indian Affairs, 1824–1977,* pp. 89–98. Lincoln: University of Nebraska Press, 1979.

Kidwell, Clara Sue. "The Choctaw Struggle for Land and Identity in Mississippi, 1830–1918." In: *After Removal: The Choctaw in Mississippi.* Samuel J. Wells and Roseanna Tubby, Eds. Jackson: University Press of Mississippi, 1986.

King, Duane H. "The Origin of the Eastern Cherokees as a Social and Political Entity." In Duane H. King, Ed., *The Cherokee Indian Nation: A Troubled History*. Knoxville: University of Tennessee Press, 1979.

Larsen, Lawrence H. "Draft Riot in Wisconsin." *Civil War History* 7 (1961): 421–427.

Lee, Keun Sang. "The Capture of the J. R. Williams." *Chronicles of Oklahoma* 55 (Spring 1982): 22–33.

Lee, R. Alton. "Indian Citizenship and the Fourteenth Amendment." *South Dakota History* 4 (1974): 198–221.

Levine, Peter. "Draft Evasion in the North During the Civil War, 1863–1865." *Journal of American History* 67 (March 1981): 816–834.

Manley, Henry S. "Buying Buffalo from the Indians." *New York History* 28 (July 1947): 313–329.

McBride, Kevin A. "The Historical Archaeology of the Mashantucket Pequots, 1637–1900: A Preliminary Analysis." In Laurence M. Hauptman and James D. Wherry, Eds., *The Pequots in Southern New England: The Fall and Rise of an American Indian Nation*. Norman: University of Oklahoma Press, 1990.

McClurken, James D. "Strangers in Their Own Land." *Grand River Valley Review* 6 (1985): 2–25.

———. "Ottawa Adaptive Strategies to Removal." *Michigan Historical Review* 12 (1986): 26–55.

McClurken, James M. "Augustin Hamlin, Jr.: Ottawa Identity and the Politics of Persistence." In James A. Clifton, Ed., *Being and Becoming Indian: Biographical Studies of North American Frontiers*. Chicago: Dorsey Press, 1989.

McConnell, Stuart. "Who Joined the Grand Army? Three Cases in the Construction of Union Veteranhood, 1866–1900." In Maris A. Vinovskis, Ed., *Toward a Social History of the American Civil War: Exploratory Essays*. New York: Cambridge University Press, 1990.

McCrady, Edward. "Gregg's Brigade of South Carolinians in the Second Battle of Manassas." *Southern Historical Society Papers* 12 (1985).

McLoughlin, William G., and Walter H. Conser, Jr. "The Cherokees in Transition: A Statistical Analysis of the Federal Cherokee Census of 1835." *Journal of American History* 44 (December 1977): 678–703.

McMaster, F. W. "The Battle of the Crater, July 30, 1864." *Papers* of the Southern Historical Society 10 (1882): 119–130.

McNeil, Kenneth. "Confederate Treaties with the Tribes of Indian Territory." *Chronicles of Oklahoma* 42 (Winter 1964–1965): 408–420.

Merrell, James H. " | 'Their Very Bones Shall Fight': The Catawba-Iroquois Wars." In Daniel K. Richter and James H. Merrell, Eds., *Beyond the Covenant Chain: The Iroquois and Their Neighbors, 1600–1800*. Syracuse, N.Y.: Syracuse University Press, 1987.

Millbrook, Minnie D. "Indian Sharpshooters." In Minnie Dubbs Millbrook, Comp. *Twice Told Tales of Michigan and Her Soldiers in the Civil War*. Ann Arbor: Michigan Civil War Centennial Observance Commission, 1966.

Mitchell, Reid. "The Northern Soldier and His Community." In Maris A. Vinovskis, Ed., *Toward a Social History of the American Civil War: Exploratory Essays*. New York: Cambridge University Press, 1990.

Mooney, James. "The Powhatan Confederacy: Past and Present." *American Anthropologist* 9 (1907): 129–152.

Morrison, James D. "Capture of the J. R. Williams." *Chronicles of Oklahoma* 43 (Summer 1964): 105–108.

Moulton, Gary E. "John Ross and W. P. Dole: A Case Study of Lincoln's Indian Policy." *Journal of the West* 12 (July 1973): 414–423.

Nash, Gary B. "The Image of the Indians in the Southern Colonial Mind." *William and Mary Quarterly*, 3d ser., 29 (April 1972): 197–230.

Neet, J. Frederick. "Stand Watie; Confederate General in the Cherokee Nation." *Great Plains Journal* 6 (Fall 1966): 36–51.

Otterbein, Keith F. "Why the Iroquois Won: An Analysis of Iroquois Military Tactics." *Ethnohistory* 11 (Winter 1964): 56–63.

———. "Huron v. Iroquois: A Case Study in Inter-tribal Warfare." *Ethnohistory* 26 (Spring 1979): 141–152.

Parker, Arthur C. "The Senecas in the War of 1812." *Proceedings* of the New York State Historical Association 15 (1916): 78–90.

Peterson, Jacqueline. "Many Roads to Red River: Métis Genesis in the Great Lakes Region, 1680–1815." In Jacqueline Peterson and Jennifer S. H. Brown, Eds., *New Peoples: Being and Becoming Metis in North America*. Lincoln: University of Nebraska Press in cooperation with the University of Manitoba Press, 1985.

Porter, Horace. "The Surrender at Appomattox Court House." In Clarence C. Buel and Robert U. Johnson, Eds., *Battles and Leaders of the Civil War*. Vol. IV. New York: Century Co., 1888; reprint, New York: Thomas Yoseloff, 1956.

Powell, William H. "The Battle of the Petersburg Crater." In Clarence C. Buel and Robert U. Johnson, Eds., *Battles and Leaders of the Civil War*, Vol. IV. New York: Century Co., 1888; reprint, New York: Thomas Yoseloff, 1956.

Richter, Daniel. "War and Culture: The Iroquois Experience." *William and Mary Quarterly* 40 (1983): 537–544.

Roberts, Gary L. "Dennis Nelson Cooley, 1865–1866." In Robert Kvasnicka and Herman Viola, Eds., *The Commissioners of Indian Affairs, 1824–1977*. Lincoln: University of Nebraska Press, 1979.

Ronda, James, and Jeanne Ronda. "As They Were Faithful: Chief Aupaumat and the Struggle for Stockbridge Survival, 1757–1830." *American Indian Culture and Research Journal* 3 (1979): 43–55.

Rorabaugh, W. J. "Who Fought for the North in the Civil War? Concord, Massachusetts Enlistments." *Journal of American History* 73 (December 1986): 695–701.

Rountree, Helen C. "Ethnicity Among the 'Citizen' Indians of Tidewater Virginia, 1800–1930." In Frank Porter, Ed., *Strategies for Survival: American Indians in the Eastern United States*. Westport, Conn.: Greenwood Press, 1986.

———. "The Indians of Virginia: A Third Race in a Biracial State." In Walter L. Williams, Ed., *Southeastern Indians Since the Removal Era*. Athens: University of Georgia Press, 1979.

Satz, Ronald N. "The Mississippi Choctaw: From the Removal Treaty to the Federal Agency." In Samuel J. Wells and Roseanna Tubby, Eds., *After Removal: The Choctaw in Mississippi*. Jackson: University Press of Mississippi, 1986.

Seraile, William. "The Struggle to Raise Black Regiments in New York State, 1861–1864." *New-York Historical Society Quarterly* 58 (July 1974): 215–233.

Shoemaker, Arthur. "The Battle of Chustenahlah." *Chronicles of Oklahoma* 38 (Summer 1960): 180–184.

Shoemaker, Nancy. "From Longhouse to Loghouse: Household Structure Among the Senecas in 1900." *American Indian Quarterly* 15 (Summer 1991): 329–338.

———. "The Rise and Fall of Iroquois Women." *Journal of Women's History* 2 (Winter 1991): 39–57.

Simmons, William S. "Cultural Bias in the New England Puritans' Perceptions of Indians." *William and Mary Quarterly*, 3rd ser., 38 (January 1981): 56–72.

Smith, Robert, and Loretta Metoxen. "Oneida Traditions." In Jack Campisi and Laurence M. Hauptman, Eds., *The Oneida Indian Experience: Two Perspectives*. Syracuse, N.Y.: Syracuse University Press, 1988.

Snyderman, George S. "Behind the Tree of Peace: A Sociological Analysis of Iroquois Warfare." *Pennsylvania Archaeologist* 38 (Fall 1948): 3–93.

Stern, Theodore. "Chickahominy: The Changing Culture of a Virginia Indian Community." *Proceedings* of the American Philosophical Society 96 (April 21, 1952): 157–225.

Stevenson, Carl Rush, Ed. "Diary of William Grafton Stevenson Captain C.S.A." *Alabama Historical Quarterly* 23 (1961): 45–72.

Stringfield, William W. "Sixty-Ninth Regiment." In Walter Clark, Ed., *Histories of the Several Regiments and Battalions from North Carolina in the Great War 1861–'65*, Vol. III. Raleigh, N.C.: Nash Bros. Book and Job Printers for the State of North Carolina, 1901.

———. "North Carolina Cherokee Indians." *The North Carolina Booklet* [Daughters of the American Revolution] 3 (July 1903): 5–24.

Thomas, Henry G. "The Colored Troops at Petersburg." In Clarence C. Buel and Robert U. Johnson, Eds., *Battles and Leaders of the Civil War*. Vol. IV. New York: Century Co., 1888; reprint, New York: Thomas Yoseloff, 1956.

Tooker, Elisabeth. "Ely S. Parker, Seneca, ca. 1828–1895." In Margot Liberty, Ed., *American Indian Intellectuals*. St. Paul, Minn: West Publishing Co. for the American Ethnological Society, 1978.

———. "The League of the Iroquois: Its History, Politics, and Ritual." In Bruce G. Trigger, Ed., *Handbook of North American Indians*. Vol. 15: *Northeast*. Washington, D.C.: Smithsonian Institution, 1978.

———. "Woman in Iroquois Society." In Campisi et al., Eds. *Extending the Rafters: Interdisciplinary Approaches to Iroquoian History.* Jack Albany: State University of New York Press, 1984.

———. "On the Development of the Handsome Lake Religion." *Proceedings* of the American Philosophical Society 133 (March 1989): 35–50.

Vaughan, Alden T. "Pequots and Puritans: The Causes of the War of 1637." *William and Mary Quarterly* 21 (April 1964): 256–269.

Vinovskis, Maris A. "Have Social Historians Lost the Civil War? Some Preliminary Demographic Speculations." *Journal of American History* 76 (June 1989): 34–58.

Wallace, Anthony F. C. "Origins of the Longhouse Religion." In Bruce G. Trigger, Ed., *Handbook of North American Indians.* Vol. 15: *Northeast.* Washington, D.C.: Smithsonian Institution, 1978.

Waltmann, Henry G. "Ely Samuel Parker, 1869–1871." In Robert Kvasnicka and Herman Viola, Eds., *The Commissioners of Indian Affairs, 1824–1977.* Lincoln: University of Nebraska Press, 1979.

Wheeler, Gerald E., and A. Stuart Pitt. "The 53d New York: A Zoo-Zoo Tale." *New York History* 37 (October 1956): 415–420.

Willey, William J. "The Second Federal Invasion of Indian Territory." *Chronicles of Oklahoma* 44 (Winter 1966/1967): 420–430.

Young, Mary. "The Cherokee Nation: Mirror of the Republic." *American Quarterly* 33 (Winter 1981): 502–524.

DISSERTATIONS

Abler, Thomas S. "Factional Dispute and Party Conflict in the Political System of the Seneca Nation." Ph.D. dissertation, Toronto: University of Toronto, 1969.

Balman, Gail Eugene. "Douglas Hancock Cooper: Southerner." Ph.D. dissertation, Stillwater: Oklahoma State University, 1976.

Brown, Walter L. "Albert Pike, 1809–1891." Ph.D. dissertation, Austin: University of Texas, 1955.

Bryan, Charles Faulkner, Jr. "The Civil War in East Tennessee: A Social, Political and Economic Study." Ph.D. dissertation, Knoxville: University of Tennessee, 1978.

Campisi, Jack. "Ethnic Identity and Boundary Maintenance in Three Oneida Communities." Ph.D. dissertation, Albany: State University of New York, 1974.

Cissna, Paul Byron. "The Piscataway Indians of Southern Maryland: An Ethnohistory from Pre-European Contact to the Present." Ph.D. dissertation, Washington, D.C.: American University, 1986.

Cotton, William Donaldson. "Appalachian North Carolina: A Political Study, 1860–1889." Ph.D. dissertation, Chapel Hill: University of North Carolina, 1954.

Fogelson, Raymond. "The Cherokee Ball Game: A Study in Southeastern Ethnology." Ph.D. dissertation, Philadelphia: University of Pennsylvania, 1962.

McClurken, James M. "We Wish to Be Civilized: Ottawa-American Political Contents on the Michigan Frontier." Ph.D. dissertation, Lansing: Michigan State University, 1988.

Peterson, John H. "The Mississippi Band of Choctaw Indians: Their Recent History and Current Social Relations." Ph.D. dissertation, Athens: University of Georgia, 1970.

Reed, Gerald A. "The Ross-Watie Conflict: Factionalism in the Cherokee Nation, 1839–1865." Ph.D. dissertation, Norman: University of Oklahoma, 1967.

Sterling, Robert. "Civil War Draft Resistance in the Middle West." Ph.D. dissertation, Normal: Northern Illinois University, 1974.

Tolbert, Charles Madden. "A Sociological Study of the Choctaw Indians in Mississippi." dissertation, Baton Rouge: Louisiana State University, 1958.

Valuska, David L. "The Negro in the Union Navy." Ph.D. dissertation, Lehigh, Pa.: Lehigh University, 1973.

Van Hoeven, James W. "Salvation and Indian Removal: The Career Biography of Rev. John Freeman Schermerhorn, Indian Commissioner." Ph.D. dissertation, Nashville, Tenn.: Vanderbilt University, 1972.

Index

291

304   *Index*

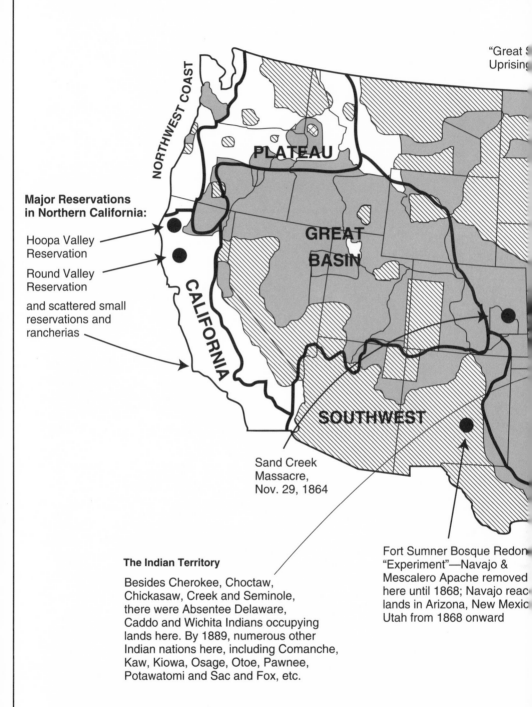

NORTHWEST COAST

PLATEAU

GREAT BASIN

CALIFORNIA

SOUTHWEST

"Great Uprising

Major Reservations in Northern California:

Hoopa Valley Reservation

Round Valley Reservation

and scattered small reservations and rancherias

Sand Creek Massacre, Nov. 29, 1864

The Indian Territory

Besides Cherokee, Choctaw, Chickasaw, Creek and Seminole, there were Absentee Delaware, Caddo and Wichita Indians occupying lands here. By 1889, numerous other Indian nations here, including Comanche, Kaw, Kiowa, Osage, Otoe, Pawnee, Potawatomi and Sac and Fox, etc.

Fort Sumner Bosque Redon "Experiment"—Navajo & Mescalero Apache removed here until 1868; Navajo reac lands in Arizona, New Mexic Utah from 1868 onward

Indian Land Cessions 1860–1869

with American Indian communities discussed in the book. (Most reservations not shown.)